Privatizing Policing

D1613209

Promotiecommissie

| | |
|---|---|
| Promotor: | prof.dr. L.W.J.C. Huberts |
| Overige leden: | prof.dr. J.C.J. Boutellier |
| | dhr. T.D. Jones |
| | prof.dr. J. Naeyé |
| | prof.dr. R. Sarre |
| | dr.ir. J.B. Terpstra |
| | prof.dr. C.D. van der Vijver |

ISBN 978-90-5454-953-6
NUR 820

www.bju.nl

VRIJE UNIVERSITEIT

# PRIVATIZING POLICING
Describing and explaining the growth of private security

ACADEMISCH PROEFSCHRIFT

ter verkrijging van de graad Doctor aan
de Vrije Universiteit Amsterdam,
op gezag van de rector magnificus
prof.dr. L.M. Bouter,
in het openbaar te verdedigen
ten overstaan van de promotiecommissie
van de faculteit der Sociale Wetenschappen
op donderdag 20 december 2007 om 13.45 uur
in de aula van de universiteit,
De Boelelaan 1105

door

Ronald van Steden

geboren te Amsterdam

promotor: prof.dr. L.W.J.C. Huberts

# Acknowledgement

It is perhaps one of the best-kept secrets that academia, far from being an ivory tower populated by unworldly eccentrics (as is stereotypically thought), is in reality filled with researchers working with a diversity of people inside as well as outside the university. Where would I be without so many others? The first to set me on the right track were academic scholars to whose publications I frequently refer for an up-to-date overview of current knowledge about private security around the globe. To name in random order a few, Les Johnston, Alison Wakefield, Trevor Jones, Tim Prenzler, Mark Button, George Rigakos, Tim Newburn, Ian Loader, Adam Crawford, Philip Stenning, Rick Sarre and Clifford Shearing. Nevertheless, because theoretical insights cannot do without practical knowledge (and vice versa), I also owe much to my respondents. Without them, obviously, there would be no content. Therefore, I thank them sincerely for their openness and hospitality. A big thank you also to Leo Huberts, my supervisor, and Hans Boutellier, my sparring partner, from both of whom I learned so much. I truly appreciate our amiable working relationships. My gratitude also to my colleagues, the Ph.D. commission and all others involved. In addition, my thoughts go to friends, family and in-laws – my parents, Kirsten, Edwin and little Daniël. I am so grateful to have you in my life. And finally, to Dorien Keus, I thank you for your time and being – I love you.


Ronald van Steden
Amsterdam, June 2007

# Contents

**1**  **Introduction: The Growth of Dutch Private Security**    **1**
1.1 Research questions and aims    4
1.2 Research methods    5
1.3 Relevance    6
1.4 Outline    7

**Part 1: Theory and Methodology**

**2**  **On Police, Policing and Private Security: A Brief Overview**    **11**
2.1 Essentially contested concepts    11
    2.1.1 The etymology of policing    11
    2.1.2 Policing and authority    12
    2.1.3 Decoupling 'police' from 'policing'    13
    2.1.4 A definition of policing    14
2.2 The fuzziness of public versus private    15
    2.2.1 Disentangling the public and the private    15
    2.2.2 Classifying Dutch policing    16
    2.2.3 A definition of private security    17
2.3 Understanding public and private policing    18
2.4 Conclusion    21

**3**  **Widening Networks: Security Governance**    **23**
3.1 Nodal governance    24
3.2 The formalization of social control    26
3.3 The culture of control    27
3.4 Trapped in downward circles?    27
3.5 The inverted safety paradigm    28
3.6 Relationships within extended police families    31
3.7 Conclusion    34

**4**  **Theorizing Private Security: The Explanatory Framework**    **35**
4.1 Rising crime and related problems    36
    4.1.1 Crime and fear    37
    4.1.2 Disorder    38
4.2 Growth of mass private property    38
    4.2.1 Mass private property    39
    4.2.2 Communal spaces    39
4.3 Economic rationalities    40

| | | |
|---|---|---|
| | 4.3.1 External incentives | 40 |
| | 4.3.2 Intrinsic motivations | 41 |
| | 4.4 Government policy toward private sector participation | 42 |
| | 4.4.1 Top-down privatization | 42 |
| | 4.4.2 Bottom-up privatization | 43 |
| | 4.5 An overburdened police force | 43 |
| | 4.5.1 A limited police budget | 44 |
| | 4.5.2 Two schools of thought | 44 |
| | 4.6 Professionalization of private security | 45 |
| | 4.6.1 External incentives | 46 |
| | 4.6.2 Intrinsic motivations | 46 |
| | 4.7 Conclusion | 47 |
| | | |
| **5** | **Studying Private Security: Research Methods** | **49** |
| | 5.1 Case study research | 49 |
| | 5.1.1 The problem of causality | 50 |
| | 5.1.2 The problem of generalization | 51 |
| | 5.2 Case selection | 52 |
| | 5.3 Data collection tools | 53 |
| | 5.3.1 National level | 54 |
| | 5.3.2 Local level | 55 |
| | 5.4 Data analysis | 56 |
| | 5.4.1 National level analysis | 56 |
| | 5.4.2 Within-case analysis | 56 |
| | 5.4.3 Cross-case analysis | 57 |
| | 5.5 Ethical considerations | 57 |
| | 5.6 Conclusion | 58 |
| | | |
| **Part 2: A National Case Study** | | |
| | | |
| **6** | **Growing Private Security: A Market in Motion** | **61** |
| | 6.1 Measuring the private security 'industry' | 61 |
| | 6.2 The Dutch private security industry | 62 |
| | 6.2.1 The census | 64 |
| | 6.2.2 Security yearbooks | 65 |
| | 6.2.3 Quickscans | 66 |
| | 6.2.4 Personal research | 67 |
| | 6.2.4.1 Manned guarding | 68 |
| | 6.2.4.2 Central alarm respondents | 69 |
| | 6.2.4.3 Armored couriers | 70 |
| | 6.2.4.4 Private investigators | 70 |

|  | 6.2.4.5 Technical equipment services | 71 |
| --- | --- | --- |
|  | 6.3 An international perspective | 72 |
|  | 6.4 Summary | 75 |

| 7 | **Private Security Growth: Exploring Explanatory Factors** | **77** |
| --- | --- | --- |
|  | 7.1 Rising crime and related problems | 77 |
|  | 7.1.1 Crime and business losses | 78 |
|  | 7.1.2 Crime and fear | 78 |
|  | 7.2 Growth of mass private property | 79 |
|  | 7.2.1 Business, retail and leisure facilities | 79 |
|  | 7.2.2 Communal spaces: Residential areas | 81 |
|  | 7.3 Economic rationalities | 81 |
|  | 7.3.1 Public-private partnerships | 82 |
|  | 7.3.2 Spillover effects? | 83 |
|  | 7.4 Government policy toward private sector participation | 83 |
|  | 7.4.1 A working group on private security | 83 |
|  | 7.4.2 Crime prevention and integral safety policy | 84 |
|  | 7.4.3 Direct privatization | 85 |
|  | 7.4.4 Stricter law enforcement | 85 |
|  | 7.5 An overburdened police force | 86 |
|  | 7.5.1 The Dutch police in brief | 86 |
|  | 7.5.2 Mounting criticism | 87 |
|  | 7.5.2.1 Bureaucratic obstacles | 89 |
|  | 7.5.2.2 Public pressure on criminal justice | 89 |
|  | 7.5.2.3 Dissatisfied citizens | 92 |
|  | 7.5.2.4 A business perspective | 92 |
|  | 7.5.2.5 Recent developments in police policy | 92 |
|  | 7.6 Professionalization of private security | 93 |
|  | 7.6.1 A struggling industry | 93 |
|  | 7.6.2 Legislation and training | 94 |
|  | 7.6.3 An international perspective | 95 |
|  | 7.7 Analysis | 97 |
|  | 7.7.1 Shifts in the size and organization of private security | 97 |
|  | 7.7.2 Rising crime and related problems | 97 |
|  | 7.7.3 Growth of mass private property | 99 |
|  | 7.7.4 Economic rationalities | 99 |
|  | 7.7.5 Government policy toward private sector participation | 99 |
|  | 7.7.6 An overburdened police force | 100 |
|  | 7.7.7 Professionalization of private security | 100 |
|  | 7.8 Preliminary conclusions | 100 |

**Part 3: Local Case Studies**

**8      Efteling: World of Wonders                                        105**
8.1 The forerunner of Efteling (1933–1952)                              105
8.2 Period 1: Anton Pieck's dream (1952–1980)                           106
8.3 Period 2: The Fairy Tale Forest and beyond (1980–1985)             107
8.4 Period 3: 'We sell memories and emotions' (1985–1990)              108
8.5 Period 4: A jester's dance (1990–2005)                              110
8.6 Recent developments: Toward an integral safety policy              113
8.7 Analysis                                                            114
    8.7.1 Shifts in the extent and nature of private security        114
    8.7.2 Rising crime and related problems                          115
    8.7.3 Growth of mass private property                            115
    8.7.4 Economic rationalities                                     115
    8.7.5 Government policy toward private sector participation      115
    8.7.6 An overburdened police force                               116
    8.7.7 Professionalization of private security                    116
    8.7.8 Changes in labor law: A new factor                         116
8.8 Summary                                                             116

**9      Stadium Feyenoord: 'Hand in Hand, Comrades!'                        117**
9.1 The early history of Feyenoord (1908–1945)                          117
9.2 Period 1: A stadium for the working class (1945–1974)              118
9.3 Period 2: Football hooliganism (1974–1990)                         119
9.4 Period 3: Reducing hooliganism (1990–1997)                         122
9.5 Period 4: Carlo Picornie and beyond (1997–2005)                    124
    9.5.1 Integral safety policy                                     125
        9.5.1.1 Stadium Feyenoord                                126
        9.5.1.2 Municipality of Rotterdam                        126
        9.5.1.3 Rotterdam-Rijnmond police force                  126
        9.5.1.4 Public prosecution service                       127
    9.5.2 Commercialization of in-house security                     127
9.6 Recent developments: Toward repression and prevention              128
9.7 Analysis                                                            129
    9.7.1 Shifts in the extent and nature of private security        129
    9.7.2 Rising crime and related problems                          130
    9.7.3 Growth of mass private property                            130
    9.7.4 Economic rationalities                                     130
    9.7.5 Government policy toward private sector participation      131
    9.7.6 An overburdened police force                               131
    9.7.7 Professionalization of private security                    132

9.7.8 Changes in labor law: A new factor     132
9.8 Summary     132

**10    Hoog Catharijne: Retail Heart of the Netherlands     133**
10.1 Hoog Catharijne's early history (1962–1973)     133
10.2 Period 1: A magnet for the homeless (1973–1982)     134
10.3 Period 2: Rising tensions (1982–1987)     135
10.4 Period 3: Policy experiments (1987–2001)     136
    10.4.1 Private funding of public police patrollers     138
    10.4.2 Ongoing struggles     139
10.5 Period 4: An integral safety approach (2001–2005)     140
10.6 Recent developments: A drastic facelift for Hoog Catharijne     141
10.7 Analysis     142
    10.7.1 Shifts in the extent and nature of policing     142
    10.7.2 Rising crime and related problems     142
    10.7.3 Growth of mass private property     143
    10.7.4 Economic rationalities     143
    10.7.5 Government policy toward private sector participation     143
    10.7.6 An overburdened police force     143
    10.7.7 Professionalization of private security     144
10.8 Summary     144

**Part 4: Analysis, Conclusions and Discussion**

**11    Dutch Private Security: An Analysis     147**
11.1 Shifts in the extent and nature of private security     147
11.2 The original model     148
    11.2.1 Rising crime and related problems     149
    11.2.2 Growth of mass private property     149
    11.2.3 Economic rationalities     150
    11.2.4 Government policy toward private sector participation     150
    11.2.5 An overburdened police force     151
    11.2.6 Professionalization of private security     151
    11.2.7 Changes in labor law: A new factor     152
11.3 Summary     152

**12    Conclusions and Discussion: Explaining Private Security     155**
12.1 The intellectual puzzle     155
    12.1.1 Shifts in private security     156
    12.1.2 The explanatory model revisited     157
12.2 Reflections on flourishing private security     157

12.3 Reflections on explanatory factors                      158
12.4 Theoretical and research implications                   159
12.5 Consequences of private security                        160
12.6 Final remarks                                           162

**References**                                               **165**

Appendix 1: Questionnaire survey and interview protocol
Appendix 2: Qualitative data matrices
Appendix 3: Summary in Dutch (samenvatting)

# 1 Introduction: The Growth of Dutch Private Security

In 1642, renowned Dutch artist Rembrandt van Rijn finished his masterpiece, the Company of Frans Banning Cocq and Willem van Ruytenburch, better known as the Night Watch (*De Nachtwacht*).[1] The militiamen portrayed symbolize the power of Amsterdam during its glorious 'golden age' of commercial success. As the canvas shows, captain Frans Banning Cocq orders his lieutenant to march the guardsmen off, a snapshot of a militia group in action that radically differentiates the Night Watch from the regularly commissioned seventeenth century militia portraits showing static rows of men. Rembrandt painted the most glamorous and wealthy members of a watch decked out in richly decorated uniforms, in fulfillment of the requirement that every healthy male citizen support the authorities by keeping public order at night.

These old night watch militia were the forerunners of the Netherlands' contemporary police system in which every region and municipality hold powers over local forces (Elzinga et al., 1995). After the Kingdom of the Netherlands was founded in 1814, night watches slowly disappeared as the providers of safety and security. Specifically, because of malpractice, drunkenness on duty, the blackmail of arrested persons and business contact with prostitutes, from 1843, the government disqualified civil guards from employment and transferred their tasks to professional police forces. However, despite official state policy, several night watches continued their activities and began selling their services to paying customers. The first official Dutch private security company was begun by Isaac Beuth in 1902 (Verhoog, 2002).

Somewhat ironically, while often overlooked, there are valid arguments in support of both the Dutch police and the private security industry being rooted in the same tradition of night watches (Van Steden, 2002: 13). The most probable reason for not recognizing this shared history between the police force and paid private security is that it was long hidden from public view. That is, Dutch security companies operated on a small scale for many decades, without much attention given to the industry's past, present or future. Remarkably, however, within just 30 years, private security has undergone swift growth, and, although the upsurge of contract guards should not be overstated compared to the increasingly varied and large numbers of public law enforcers (Nalla and Newman, 1991), a steadily growing arsenal of paid security staff has entered the arena. What is taking place is a rebirth of private policing (Johnston, 1992a) in

---

[1]     For more information, see www.rijksmuseum.nl

the sense that, in addition to the criminal justice apparatus, corporations and civilians increasingly occupy a place in security governance. From an international perspective, this renaissance is not exceptional – many scholars have recognized a worldwide resurgence of private (mostly commercial) security activities.[2] As a result, a plethora of firms now offer a kaleidoscope of services and products ranging from staffed services, alarm-monitoring services and cash and transit services to the production of security equipment, white-collar crime investigation and consultancy on such issues as risk management.[3]

In the early 1970s, social scientists began to take an interest in the place of private police in society (Becker, 1973) and announced it to be a new research area. In the United States, a number of reports were published on the nature and extent, as well as the perils and rewards, of commercial security,[4] followed soon after by reports, books and articles from Canada[5] and the United Kingdom.[6] Since then, the body of knowledge on private security has been slowly developing, although it still lags much behind research on public policing. Shearing (in his preface for Wakefield, 2003: xvii) observed that

> [w]hile private security is certainly no longer a subject that languishes on a forgotten scholarly back burner, it remains surprisingly under researched. Despite its obvious importance to the governance of security, scholars continue to focus far more attention on the police than they do the various other agents and agencies that provide for security.

Thus far, diverse, predominantly Anglo-Saxon, publications have placed private security workers in plural or fragmented organizational landscapes of police(like) actors such as city wardens, neighborhood watches, regulatory and

---

[2] See Grabosky (1996) and Wood and Kempa (2005) for useful synopses of discussions on the theoretical and normative dimensions of enlisting nongovernmental organizations as partners in crime control.

[3] The security market also expands into other areas, such as the private military industry (Singer, 2003), private adjudication (Russell, 2001), private prisons (Jones and Newburn, 2004), private jails (Kiekbusch, 2001) and bounty hunters (Burns et al., 2004). However, this research, while recognizing that these emerging research areas are fascinating, will leave them mostly untouched.

[4] The key reports among these are Kakalik and Wildhorn (1971, 1977) (Rand Reports), Cunningham and Taylor (1985) and Cunningham et al. (1990) (Hallcrest Reports I and II). Other American studies reviewing the characteristics of private security are O'Toole (1978) and Albanese (1989).

[5] Shearing et al. (1980) and Shearing and Stenning (e.g., 1981, 1983a, 1983b, 1985, 1987a, 1987b) have published groundbreaking studies on private security in Canada.

[6] Draper (1978) and South (1988) have published initial studies on private security in Britain.

investigatory bodies, inspectorates and, of course, regular police forces.[7] Further studies have described the structure and organization of the private security industry[8] and have delved into the working practices of its personnel.[9] Subsequently, some researchers have drawn general international comparisons of expanding national private security industries,[10] while others have published various comprehensive country studies on private security, often with reference to its relationships with public policing agencies.[11]

In contrast, little detailed information is available about the Dutch private security industry. [12] To fill this void, this present study aims not only to give an in-depth overview of the nature of private security but to incorporate its findings into a theoretical framework for *explaining* the growing number of private security guards in the Netherlands. This goal is important because the particularized accounts of scholarship on social, economical, legal, geographical and political factors for privatization trends in policing do not offer a convincing overall picture of current developments (Johnston, 1996a). Rather, explanations for the growth of private security remain multifarious, while debates about the upcoming industry are often ideological not scientific. Essentially, the academic

---

[7]     For overviews of the British policing landscape, see Button (2002), Crawford et al. (2005), Jones and Newburn (1998) and Johnston (1992a, 2000a).

[8]     See George and Button (2000) for an oversight of the British private security industry and Van Steden (2004) for an oversight of the Dutch private security industry.

[9]     For research on the tasks, competencies, working methods and mentalities of private security guards, see McManus (1995), Micucci (1998), Michael (1999), Rigakos (2002), Pastor (2003), Wakefield (2003, 2005), Button (2003, 2007a) and Hutchinson and D. O'Conner (2005).

[10]    For international comparisons of private security industries, see South (1994), De Waard (1999), Ottens et al. (1999), Van Outrive (1999), Van Steden and Huberts (2005), and Van Steden and Sarre (2007).

[11]    Such research includes studies on Belgium (Cools and Verbeiren, 2004), Britain (Jones and Newburn, 2006a), Germany (Nogala and Sack, 1999), Greece (Rigakos and Papanicolau, 2003; Papanicolau, 2006), France (Ocqueteau, 2006), Spain (Giménez-Salinas, 1999, 2004), South East Europe, including the Balkan (SEESAC, 2005), Bulgaria (Gounev, 2006), Russia (Volkov, 2002; Favarel-Garrigues and Le Huérou, 2004), Ukraine and Georgia (Hiscock, 2006), Japan (Yosida, 1999; Yoshida and Leishman, 2006), China (Guo, 1999), South Korea (Lee, 2004; Button et al., 2006; Nalla and Hwang, 2006), Saudi Arabia (De Jong, 2002), Sub-Saharan Africa (Abrahamsen and Williams, 2005a, b, c), South Africa (Minnaar, 2005; Shearing and Berg, 2006), Australia (Prenzler, 2005), the United States (Manning, 2006), Canada (Rigakos and Leung, 2006), Mexico (Reames, 2005), Brazil (Wood and Cardia, 2006) and other Latin American countries (Abelson, 2006).

[12]    Early research has been carried out by Hoogenboom (e.g. 1986, 1991a, 1991b, 1994), but he has recently focused mainly on private investigation rather than on private guarding that is the focus of my own research. Given that uniformed guards are, by far, the largest and most visible element of the private security industry and that their presence has been considerably intensified, it is this development that calls especially for illumination and comprehension.

community lacks an integrated model for explaining the expanding role of private security (Kempa et al., 2004: 574–576). Therefore, now is the time to clarify *why* policing has been privatized during previous years.

It should also be noted that many of the suggested explanations are based primarily on the North-American experience. Predominant among these is Shearing and Stenning's (1981, 1983a) proposal that the ascendancy of private security guards resulted from the spreading-out of mass private property like shopping centers, amusement parks, football stadiums, holiday resorts, office parks, airport terminals and zoos. Despite being convincingly argued, their thesis that the proliferation of such publicly accessible but privately owned and managed spaces has contributed significantly to the demand for private security has come under fire. For example, Jones and Newburn (1998, 1999, 2002) have criticized the assumption that changes in property relations are *the* explanatory factor for the resurgence of paid security guards. Moreover, the universal generalization of privatization patterns in the United States and Canada is questionable. Rather, while European private security shows a trend that mirrors events in North America, it has its own idiosyncrasies.[13] Therefore, commentators have been pleading for detailed research on the tenability of the factors suggested to explain the rise of private security industries around the world.

In sum, the academic literature on private security suffers from three blind spots. First, there is little systematic research that deals with the size, shape, nature, growth and implications of private security in non-English language countries (in this case, the Netherlands). Second, there is no coherent set of theoretical concepts that can explain the developing private security market. Third, theoretical debates on private security have been dominated by the North-American experience and have overlooked the situation elsewhere. This book aims to tackle these blind spots by focusing on both the theoretical and empirical side of mushrooming private security sectors – particularly manned guarding services – with a key objective of explaining the rise of private security in the Netherlands.

## 1.1 Research questions and aims
The main research question generated for the study is the following: *How can the growth of private manned guarding services in the Netherlands over the past three decades be explained?* This question breaks down into the following two subquestions:

---

[13]        South (1994) and Jones and Newburn (2006b).

1.  To what extent have Dutch private manned guarding services expanded over the past three decades?
2.  What explains the growth of private manned guarding services in the Netherlands over the past three decades?

The research aims are twofold. The first is to create detailed knowledge about the size and organization of private security in the Netherlands; specifically, how the industry has evolved, what private guards do in practice and how they relate to public police officers. The second is to elucidate why private security has grown so large; that is, what factors are important to explaining the rise of the industry.

## 1.2 Research methods
The literature on private security proposes a somewhat chaotic list of explanations for the industry's expansion, which in this book are clustered into a framework of six, sometimes overlapping and interconnecting, theoretical factors:

1.  Rising crime and related problems;
2.  Growth of mass private property;
3.  Economic rationalities;
4.  Government policy toward private sector participation;
5.  An overburdened police force; and
6.  Professionalization of private security.

Since so little information is available on the Dutch private security industry, this research draws on a combination of case studies at both the national and local level of analysis. At the national level, first impressions are formed by describing, analyzing and explaining general trends in private security to provide an overarching context for interpreting the subsequent local case studies. These case studies of *Efteling* (an amusement park), *Stadium Feyenoord* (a football stadium) and *Hoog Catharijne* (a shopping mall) – all typical of the privately-owned facilities in which security guards traditionally work – in turn throw further light on the factors that drive such trends in manned guarding services. Most particularly, all three locations represent quasi-public sites about which, despite great emphasis on freedom and fun, debate continues about demarcations between state and nonstate responsibilities for peacekeeping and the maintenance of order.

## 1.3 Relevance

The relevance of this study is clear. Over the last 30 years, an irreversible restructuring of policing in the Netherlands (and abroad) has led to increased reliance on the private security industry. Within this context, actors other than the police have become increasingly more accepted as crime stoppers and maintainers of order (McLaughlin, 2007). This situation traps police authorities, once privileged if not monopolistic providers of public security, in a multifarious interlocking of nonstate, especially profit-oriented, organizations (Winkel et al., 2005). Thus, it would be a mistake to dismiss this upsurge in private security lightly, for it represents nothing less than a 'quiet revolution' (Shearing et al., 1980: 1) that is growing ever noisier in its quest to participate in what to date has been government's primary responsibility – ensuring and guaranteeing public order. Thus, the phenomenon of private security, and what it can and cannot offer society in terms of policing, warrants much more scholarly attention, which requires first that the growth of private security and its place and role over the years be described and explained.

That said, it is incorrect to presume that only the academic community has relatively limited acquaintance with the unobtrusive but steady infiltration of private security into public life. Politicians, policy-makers, police leaders and ordinary citizens also frequently encounter this industry yet know little about it. That is, both citizens and practitioners seldom ask themselves where security guards come from, who they are and what tasks they perform. In fact, given the commonly held prejudice that paid guards are incompetent, amoral, shady and unsavory 'wannabe cops' (Livingstone and Hart, 2003: 161), private security still has a fairly negative image worldwide.[14]

Thus, this study has practical relevance in that it sheds light on the Dutch private security industry, which, given its rapid development over the last three decades, deserves careful analysis and reflection. Nonetheless, because the focus on the Netherlands somewhat limits generalization of the findings, this book must not be read as an all-encompassing study. Rather, its predominant academic aims are to offer an integrated explanatory framework and challenge the currently touted explanations for the growth of private security. Hopefully,

---

[14]  Nalla and Hereaux (2003) softened this negative perception with their finding that, in a survey of U.S. college students, respondents generally held a positive attitude toward private security staff. Although these findings are limited by the participation of only a small subgroup of the American population, they may be a signal of greater acceptance of private security among the younger generations. Other research has shown that such a negative image is not necessarily of concern to security guards themselves (Manzo, 2006); rather, the guards note that, as for fully-fledged police officers, public disrespect is part of the job. They therefore cope with it as a type of challenge.

doing so will provide a starting point for a more subtle understanding of the industry's expansion elsewhere.

**1.4 Outline**
The book is organized into four parts, each containing several chapters. In the opening part, 'Theory and Methodology', Chapter 2 defines policing, classifies organizations along public/private dichotomies and sets out the competing principles of state and nonstate bodies. Chapter 3 then offers a brief overview of the academic debate on the place and role of private guards in the wider security landscape, particularly the dialogue between scholars who are either skeptical or optimistic about state contributions to the governance of security. Chapter 4 focuses on the theoretical framework for explaining private security's growing role and place. Most particularly, it identifies and discusses the six explanatory categories outlined above. As a corollary, chapter 5 provides the specific building blocks of the research design by outlining the methodology adopted in this project.

The second part, 'A National Case Study', contains two chapters on the history of security in the Netherlands: the first, chapter 6, describes industry developments, which are subsequently analyzed in chapter 7. The third part, 'Local Case Studies', advances detailed knowledge of the trends under scrutiny by examining private security in three different local contexts – an amusement park (chapter 8), a football stadium (chapter 9) and a shopping centre (chapter 10). The final part, 'Analysis, Conclusions and Discussion', draws together all the research data. First, chapter 11 reviews the currently proposed explanations separately in light of the observed changes in the size and organization of Dutch private security. Finally, chapter 12 presents conclusions on which explanatory factors matter most in explaining the increased presence of paid guards, with particular reference to the practical and theoretical relevance of these results. The book closes by highlighting key issues for the future of private security.

**Part 1: Theory and Methodology**

# 2 On Police, Policing and Private Security: A Brief Overview

This chapter briefly outlines the scholarly debate on police, policing and private security, in particular manned guarding services. Because today uniformed guards represent by far the largest and most visible private protective resource in the Netherlands, their presence needs to be recognized and explained. To this end, this chapter consists of three main sections, the first of which arrives at a workable definition of policing. The second section contrasts the public/private dichotomies applied to organizational features, a classical distinction that, despite its problems, is still useful for exploring the positions of public and private sectors within the 'new policing order' (Leishman et al., 1996: 20). The final section concentrates on the dissimilarities in responsibilities, interests and principles between police officers and security guards – a controversy that is touched upon later in the book.

## 2.1 Essentially contested concepts

The concept of 'police', and in a wider sense 'policing', appears transparent but, as scholarly studies have pointed out, such ideas 'have borne a variety of meanings, reflecting the nuances and relations between police and people at different times and places' (Wright, 2002: 36). The term 'policing', like such terms as 'democracy', has so many connotations that it is inevitably subject to disagreement and dispute. Indeed, Gallie (1962) pointed out that such concepts are essentially contested because their polymorphous nature makes their exact designation difficult, if not impossible. Thus, it should not be surprising that workable definitions are scarce in the literature, and researchers often presuppose the meaning that policing evokes by simply avoiding definitional discussions. Nonetheless, it is important to specify the current focus without claiming an incontrovertible solution. Therefore, this discussion takes a more concise route by trying to find the common ground of what constitutes policing. To this end, the following paragraphs examine the semantics of this concept in detail.

## 2.1.1 The etymology of policing

The word 'policing' derives from the ancient Greek term *politeia*, an 'immanent organizing principle' or 'constitution' underlying public life in a city-state (*polis*), which, translated into modern language closely resembles 'a socio-political function [...] exercised in society' (Johnston, 1992a: 4). This concept assumes a political organization of free and equal citizens (albeit one restricted to wealthy, adult males) in which everything is decided through speech and persuasion. Thus, the Greek *polis* has nothing to do with the modern perception of a regulatory state as a means of protecting society, if necessary with coercion. Rather, this idea of government power is truly a modern invention, which as a rule became institutionalized from the sixteenth and seventeenth century onward. For example, Thomas Hobbes (1968 [1651]), a pioneer in advocating a strong state to safeguard society from any disturbances, urged the establishment of specialized officials to guarantee durable peace, justice and prosperity. Without state power, Hobbes argued, society would fall apart because of its inability to save itself from war (cf. Max Weber, 1968 [1919]). Thus, direct participation and self-government, once celebrated by the Athenians, was abandoned as a fruitful political option.

Nonetheless, popular involvement in what is now generally recognized as private policing has been routine for a long time.[1] In fact, historical research has suggested that until the nineteenth century, uniformed civil and commercial groups of, for example, night watchers in the Netherlands and thief-takers in Britain were actually the greatest experts in order maintenance. Thus, as Rawlings (1995: 130) pointed out, 'in practice, the vast bulk of policing has always been done by organizations and people other than the police'. Only since the nineteenth century has the term 'police' begun to be associated with a specialized government organization holding certain legitimate (repressive) powers to preserve internal or domestic security (as opposed to military preservation of external or foreign security). Thus, the common interpretation of policing as at the heart of the state is, at best, 200 years old.

### 2.1.2 Policing and authority

In everyday knowledge, policing is what the police do. However, because police officers perform myriad tasks simultaneously, no conclusive agreement exists on the nature of policing (Bayley, 1994). Most often, officers are on patrol, rendering assistance in a car crash, dealing with crime(-related) problems, helping elderly people who have lost their way, regulating heavy traffic, and so forth. Accordingly, following Bittner (1990: 249), police work can be summarized as responses to numerous calls from citizens about 'something-that-ought-not-to-be-happening-and-about-which-someone-had-better-do-something-now!' Or, to put it another way, the practice of policing is the art of instant problem-solving and pragmatic decision-making in sometimes bizarre circumstances.

To enable decisive action, officers are vested with a unique mandate to maintain and restore order. That is, they have the ultimate power to overthrow

---

[1]      South (1994), McMullan (1995), Rawlings (1995, 2003) and Zedner (2006a).

opposition by imposing sanctions and, ultimately, resorting to *force* against people and property: 'the policeman, and the policeman alone, is equipped, entitled and required to deal with every exigency in which force may have to be used, to meet it' (Bittner, 1990: 256). The foregoing description of policing implies that officers are, under constrictions, allowed to use (lethal) violence. Of course, police work frequently requires no repressive measures, but it is of extraordinary importance to understand that officers cope with situations in which the use of force *may* be necessary to bring about a desired outcome (Bittner, 1990: 257). Thus, Bittner hinted at the *possibility* rather than the certainty of mobilizing repressive sanctions to ensure public order.

Bittner's (1990) description of what policing entails is insightful. While admitting the enormously diverse and haphazard police role, he accentuates unity in the officers' capacity to take decisive action. That is, only police officers are in the legitimate monopolist position to end a violent riot, direct traffic and break into a house to rescue someone from a fire. Thus, the police customarily exercise what authors refer to as 'symbolic power', alternatively expressed as 'authority'.[2] Moreover, they do so not only occasionally while involved in an incident but also when simply walking down the road. Thus, uniformed police officers can basically *command* an area purely because of their mere presence, which illustrates that the capacity to vigorously enforce laws, norms and rules imbues everything that police officers do in the interest of protecting public safety. After all, *de facto*, policing involves an air of authoritative power.

### 2.1.3 Decoupling 'police' from 'policing'

People commonly intertwine policing with the police as a bureaucratically organized institution that employs 'professionally trained employees entrusted with the tasks of enforcing criminal law and maintaining order backed by the authority of the state, paid by public funds, and accountable to democratic institutions' (Joh, 2004: 61). However, scholars have called this vision into question, pointing out that policing is not an exclusive monopoly provided by the public administration.[3] In the words of Dutch sociologist Cachet (1990: 7), 'policing is not so unique as practitioners think. It belongs to a more general category of control mechanisms'.

This observation seems to imply a return to the historical idea that the concept of policing is much broader than the police force itself. That is, police officers are no longer, if they ever were, isolated and freestanding functionaries preserving peace and order. Rather, they are simply one rule enforcer among

---

[2]      Loader (1997a: 3) and Waddington (1999: 18–20).
[3]      Reiner (1997: 1003–1008), Johnston (1999a: 226–227) and Huberts and Van Steden (2001: 5).

many. From this perspective, policing is fundamentally a function of serving the community and disciplining behavior, which must be practically supported by an army of institutions like families, churches, schools and sport clubs. As Waddington (1999: 11) put it, '[t]he police cannot lay claim to be society's "thin blue line" against disorder and lawlessness, for they are supplemented by a congregation of social controls which, if absent, would leave the police virtually powerless' .

Along similar lines, Shapland and Vagg (1988) documented various ways in which villages and cities police themselves. Such policing by the public – social control activities that occur outside police involvement – frequently take place at the microscopic level of community life as active citizens watch suspicious-looking strangers, form gossip networks or reassure fearful neighbors. Nonetheless, despite these observations, critics are hesitant about the idea of policing as social control. For example, Jones and Newburn (1998) argued not only that the Shapland and Vagg study is too broad but that the notion of social control has too many connotations to be useful. Specifically, they claimed that because social control refers to almost every technique for inducing order in society, it is overly imprecise and hence meaningless. Thus, it turns out to be, as Cohen (1985: 2) commented, a confusing 'Mickey Mouse concept'.

To avoid this pitfall of concept stretching, Cohen (1985) and Cachet (1990) stress the division between informal and formal sources of social control; that is, essentially separating direct from indirect forms of influence on human behavior. The former relates to close relationships among people when, as Shapland and Vagg (1988) observed, residents exert face-to-face influence on each other to maintain a pleasant and desirable neighborhood. In contrast, formal social controls involve *organized* or *planned* responses to criminal and/or deviant behavior, which have both a public and a private face. That is, apart from the state apparatus, an assortment of specialized occupations engages in the process of order maintenance. For example, security guards, like their colleague police officers, are capable of handling and equipped to deal with violations of the perceived norm within a particular social system.[4] Hence, policing must be interpreted as an aspect of much broader social control activities.[5]

### 2.1.4 A definition of policing

Based on the previous theoretical discussions, this study, which focuses on *formalized* social control mechanisms implemented by actors who *primarily* function to assure a certain degree of order, defines policing as follows: *a regulatory function, whose central purpose is upholding generally accepted*

---

[4]      Cachet (1990: 88–89) and Huberts (1998: 3–4).
[5]      Cachet (1990: 96–102) and Button (2002: 6).

*norms and rules and protecting the order within a social system – a function vested with the authority to take coercive measures against people and property if necessary.* It should be noted that this definition covers a 'quilt' or 'patchwork' of (non)state policing bodies and agencies (Crawford and Lister, 2004a), including private security firms.

## 2.2 The fuzziness of public versus private

The expansion of paid security occupations has significant implications for the division between the public (government) and private (market) sectors. Yet what is public and what is private? Or, to use a slightly different formulation, where does the public sector end and the private sector begin? As is shown below, exact demarcations between public and private are hard to sketch because the two extremities flow into multidimensional fusions (Benn and Gaus, 1983). Indeed, some authors have even expressed doubts about the usefulness of public/private distinctions: 'the traditional public/private dichotomy has [...] lost a great deal of salience in characterizing developments in the process of policing and the organization of collective life in general' (Kempa et al., 1999: 219).

Others, being more creative, have invented new terminology such as parapolice (Rigakos, 2002) and quasi-policing (Jason-Lloyd, 2003) to denote police-like actors. Loader (2000: 326–329) even tried to construct a brand new typology that distinguishes policing by, through, beyond, below and above the state. Yet, despite such novel terms and categories, academic debate enduringly sustains the conventional public/private divide. Therefore, it is essential to formulate a sound theory about this dichotomy applied to policing.

In this regard, noteworthy contributions to the conceptualization of the public and private spheres have been made by the philosophers Weintraub (1997) and Geuss (2001), who both posited that public and private are not purely opposed to each other but rather dissolve into a number of very distinctive connotations. For example, according to Geuss (2001: 6), 'there is no single clear-cut distinction between public and private but rather a series of overlapping contrasts, and [thus] the distinction between the public and the private should not be taken to have the significance often attributed to it'. It is therefore valuable to reflect on *which* practically significant public/private divide is suitable for clarifying the observed changes in policing.

### 2.2.1 Disentangling the public and the private

A commonplace interpretation of public as contrasted to private is the liberal-economic division between states and markets. Yet the demarcation of each sector does not fully resolve the public/private dichotomy, especially because the boundaries dividing governmental and nongovernmental provisions of services and products are gradually blurring. Thus, Dijkstra and Van der Meer (2003: 90) pointed to

> widespread acceptance of public and private osmosis in public administration and management textbooks, indicating that there is a tendency to integrate private enterprises in the production of collective goods, whereas government agencies are stimulated to pursue business-like strategies. A multitude of organizations, accordingly, have an amalgam character, mixing degrees of 'publicness' and 'privateness'.

With this in mind, the authors disentangled the fluid public/private frontiers using different views of organizational features. First, they asked whether actors are considered *equal* to institutions (private) or whether there are organizations with *overruling powers* to protect collective welfare (public). Second, they examined the organizations' legal *status* – whether entities are created voluntarily (private) or on the basis of constitutional acts (public). Third, as regards public and private property relations involved in *organizational ownership*, they queried whether organizations are owned and controlled by societal or market parties (private) or are part of public administration (public). And finally, they also examined the differences in market mechanisms and allocated budgets; most especially, whether an organization generates income (or *funding*) from selling its goods (private) or from receiving government budget (public).

## 2.2.2 Classifying Dutch policing

Combining the public/private angles outlined above with police(like) agencies produces a useful classification of the contemporary policing landscape in the Netherlands.[6] As Table 2.1 illustrates, regular police forces, military police forces and specialized regulatory and investigatory bodies (or watchdogs like the Labor Inspectorate) are situated at the public extreme of the spectrum;[7] city wardens, who serve as extra eyes and ears for the police, are located somewhere in the middle; and paid security guards and voluntary neighborhood watches lie at the other, most private, end of the continuum. Yet, although civil watches fit the same profile as security guards, these latter differ radically in the sense that 'they must *sell security*' (Rigakos, 2002: 13). That is, contrary to unpaid forms

---

[6]     See Huberts and Van Steden (2005) and Van Steden and Huberts (2006) for an empirical overview of Dutch policing.

[7]     Private sector sponsorship of state-organized policing challenges the full publicness of police operations (Bryett, 1996; Grabosky, 2007). Chapter 10 offers an illustration of a private organization purchasing public police services in the Netherlands.

of private policing, paid private security employees undertake their work for profit (South, 1988).

**Table 2.1: Classifying Dutch policing**

| Category | Powers | Status | Ownership | Funding |
|----------|--------|--------|-----------|---------|
| Regular police | Pu | Pu | Pu | Pu |
| Military police | Pu | Pu | Pu | Pu |
| Regulatory and investigatory bodies | Pu | Pu | Pu | Pu |
| City wardens | Pr | Pu | Pu | Pu |
| Neighborhood watches | Pr | Pr | Pr | Pu/Pr |
| Private security companies | Pr | Pr | Pr | Pu/Pr |

### 2.2.3 A definition of private security

In specifically defining private security and more generally delineating private policing, Shearing and Stenning (1981: 196) established two criteria: guards are '(a) privately employed and (b) employed in jobs whose principal component is some security function'. Yet this definition is not watertight, primarily because security guards, in practice, are not unquestionably publicly or privately employed. Rather, security companies execute duties not only for commercial customers but also for governments, universities and other (quasi-)public institutions. Recognizing this problem, Sarre and Prenzler (2005: 4) redefined private security personnel as

> those persons who are employed or sponsored by a commercial enterprise on a contract or 'in-house' basis, using public or private funds, to engage in tasks (other than vigilante-style action)[8] where the principal component is a security or regulatory function.

This broader definition allows for a marketized workforce carrying out a range of legal duties for public (state) and private (nonstate) clients.

Somewhat earlier, Miccuci (1998) had described three competing, ideal types of security occupations in the industry; namely, crime-fighters, guards and bureaucratic 'cops'. The first two are frontline officers oriented either toward crime control and order maintenance or service and loss prevention. The third

---

[8]    Private security can, in a way, be offered through assurances or guarantees outside the legal ambit of the state, raising images of voluntary but organized and watchful citizens (Johnston, 1996b) or hard-line security firms (Sharp and Wilson, 2000), who prevent crime in neighborhoods under threat of violence. These types of extrajudicial activities are excluded from the definition used here.

type, bureaucratic 'cops', occupies higher administrative ranks and exerts influence on recruitment, training and policies. Whereas this typology is not entirely inaccurate, care must be taken not to frame Dutch private security in police language (e.g., 'crime fighters' and 'cops'); especially, as paid security workers also take on activities like inspecting buildings, closing windows and locking doors that the police have never done and will never do. Moreover, as Stenning (2000) argued, the powers of private security personnel and public police officers are not analogous. This is not to deny that security guards certainly have greater symbolic powers than ordinary citizens – for example, they wear a uniform, are affiliated with a particular organization, have the right to deny access and are trained to (forcefully) eject people from the property.[9] However, they indisputably lack the statutory authority of police officers. As Stenning (2000: 331) put it:

> By comparison to that of the public police officer, the 'tool-boxes' of private police officers[10] typically look very different. […] [T]he private 'tool-box' typically contains many fewer formal legal powers of the kind associated with the public police. Unless they are 'deputized' (to use the American term) or granted some limited official status (e.g. as a 'special constable'), private police officers usually have none of the special statutory powers enjoyed by their public counterparts, although of course they do have access to the same legal powers (e.g. to make a citizen's arrest in limited circumstances) as other private citizens enjoy.

It is thus paramount to recognize that differences between public and private policing operatives are not always as ambiguous as sometimes assumed. Yet referring to public *versus* private policing is becoming increasingly difficult. For example, a Dutch phenomenon is the introduction of privately delivered, but publicly employed (sworn-in) special constables (*Buitengewoon Opsporingsambtenaren*) working for regulatory and investigatory agencies. These form a corps of parking wardens, environmental inspectors and other supervisors with limited powers that constitute an unique crossbreed of state and market institutions.

## 2.3 Understanding public and private policing
Having defined the essence of private policing, it now becomes necessary to theoretically specify what binds and divides the market and government sectors.

---

[9]    For empirical research, see Mopas and Stenning (2001) and Button (2007).

[10]   The term 'private *security* officer' is preferable to Stenning's 'private *police* officer' because the former conveys a clear conceptual basis for understanding the differences between the police and the security industry.

Wright (2002: 44) distinguished four interlocking modes of police practice – peacekeeping, crime investigation, risk management and community justice – which are discussed below.

The first mode, *peacekeeping*, involves policing as social order provision and alludes to ways of public order maintenance. From this perspective, policing in local contexts primarily resembles the provision of security. Nonetheless, it is imperative to realize that *who* takes responsibility for peacekeeping and, closely related, order maintenance, *ipso facto* sets out *what* the precise objectives of security arrangements are. As Cain (1979) pointed out, the type of class, group or institution that sustains police (no longer 'the police') determines the type of security provided. However, a frequently raised objection to making 'policing' equivalent to 'security' provision is the vagueness of both concepts. That is, researchers are severely hampered by the question of what precisely constitutes security.[11] Therefore, Shearing (1992: 399) delineated security as the *absence* of human violence in all its cruel forms,[12] implying that policing is linked to long-lasting assurances *against* damages and losses incurred by (existential) threats both current and future.

Van Zuijlen (2004) also explored the connotations of security (Latin: *securitas*) but from another perspective. Although *securitas* can be comprehended *negatively* as defending a community against threats and dangers, on the other hand, being connotatively linked to the contiguous concept of 'safety', as well as aspects of 'health', 'stability', 'togetherness' and 'social welfare', it also involves *positive* interpretations related to citizens' happiness and prosperity. Thus, when associated with personal well-being and social relations, security issues can have a wider, and much more constructive, impact on society than often thought. Understood as such, security does not simply reside in the installation of alarms, locks, fences and gates to reduce risk and increase control but has a stark symbolic meaning that addresses the emotional human needs of belonging and flourishing (Loader and Mulcahy, 2003). Accordingly, a convenient theoretical distinction can be drawn between paid security personnel and police officers – even though security guards espouse police-like patrol strategies, their approach is arguably much more oriented toward the protection of individual goals (exclusionary or negative security) than is that of the police, who serve a more or less unequivocal collective social interest (inclusionary or positive security). As a result, the role of security guards can be interpreted as *privately* rather than *publicly* oriented policing.

---

[11]   Shearing (1992), Manunta (1999), Zedner (2003a), Johnston and Shearing (2003) and Wood and Shearing (2007).

[12]   Manunta (1999: 58) formally defined security as 'a function of the presence and interaction of Asset (A), Protector (P) and Threat (T) in a given Situation (Si)' [S = f (A, P, T) Si]. The absence of A, P or T voids security of its significance'.

The second mode of policing, which is interconnected with peacekeeping, is the practice of *detecting* and *investigating crime*, but again, the motives for and methods of crime investigation vary widely between the private security industry and the police. Whereas police officers ideally arrest offenders and bring them to court, their commercial counterparts (e.g., not only private security guards but also private investigators, store detectives and forensic accountants)[13] undertake work on behalf of clients. These clients are mostly business executives who prefer internal problem-solving to invoking the police because disclosure of (white-collar) crimes can result in damage to the corporate image and stock values. Moreover, corporations, being most concerned with issues of confidentiality, flexibility, recovering losses, minimizing future risks and administering informal disciplinary punishments rather than bringing criminal charges through trials, may have goals other than the criminal justice system. Hence, systems of private justice (Shearing and Stenning, 1983b) and commercial justice (Johnston, 1992b) have become retributive alternatives that partially supplement the public court process.

In addition, as a third mode, policing is linked with *risk management*. For example, Ericson and Haggerty (1997: 19–38) suggested that police officers are 'knowledge workers' or 'information brokers' who serve (non)state institutions through their communication systems. Thus, these authors paid special attention to computer technology and the use of (digital) databases to store information on incidents and accidents. This information is (within the standards set by privacy laws) regularly handed to external agencies, which demand the knowledge for their own risk management activities. As a result, police officers frequently cooperate with guards, detectives, insurers and other involved security operatives. Such cooperation between this multiplicity of agents may lead to a strengthening and convergence of working styles that lifts individuals out of their anonymity and subjects them to meticulous observation and regulation. Conceived thus, managing risk becomes more about prevention than cure, which has stimulated new penology techniques like increased reliance on surveillance, control and imprisonment to anticipate potentially dangerous groups and events (Feeley and Simon, 1992). Even the traditional public police function is seemingly moving toward these preventative philosophies (Johnston, 1997), although differences between the public and private sectors remain. That is, the police still tend to be universally engaged in *crime* prevention, whereas private security firms usually play a dominant role in *loss* prevention by offering their clientele tailor-made services and products (Shearing and Stenning, 1981).

Finally, as a fourth mode, policing can be viewed as *community justice*, an approach that refers to the uniting of citizens and the judicial apparatus to

---

[13]     Gill and Hart (1997a,b), Hayes (2000), Levi (2002) King and Prenzler (2003), Williams (2005) and Schneider (2006).

make neighborhoods safer. Here, justice mobilizes the community as a local partner in crime prevention and invokes restorative procedures of arbitration and reparation. Thus, victims and offenders are persuaded to mediate and perhaps forgive rather than seeking payback and sentencing. Such peacemaking networks are currently in vogue among public police agencies as tools in conflict resolution and for building hope and confidence in the community (Braithwaite, 2006). However, in the contemporary context of privatized neighborhood patrols,[14] it is debatable whether citizens and their communities will adopt such ethical responsibility. Rather, communities, especially those with strong ties, are built of insiders and thus, *inter alia*, forestall the presence of outsiders (Crawford, 1999, 2006a). This constraint is explicated in control strategies developed to ensure good and avert ill for autonomous, self-governing locales and localities (Rose, 1996). Put differently, rather than bringing people closer together, security guards' principal commission is to remove unwanted (groups of) people from publicly accessible space (Crawford and Lister, 2006). That is, they have an essentially client-centered mandate stemming from *instrumental* rather than *moral* intentions.

### 2.4 Conclusion

This chapter has demonstrated that policing is a broad concept encompassing far more than the familiar blue-uniformed police forces. Specifically, it has defined *policing* as a regulatory function whose central purpose is upholding generally accepted norms and rules and protecting the security of all individuals in a social system. Moreover, this function is vested with the authority to take coercive measures against people and property if needed. Additionally, the discussion has delineated *private policing* as the employment or sponsorship by commercial enterprise – on a contract or 'in-house' basis, using public or private funds – of those engaged in tasks (other than vigilante-style action) whose principal component is a security or regulatory function. Besides providing these clear definitions, it has identified four *modes of policing practice*: peacekeeping, crime investigation, risk management and community justice. Exercised through private (mostly commercial) policing forms, these modes tend to generate priorities that favor clients' interests rather than the interests of society as a whole.

---

[14]     Walsh and Donovan (1989), McManus (1995), Noaks (2000) and Poulin and Nemeth (2005).

# 3    Widening Networks: Security Governance

Shifts in policing have been recognized worldwide, even to the point that the state's tendency to lose its previously taken-for-granted dominance over public order maintenance has become 'conventional wisdom' (Marenin, 2005: 101). Indeed, security governance may have become a postmodern pastiche (De Lint, 1999) carried out by a mixture of professionals, including private security companies. And indeed, the profusion of authorities that now create arrangements for directing economic activity, social life and individual conduct outside the limits of national and local government tends to undercut conventional accounts of state-centered power (Rose and Miller, 1992).

As a result, more often than not, scholars commenting on such developments have expressed deep suspicion about the bastions of state power that deliver regulation and security. Specifically, they have construed the state, especially the ways that public police institutions impinge upon citizens' lives, as a repressive defense of the dominant interests and values of society's ruling classes, which discriminates against, for example, ethnic and gender minorities and delivers qualitatively poor, if not unjustified, services to its subordinates. From this perspective, the state is at best a regrettable necessity for safeguarding public peace and at worst an illegitimate aggressor against inalienable individual freedoms. As Loader and Walker (2006: 167) remarked,

> [s]cratch below the surface of many a text in policing and security studies and one tends to encounter the signs of more or less powerfully felt skepticism towards the state. [...] Much less it is assumed that the state may play a positive role in producing the forms of trust and abstract solidarity between strangers that are a prerequisite of secure, democratic and political communities.

To address the nature of security governance, this chapter illustrates three theoretical approaches – nodal governance, the culture of control and the inverted safety paradigm – on the future of policing. Specifically, through a 'friendly dialogue' (Wood and Dupont, 2006: 1) with state-skeptical theorists, it outlines how to fruitfully situate private security guards within the mixed economy of visible patrolling while esteeming security as a collective good (Loader and Walker, 2001) and accepting the notion of a virtuous state (Loader and Walker, 2006) as preconditions for reconstituting affirmative connections between policing, the state and local communities. The discussion further explores how public police constables and private security guards operate together, an issue of particular importance in academic disputes about policing bodies and agencies (Fleming and Wood, 2007). Key elements within much related discourse are the possible working relations between state and nonstate beat officers and the consequences of these ties for the cooperative endeavors of local security networks.

### 3.1 Nodal governance
Public policing has come under pressure around the globe because of the plurality of private (civil and commercial) agents and agencies entering society. One of the most powerful viewpoints in this lively debate claims a gradual erosion, or 'hollowing out' (Rhodes, 1994), of public police authorities' hegemonic presence that may pose serious challenges to the condition of the police (McLaughlin and Murji, 1999) and security governance (Johnston and Shearing, 2003). According to Reiner (1992: 779),

> [t]he rise of *the* police – a single professional organization for handling the policing function of regulation and surveillance, with the state's monopoly of force as its ultimate resource – was itself a paradigm of the modern. [...] The changes in social structure and culture, which have been labeled postmodernization, render this conception of policing increasingly anachronistic.

Other authors have extended Reiner's argument to the limit by forecasting deep-seated transformations in policing. Perhaps the most outspoken, Bayley and Shearing (1996: 585), argued that democratic countries

> have reached a watershed in the evolutions of their systems of crime control and law enforcement. Future generations will look back on our era as a time when one system of policing ended and another took its place.

These words imply a seismic upheaval of currently uncontrollable magnitude in which government has lost its *entire* policing monopoly:

> Policing has become a responsibility explicitly shared between governments and its citizens, sometimes mediated through commercial markets, sometimes arising spontaneously. Policing has become pluralized. Police are no longer the primary crime-deterrent presence in society; they have been supplanted by more numerous private providers of security. (Bayley and Shearing, 1996: 588)

This conclusion links with wider debates about trends in policing. For example, scholars have presented evidence for transnational pressures that change policing organization as intensified global relations cause governments to lose hegemony over their territorial basis to (commercial) policing institutions operating within and across national borders.[1] Central to other scholarship on neoliberal ideology (O'Malley, 1997), post-Keynesian states (O'Malley and Palmer, 1996), new regulatory states (Braithwaite, 2000) and commodified policing (Loader, 1999) is the implementation within public police organizations of business-like management techniques, including the creation of public-private partnerships for outsourcing tasks and downsizing government. In addition, authors have linked increased reliance on private security to fashions in information technology (Marx, 2005) and a move toward information-intensive preventative policing strategies (Ericson and Haggerty, 1997). Thus, police forces have stripped themselves of the blue (Den Boer, 2004) as they are increasingly sharing their duties with a range of specialist agencies outside state parameters.

In a far more radical argument, however, Bayley and Shearing (1996, 2001) claimed that the proliferation of nonstate security services is not only confined to a mounting number of providers but also to auspices that control their own policing. This observation is significantly reflected in the growing importance of private governments (Macaulay, 1986) capable of determining the very definition of order to be upheld (Shearing, 1996, 2006). Such a development suggests a pluralization or mulilateralization process that dramatically alters the privileged status of regular police forces; for example, owners of mass private properties like shopping malls, leisure parks and sports stadiums would actively start to govern and regulate themselves (Shearing and Stenning, 1981, 1983).

Not surprisingly from the above perspective, transformation theorists give no priority to dominant auspices and/or security providers. Although they do not believe that public police forces collapse entirely, they see no reason to assume *a priori* that these forces should take on the primary social responsibility. Consequently, Shearing (2001, 2005) and others (e.g., Johnston, 2006) have introduced a new morphology of security governance that stresses the emergence of polycentric or nodal networks (Johnston and Shearing, 2003) of security arrangements that may be public, private or amorphous. Within these networks, policing is neither unquestionably state led, nor is the state exclusively preoccupied with crime fighting and reactive law enforcement. Rather, it focuses also on preventative strategies while allowing private

---

[1]     Johnston (2000b, 2006), Sheptycki (2002), Walker (2003) and Marenin (2005).

organizations to occupy an increasingly dominant share in carrying out duties that were once the police's eminent domain.

Shearing and his colleagues expressed little regret over this tendency toward policing diversification.[2] Instead, while acknowledging and criticizing the unfettered expansion of private governance in favor of privileged (corporate) auspices, they suggested that nodal policing conceptions should facilitate the interests and abilities of less advantaged groups (Shearing and Wood, 2003). From this viewpoint, state-led security provision is too ill-equipped to endorse such ideals because police agencies are likely to behave bureaucratically, inefficiently and even oppressively. Thus, communities seem better off with locally designed and organized interventions as a means to promote accountable and democratic policing.

### 3.2 The formalization of social control

Bayley and Shearing's (1996) transformation thesis has faced sharp opposition from their fellow police scholars. For example, from a historical perspective, Jones and Newburn (2002) pronounced it problematic to appraise the contemporary upheavals in security governance as a fundamentally disintegrating (i.e., postmodern) break with the past. Whereas they recognized the changes in criminal justice systems, they rejected provocative declarations of imploding public policing. Above all, they argued that the belief in a public monopoly over law and order and crime control is fictional and police have never been able to give citizens complete assurances against disorder. As Bayley (1994: 3) bluntly declared, 'the police do not prevent crime. [...] This is a myth'. In reality, police officers have always depended heavily on warning signals from and the preventive initiatives of citizens and organizations.

Moreover, according to historical research, the private security industry has been operating on a less visible and sizable scale for over a hundred years. As early as the nineteenth century, large corporations often administered formal social control over their workers by employing in-house security staff. Other early antecedents of contemporary crime control include thief-takers, prosecution associations and communal self-help (Zedner, 2006a). Thus, privatization, in broader terms pluralization, processes are not as novel as they may seem: plural policing 'has been with us for some time' (Jones, 2005: 5).

Yet in what direction is today's policing landscape evolving? According to Jones and Newburn (2002: 139), the growth of paid private security (and other nonstate policing forms), rather than representing the inevitable fragmentation of state institutions, reflects 'a general trend towards the formalization of social control'. These authors argued persuasively that the

---

[2]        Johnston and Shearing (2003) and Wood and Shearing (2007).

decline of eyes and ears 'on the street' relates strongly to the upsurge of (commercial) functionaries whose social control activities are a principal defining characteristic of their occupation. Thus, caretakers, park keepers, milk deliverers, bus conductors and railway masters have quietly been replaced by security guards, citizen patrols, risk managers and the like. At the root of this development lies a neoliberal policy of economizing on public expenditures.

### 3.3 The culture of control

Garland (2001) recorded a similar if somewhat ambivalent change, pointing out that over the past 25 years, as a result of a 'responsibilization policy' that encourages citizens and organizations to start their own anticrime measures, an entire preventative community infrastructure has grown up *in addition to* police and criminal justice services:

> This new sector occupies an intermediate, borderline, position poised between the state and civil society, connecting the criminal justice agencies with the activities of citizens, communities and corporations. And while its budgets, staff lists, and organizations are relatively small (particularly compared to overall police or prison expenditure) the development of this new infrastructure significantly extends the field of 'formal' crime control and its potential for organized action. (Garland, 2001: 170)

Yet, paradoxically, perhaps even schizoidly, simultaneous with such responsibilization strategies, the government has also clung to a repressive mode of punishment and harsh sentencing. In other words, its overall political orientation has been toward minimizing criminal opportunities, reducing harm and managing risk in conjunction with law enforcement, retaliation and long-term sentencing. Whereas Garland did not specifically explore the nature of the public-private entanglement, he did insist that the state's criminal justice apparatus is unlikely to deteriorate within the foreseeable future. On the contrary, he pointed to a fairly sinister 'culture of control' of interrelated public and private responses to crime 'with immediate consequences for those caught up in its repressive demands, and more diffuse, corrosive effects for the rest of us' (Garland, 2001: 194).

### 3.4 Trapped in downward circles?

To date, it has been very tempting in the theoretical debate to describe today's fearful society in cynical terms, painting security as axiomatic and policing as ambient. Indeed, Loader (2006: 216) distinguished two insecurity-sustaining 'vicious circles', one *fragmented* and the other *authoritarian*. The first spiral, which coincides with the pluralization hypothesis, occurs when people or groups that feel insufficiently protected by the state turn to commercial firms and communal initiatives for security. These citizens fortify themselves in closed and heavily protected enclaves or make use of local knowledge and the capacities of indigenous communities to realize their collectively shared security interests. This striving for autonomous policing may appear harmless on the surface, but, at a certain stage, it can undermine political communities that foster trust and solidarity. 'Society fractures', Loader (2006: 217) gloomily concluded, 'into a world of markets and tribes'.

The second spiral, which coincides with the culture of control hypothesis, feeds itself with more police, more guards, stiffer controls, harsher penalties, and so on. Moreover, 'if such actions are perceived to have failed, or are ideologically depicted in these terms, [...] this overwhelmingly prompts calls for still "tougher" measures – only this time with a heavier dosage' (Loader, 2006: 216). In other words, there is no doubt that criminal law policy, crime control and expulsion potentially represent an endless ratcheting up of precautions having serious ramifications for personal privacy and civil liberty.

Nonetheless, to escape such a dystopian future, it must be recognized both empirically and normatively that such negative interpretations are one sided and unidimensional. In reality, the search for security in modern times has become not only a threatening but a *motivational* theme by which public authorities perpetuate hierarchy, command and interventionism.[3] Therefore, too much weight should not be given to the impacts of commercial and civil security provision on the pivotal position of government institutions. Rather, there is more truth in the observation that the role of the state is *shifting* not *shrinking*. Thus, government reshuffling and outsourcing tasks does not necessarily render their traditional intervention powers obsolete.[4]

### 3.5 The inverted safety paradigm
Taking the above criticisms seriously, Boutellier (2004, 2005) adopted a third stance in the governance debate. Rejecting the 'seismic' theory and perspective, he argued that in lieu of an alternative (postmodern) security paradigm, an *inverted* paradigm has developed. In contrast to the classical assumption of solid civil institutions capable of socialization, social control and self-regulation in which the police and judicial system barely need to intervene and coercive measures need only be used as a *last* resort against deviants, this alternative paradigm sees disciplinary intervention not so much as an end point but as a *starting point* for social and normative order. As Boutellier (2004: 96) also

---

[3]    For further debate, see Loader and Walker (2001, 2006), Boutellier (2005) and Crawford (2006b).
[4]    Kooiman (2003: 3), Crawford (2006b: 471) and Jones (2007: 843–844).

argued, 'the purpose of criminal justice is not to confirm an existing communality but to construct a community that does not yet exist or never has or will. [...] [In so doing], criminal justice operates from the perspective of expedience. It intervenes at the places where and the moments when the norm most emphatically needs to be set'.

Within this new paradigm, security guards are part of extended police families[5] of sworn police officers and '(not-too-distant) cousins' like city wardens and neighborhood watches, as well as other *non*-policing associations like social work and housing.[6] The model thus assumes that regular police forces, while they recognize declining autonomy and the increasing competence of nonstate security providers, continue to be the chief producers, or at least facilitators, of public order. Moreover, despite the mounting visibility of private security services, the government has not even been transformed let alone abolished. On the contrary, the scale of government's crime control apparatus has been greatly expanded, with the police and judicial system operating in a defensive mode. Nonetheless, this development is not automatically restricted to punitive state power and watchful private eyes. As already indicated, criminal law policy has also opened up to sectors beyond the conventional ambit of police(-like) forces. In Boutellier's (2001: 373) words,

> [t]he social sector – education, social services, youth care, welfare work – increasingly realizes that the demand for safety is also relevant to their own type of work. In addition, the police and judicial authorities increasingly define themselves in terms of social objectives that are broader than maintaining public order and enforcing the criminal law. Recently, the cooperation between 'both worlds' has been intensified, e.g. by exchanging cases between police, judicial authorities and youth care.

As a result of this cooperation, collaboration between civil society and the state has been gradually strengthened, which may have ramifications for citizen freedom. Nonetheless, according to Loader and Walker (2006), if *democratically anchored*, mixed security provision can also have great advantages, which casts doubt on the idea that nodal governance offers the best hope for security organization. In their view, as a baseline, state presence is of fundamental importance to ensuring that citizens and communities do not act inconsistently with the irreducible *social* and *constitutive* dimensions of security and policing (Loader and Walker, 2001: 26). That is, only the state can help construct and sustain local conditions for a well-ordered society and shared

---

5       Johnston (2003) and Crawford and Lister (2004b).
6       Terpstra and Kouwenhoven (2004) and Terpstra (2005).

feelings of 'we'. Thus, rather than further dissolve sovereignty, public police and justice authorities should remain vital background players within networked governance regimes to advance beneficial outcomes for society as a whole.

To illustrate an ideal scenario, Boutellier (2005: 22–24) used the metaphor of a soccer team working outward in concentric defense lines (see Figure 3.1). The public prosecutor, like a goal keeper, stands between his goal post receiving the many balls (i.e., criminal cases) directed toward him (the fourth line). He therefore tries to coach a defense line of risk-managing institutions (the third line) such as police forces, private security companies and neighborhood watches in an attempt to reduce dangers and vulnerabilities. These institutions fulfill a crucial role in stopping deviant and criminal behavior before a forceful criminal law reaction becomes necessary. At the same time, risk-managing institutions are surrounded by normative institutions (the second line) like schools, welfare services, housing associations and churches. These institutions have a pedagogic function in guiding and supporting moral consciousness among citizens. Thus, their main tasks are to instill ethics, correct deviant behavior and settle conflicts. Finally, the forefront players are ordinary citizens and their social bonds (the first line), and it is at this crossroads of social activities that the ball must really 'be rolling'. Here, individuals find bonds of trust, friendship, fraternity and reciprocity that ideally add up to safe and secure living spaces.

**Figure 3.1: The inverted safety paradigm** (source: Boutellier, 2005)

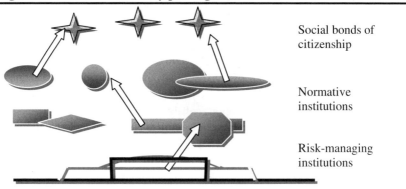

Social bonds of citizenship

Normative institutions

Risk-managing institutions

The above model implies that society should be responsible for security matters but the government should offer backup when required. Specifically, police officers should adopt a 'libero position' (Boutellier, 2005: 27) in which they *support* organizations and citizens with preventive practices and constraint interference, sometimes making use of their authority to firmly restore public order. Nonetheless, security is more than an end in itself. It is a prerequisite for meeting the challenge of rediscovering the multiple normative functions performed by institutions that teach people about right and wrong and create some sense of belonging. According to this perspective, the search for safety and security comes with a *moral appeal* because the concepts have a wider connotation than the merely negative one of shielding people against risks and dangers (Boutellier, 2005). Safety and security can also provide reassurance in the positive sense of a virtuous society, one of internalized democratic morals, loyalty and kinship. Thus, the desire for shelter and protection does not have to assume a rigid culture of control that enlivens the rationale and actions of the police, judiciary and affiliated private actors. Rather, it might be interpreted as a hopeful sign of a revitalizing civil society.

### 3.6 Relationships within extended police families
Following from the ideas discussed above, researchers have been interested in understanding how public and private policing fit together.[7] Most particularly, the frequent inconsistency of the goals, mentalities, instruments, outlooks and interests of the mixed network raises the question of whether there is harmony or competition among the partners involved. To capture what happens between public and private operatives, Sarre and Prenzler (2005) theorized on 'ideal-type' organizational models. Specifically, they offered the following descriptive hypotheses:

1. Classical divisions between public and private policing related to their responsibilities for protecting *property* remain. As before, the police patrol roads, streets, footpaths, squares and other public spaces, whereas private security operates in shopping centers, holiday resorts, industrial complexes and the like.
2. The classical *division of labor* between the police and private security is left untouched. Like the previous model, there is nothing new about the present policing order. Private security contributes to order maintenance through its fixation on loss prevention, while the police have more outspoken crime fighting purposes.
3. Private security and the police have quite similar capacities in their responses to crime. There is thus *strong rivalry* for market shares.
4. Private security and police forces cooperate in society, but the police take precedence. From this standpoint, private security is a *supplementary* partner of the police.

---

[7]    Shearing (1992: 403–426), Johnston (1998: 209–212) and Crawford (2003a: 156–161).

5. The public and the private sector are separate worlds, but they work together in a crisis situation. Based on this assumption, public-private partnerships are formed on an *ad-hoc basis* as needed.

6. Public-private partnerships *combine* their strengths. The two sectors have corresponding interests and develop symbiotic links at executive and operational levels to maximize their collaborative efforts.

7. Public-private partnerships are *unholy alliances*. Contrary to the previous models, partnerships between police forces and private security teams are 'a bridge too far'. It is a pathological development, because, when working too closely together, both sectors face temptation to illegal practices and misuses of power. (Adapted from Sarre and Prenzler, 2005: 197–198)

Some aspects of these hypotheses can be linked to empirical findings, but none fully portrays the diversity and complexity of (present and future) intersectoral relationships. Hypotheses 1 and 2 may even be redundant, because, as Johnston and Shearing (2003) indicated, the organizational and operational principles of some private security firms are barely distinguishable from the public police and vice versa. A similar position is taken by the Law Commission of Canada (2002: 15):

> Complex *networks* of policing that reflect a mix of public and private security providers are emerging. In many urban areas, we are witnessing not simply two-tiered policing but multi-level policing: the public police contract out patrol services to private security firms; in some instances, private security firms help fund public police investigations: private police resolve complaints that were once within the exclusive domain of the public police; public police and private security firms cooperate in investigations; and private organizations hire public police to provide security for private functions.

According to this view, it is progressively more difficult to draw a clear line between public and private policing responsibility. That is, rather than establishing a pragmatic 'cross-fertilization' between working practices, strategies and styles, public and private agencies increasingly *merge* into symbiotic entities (hypothesis 6).

Such far-reaching public/private associations may also develop in the Netherlands. For example, Hoogenboom (1991a: 24), observing the formation of what he termed a 'policing complex', predicted that the private security industry will progressively intermingle with the public crime control apparatus. His prediction was inspired by the government's policy-wish to solve the capacity restrictions of the police force and criminal justice system by giving more space to private policing bodies. To this end, policymakers ventilate their own wishes to reorganize the police within clear limits and tighten relations with inspectorates, private security firms and detective agencies whose information resources may contain valuable evidence. The resulting (informal) integration of 'different departments, policies, bureaupolitics and commercial interests' (Hoogenboom, 1991a: 25), is worrisome because it potentially makes established democratic mechanisms of accountability obsolete (hypothesis 7). Thus, citizens should not be blind to the dangers of elusive 'grey policing' networks.

Nonetheless, it is uncertain whether 'extended police families' are really so incestuous. Despite overlapping concerns, the *absence* of conformity between public and private interests and goals suggests the doubtfulness of 'a "Big Brother" society, to the extent that Orwell's literary metaphor implies an overarching police structure with central coordination' (Joh, 2004: 90). For example, in a study of British neighborhoods, Crawford et al. (2005) found that security and police come close together but do not intermingle. Rather, whereas the government and commercial sector have primarily converging agendas on better *cooperation*, the police hold the dominant steering position (hypothesis 4). Moreover, ethnographic research by Noaks (2000), also on a British residential area, emphasized quite substantial *competition* (hypothesis 3) between police patrols and private security patrols. While residents ascribed a positive value to private schemes, the police were reluctant to collaborate with commercial guards. Such reluctance was partly justified by the dubious image of some security services, but the police also had cause for concern in terms of comparative satisfaction levels with the private sector. Other research on policing in the London Borough of Wandsworth (Jones and Newburn, 1998) confirmed these findings or indicated situations in which police officers and private security guards peacefully *coexisted* while having little contact with each other. That is, police officers and private security guards operated largely in separate spheres, only having contact in case of an incident (hypothesis 5).

The precise distribution of public and private responsibilities within local security networks is important to this study because it should throw light on security guards' relationships with the police. Therefore, the local case studies will include brief comments on the working of multiagency partnerships in the Netherlands.

## 3.7 Conclusion

The pluralization, and correspondingly, the privatization, of policing are major topics in academic debate. Authors have reflected especially on the possible implications of increased private security for the sovereignty of state police forces. Some writers have even heralded it dramatically as the end of public policing as we know it (McLaughlin and Murji, 1999), while others have stressed that, far from withdrawal or implosion, the state 'is engaged in ambitious projects of social engineering' (Crawford, 2006b: 449) that include strengthened relations between nonstate security agencies, police forces, judicial authorities and the social sector. Nonetheless, even though public-private policing arrangements loom large in society, it seems exaggerated to proclaim a culture of control, because, together with an expanding 'safety state' that relies on criminal law approaches, a moral élan of community safety has developed. As a result, social policy and criminal justice are gradually converging, which implies that private security companies increasingly work with police forces and public prosecution agencies, as well as with normative institutions (e.g., schools, welfare services, housing corporations), to tackle crime and disorder problems. In this way, they form defense lines around state authorities, uniting penalty and prevention strategies that should not be merely explained in negative terms of power and repression. In a more positive light, the collaboration between different actors also reveals a moralizing trend towards livability, care and alternative (social and pedagogical) routes of correction. Consequently, much discussion focuses on the types of policing relationships within local communities. To date, scholars have identified conflicting, coexistent and cooperative associations, themes touched on in later chapters of this book.

# 4 Theorizing Private Security: The Explanatory Framework

Dutch private security has grown significantly over the past three decades, raising the question of how the industry has become so successful. To answer this question, this chapter presents a review of the literature that theoretically examines possible explanations. The first comprehensive studies on private security in the United States, conducted by the Rand Corporation, suggested that the industry has boomed most particularly because of rising (fear of) crime, business losses, the threat of hijack, violent demonstrations and bombings, advancing surveillance technology, business trends toward purchases of specialized services, insurer demands, general increases in corporate income and disappointment with police productivity (Kakalik and Wildhorn, 1971: 13–15). In addition, the Hallcrest I and II reports published later,[1] claimed that crime and terrorism, whether real or perceived, together with the privatization of law enforcement activities (contracting out and transfer of police tasks) have been directly involved in boosting the security industry.

Other early literature relates the arrival of private security guards to the mushrooming of mass private property – quasi-public spaces like shopping centers, business complexes, holiday resorts, airport terminals and sports stadiums (Shearing and Stenning, 1981, 1983a). This argument claims that private security is principally a result of corporate governance deploying all means necessary to prevent losses. Thus, in reality, it represents an evolution of multifarious corporate and social structures that are likely to take regular police work in their own hands.

Drawing on such theories, researchers in the field – especially, Hoogenboom (1986), Johnston (1996a, 1999b), Jones and Newburn (1998, 2006c), George and Button (2000), Bayley and Shearing (2001), Newburn (2001), Van Dijk and De Waard (2001), Pastor (2003), Prenzler and Sarre (2004), and Lee (2004) – have proposed a wealth of criminological, sociological, political, legal, economic and geographical determinants of private security growth. They can be categorized into six viable explanatory factors: (1) rising crime and related problems, (2) growth of mass private property, (3) economic rationalities, (4) government policy toward private sector participation, (5) an overburdened police force and (6) professionalization of private security. For theoretical clarity, these proposed factors are discussed separately in the following section.

---

[1]     Cunningham and Taylor (1985) and Cunningham et al. (1990).

## 4.1 Rising crime and related problems

Many scholars have coupled the strengthened stature of private security with a universal sensitivity toward lack of safety and insecurity, a sensitivity that private security firms (and also such sectors as the pharmaceutical industry) eagerly play on via advertisements (George and Button, 2000). Indeed, endemic existential *Unsicherheit* (German for 'uncertainty', 'insecurity' and 'unsafeness') can even be considered a common denominator in contemporary society, as risk, fear and precaution define guidelines in the western world (Bauman, 2000). From this perspective, contemporary Westerners live in a culture of fear (Furedi, 2002) that, somewhat incongruously, finds far more to worry about than did their classical predecessors or currently developing countries. This is not to make light of threats, but from a historical and international perspective, those living in the West are actually relatively safe.

Various authors have made thoughtful contributions that advance the understanding of today's pressing anxieties and emotions. For example, Giddens (1990: 7) argued that living in the western world is 'a double-edged phenomenon.' On the one hand, citizens enjoy, to some extent, greater opportunities than ever before to create their own life project with little restriction from the social bonds of tradition, family and religion that shaped public life until the second half of the twentieth century. On the other, society has paid a price through the 'disembedding' of human associations and the altering of trust relations, which has resulted in a heightened sense of unpredictability and vulnerability (Giddens, 1990: 17). Thus, people's general sense of ontological well-being has diminished owing to the increased pace of sociocultural restructuring, in which *(in)security* is frequently used as a 'semantic net' (Boutellier, 2005: 6) to grasp events and commence appropriate action.

Along similar lines, Boutellier (2004: 2) hinted at what he termed 'vital drives' of carefree lightness and carnivalesque thrills within the context of 'an unprecedented and uninhibited sense of freedom'. However, even *positive* forms of intoxicating freedom and vitality have their *negative* counterparts of unforeseen chaos and distress. For example, Van den Brink (2001) pointed to the increased violence among ego-focused youth, Hobbs et al. (2005) alluded to the broad phenomenon of alcohol and drug-soaked partygoers, while Frosdick and Marsh (2005) cited football matches wrecked by hooligans and aggressive affinity groups. Thus, the pursuit for personal safety should be seen as deriving from a culture of creativity, self-realization and hedonism that bumps up against its own restrictions. As Boutellier (2004: 2) noted,

[v]itality and safety are two sides of the same coin: a liberal culture that has elevated self-fulfillment to the true art of living also has to make every effort to stipulate and maintain the limitations of individual freedom. A vital society generates a great need for safety and thus comes up with an undeniable paradox: if liberal freedom is to be unreservedly celebrated, its boundaries need to be set.

This vicious and perverse side of our paradoxical societies can perhaps best be expressed by the influential phrase 'risk society' (*Risikogesellschaft*), one in which many are, as Beck (1992) argued, obsessed with risk avoidance and risk management because incidents and accidents, as well as conflicts and threats, are implicit in the logic of western culture. As a result, such occurrences are by no means seen as unusual calamities but rather as unintended side effects of modernity, which gradually reach a critical mass of societal acceptability. Apart from the physical dangers of explosion, there is a substantial presence of political explosiveness, as an assertive population demands that the risks of victimization be reduced as much as is reasonably practical (preferably zero) and loses faith in a state ostensibly incapable of controlling the destructive potential in a global risk society. This 'legitimacy crisis' of government authorities may well underlie people's search for alternative, often commercial solutions, to ease their fears.

### 4.1.1 Crime and fear
Given the above discussion, it is important to stress that skyrocketed crime rates have specifically triggered peoples' emotions. Admittedly, population growth and improved quality of police recording practices may be biasing this observation, but there is little disagreement about the inexorable explosion of crime-evoked victimization. In this context, Garland (2000: 359) pointed out that

> [f]rom being a problem that mostly affected the poor, crime (and particularly vandalism, theft, burglary and robbery) became a daily consideration for anyone who owned a car, used the subway, left their house unguarded during the day, or walked the city streets at night.

High crime levels thus epitomize only half the problem. The constant *awareness* of criminals (and terrorists) ready to strike seems to be equally, if not more, important as an objective measure. Thus, actual crime is mediated by feelings of unrest and fear, which, in the words of Skolnick and Bayley (1986: 2), 'disrupts patterns of daily life, immures people, especially the elderly in their homes, creates debilitating stress, contributes to the deterioration of neighborhoods, causes economic loss to merchants, and leaves portions of cities abandoned to the very criminals everyone fears'. Nor are the media neutral actors in creating such moral panic over crime. Facing fierce rivalry in a competitive communications market and realizing that scary stories sell, journalists tend to exacerbate and sensationalize threats. This exaggeration in turn cultivates mutual distrust, social unrest and populist calls for a maximum security society (Norris and Armstrong, 1999) that is prison-like in its character. Thus, fear initiates a self-perpetuating process – 'it is', as Jones and Newburn (2006c: 8) commented, 'like scratching an itch that simply gets worse'.

### 4.1.2 Disorder
Such fear goes further than fear of crime (and terrorism) alone. People and organizations are frightened partly because levels of victimization have risen but also because they feel threatened and vulnerable. In this respect, as Pastor (2003: 55-57) suggested, signs of *disorder* in the areas where people work, live and spend their leisure time heightens their sensitivity to danger. In such an environment, it is unpredictable groups (e.g., drug addicts, youth, the mentally ill and panhandlers), and incivilities like street litter, abandoned buildings and graffiti, that scare people off (cf. Wilson and Kelling, 1982). Although not inevitably dangerous, these incivilities foster the *impression* that something nasty can occur and can have serious implications for cities in general and local areas in particular. By word-of-mouth, and united by a fascination with shadowy events, individuals notify each other of occurrences, point at suspicious others, try to organize protection or merely turn their back to so-called troubled urban areas. Hence, even though police officers are the key to restoring public order, citizens and organizations may precipitously fall back on 'cost-effective' paid security personnel to reduce their feelings of uneasiness and minimize the probability of harm.

### 4.2 Growth of mass private property
Rising private security has often been coupled with changes in spatial ordering. That is, modern societies are increasingly formed through spatially separated airport terminals, business parks, shopping centers, entertainment districts and residential areas having heterogeneous security needs. This process interrelates with globalization, individualization and urbanization waves that have profound consequences for society as a whole. For example, even though city life can lead to closer contacts, it also causes isolation, alienation and anonymity because residents feel afloat in a world of strangers (Lofland, 1973) without trustworthy clues and contacts to rely on. Specifically, Jacobs (1962) pointed to the corrosive impact of suburbanization – the separation between work, leisure and residence – which leaves large urban areas deserted at various times of the day.

Additionally, in a much wider sense, Putnam (2000: 19) warned that society's stock of "social capital" – namely 'connections among individuals [...] and the norms of reciprocity and trustworthiness that arise from them' – is in malaise. Yet, to secure themselves, humans seek to reduce the unfriendliness and (perceived) threats of the world they live in. They colonize openly accessible territories and reshape them into defensible spaces (Newman, 1972) designed to improve opportunities for surveillance and control.

### 4.2.1 Mass private property

Shearing and Stenning (1981, 1983a) are leading advocates of a relationship between the upsurge of privatized policing and changes in spatial ordering. These authors, drawing their arguments from Spitzer and Scull (1977), pointed out that early private security initiatives in the United States coincided with nineteenth-century industrialization and the building of company towns, which brought together large workforces under a system of paternalistic, commercially organized control. Although these towns belong to history, Shearing and Stenning extrapolated connections between changes in spatial ordering and paid policing that apply to the modern metropolis. Today's cities, they claimed, are increasingly dominated by mass private property that is *publicly* accessible but *privately* owned and managed. A direct result of this shift in property relations is that policing falls into the hands of private governments (Macaulay, 1986) who control large tracts of space. Such governance overthrows the old Hobessian-Weberian framework in which the public sphere is the sphere of governors and the private sphere is the sphere of the governed (Shearing, 2006: 31). As a result, there is a growing emergence of private, notably corporate, organizations that, in practice, have their own security team working to reduce disorder, crime and economic losses.

### 4.2.2 Communal spaces

Accepting Shearing and Stenning's observations, Kempa et al. (2004) refined the original mass private property thesis proffered in the 1980s by positing that shifts in policing can be tied to physical spaces other than mass private property. They thus introduced the term 'communal spaces' as an umbrella concept for large-scale property supervised by state and/or nonstate agencies. What has actually developed is a continuum of heavily protected spaces that range from 'capsular' residential areas (known as 'gated communities') to 'restrictive' clubs and pubs (Crawford, 2003a: 151–152)[2] that, in contrast to mass private property,

---

[2]     Crawford (2003a) also pointed to the Internet as a digital space regulated by professional police forces and commercial providers in their fight against illegal practices like child pornography.

are only available to members and/or paying visitors. Thus, the quest for private security must be understood beyond shopping malls and business parks.

## 4.3 Economic rationalities

The hypothetical link between economic growth and flourishing private security is not hard to draw. More *wealth* logically creates more criminal opportunities to steal or damage properties and broadens the consciousness of risk. The resulting desire to reduce such risk explains the call for protection, while a general rise in affluence generates additional *income* to pay for it (Kakalik and Wildhorn, 1977: 19). Obviously, urban surroundings like shopping centers, office parks, leisure zones and university campuses are highly vulnerable to crime and disorder: their goods and commodities are within easy reach of many, not always kind-hearted, visitors, some of whom make use of the occasion to steal, damage and sabotage.

The demand for guards, door supervisors (or bouncers), stewards and other paid security personnel is further fueled by the hedonistic velocity of modern-day societies. In a pulsating experience economy in which temptation and seduction are the norm (Pine and Gillmore, 1999), society must shoulder extra responsibility for controlling manifest lawless and undesirable behavior. Moreover, accepting this responsibility represents more than simply reacting to stakeholder requirements (external incentives). Property owners who employ paid watchers at their premises also have their own economic interests of customer care, image and reputation (intrinsic motivation).

### 4.3.1 External incentives

Scholars have identified several external incentives for commercial property owners to rely on security companies. First, *police officers* may withdraw from quasi-public spaces and persuade the business community to let paid security guards execute patrol duties on their property instead (Shearing and Stenning, 1983a: 496–497). In this situation, the buzzwords are 'responsibilization' and 'activation'. In addition, *insurance companies* may significantly influence an entrepreneur's decision on whether or not to use a security branch (George and Button, 2000) by demanding security measures before coverage is issued and offering premium discounts to customers who purchase preventative technologies. Finally, in a North-American context, *lawsuits* have motivated business owners to safeguard their clients, staff and property (Pastor, 2003). Based on the assumption that offenders commit their crimes rationally – a view partly influenced by protection levels in specific locations – courts have accepted the counterintuitive proposition that entrepreneurs who fail to offer adequate safeguards must bear the (material and immaterial) costs of criminal deeds. Concerned with the prospect of being sued, these owners turn to private security companies whose guards and technologies are then deployed to forestall any problems.

### 4.3.2 Intrinsic motivations

Because entrepreneurs want to establish, maintain and sustain good customer relations, internal corporate management strategies are probably no less decisive than external incentives for higher spending on private security guards. An excellent discussion of the reasons is provided in Bryman's (2004) *Disneyization of Society*, in which the author argued that modern societies progressively display features of Disney's Magic Kingdom, characteristics geared towards the ideology of capitalism, commercialization and consumption. This development manifests along four dimensions: theming, hybrid consumption, merchandizing and performative labor. Most interesting, however, one decisive aspect underlies all the principles – the growing importance of surveillance and with it, control. Control, Bryman (2004: 131) noted, *enables* Disneyization 'to operate to its full capacity', a conclusion echoed by Shearing and Stenning (1987b: 317):

> [T]he Disney order is no accidental by-product. Rather, it is a designed-in feature that provides – to the eye that is looking for it, but not to the casual visitor – an exemplar of modern private corporate policing.

For Disneyized sites to run smoothly, they must keep visitors' behavior under soft-handed but strict surveillance through security guards, cameras and park layout. That is, visitors must feel safe so they are inclined to stay for longer and consume more. Evidently, troublemakers do not fit into this picture because, by threatening the 'safety and security [that] are big sellers for a family day out' (Shapland, 1999: 157), they disrupt the peace and harmony essential to high levels of customer satisfaction. Thus, without widespread supervision, control and regulation, the attractiveness of private worlds would soon diminish.

The above analysis of Disneyization emphasizes the significance of policing at mass private property, in which keeping people under surveillance for the purpose of discipline is principally determined by commercial objectives. That is, the main concern is not so much reducing crime and doing justice but *making a profit*. As a result, (quasi-public) spaces are increasingly constructed and managed to 'please the client' and intensify consumption, giving visitors the feeling that they can relax and have fun in spaces within which a 'controlled suspension of constraints' or a 'controlled sense of decontrol' can be 'purchased, experienced and played with' (Hayward, 2004: 191). Because general apprehension about *real* disorder and dangers may disturb commercial objectives, entrepreneurs do everything possible to ensure that thrills are predictable. Indeed, as Bryman (2004: 144) summarized, the risks 'dangled in front of visitors as lures' are still 'safe risks' or 'riskless risks'.

## 4.4 Government policy toward private sector participation

Scholars in criminology have given considerable attention to what they have described as neoliberal policies aimed at the privatization of policing. Such privatization is part of a much broader responsibilization process that activates citizens and organizations to take responsibility for crime prevention and crime control (Garland, 1996). Nonetheless, it should be emphasized that this privatization trend does not equate with a literal selling-off of services as happened to public utilities like electricity, telephone and cable television. On the contrary, so far, there are no signs of a 'free market police' (Rothbard, 1978: 222) that could wipe out even the most humble plea for state intervention. Rather, the focus is on a multiplicity of policies that have encouraged diversification of nonstate policing agents and agencies.

One key recommendation for such government reforms, which are frequently grouped under the rubric 'new public management' (NPM), is to 'steer' rather than to 'row' (Osborne and Gaebler, 1992: 35). Specifically, the government should decide on future polity goals and thereby empower or lead civil society and markets to embrace public goals and interests. At the practical level of policing, NPM strategy implies the stimulation of diverse interest groups to anticipate crime and disorder problems by, for example, employing private security patrols, while, contrary to the invisible government that might be expected, state authorities should increasingly seek a strong presence. In reality, this aim produces a somewhat contradictory situation. That is, the moment that national campaigns induce individuals, communities and organizations to take responsibility for crime prevention, criminal justice authorities impose lower (or even zero) tolerance limits, stricter controls, harsher sanctions and longer imprisonments to restore people's confidence in the government (Garland, 2001). Thus, responsibilization and penalization are closely interrelated.

### 4.4.1 Top-down privatization

As regards neoliberal privatization agendas specifically, governments use assorted tactics to reduce their own span of activities. One strategy is to *offload* ancillary tasks such as responses to (false) intruder alarms, which the police then totally abandon to private security. In a second ploy, privatization connotes the *contracting out* of police duties other than (not so clear-cut) core functions (Van der Vijver et al., 2001), whereby the government retains control over funding and policy. Widely recognized examples include the disposal of custodial and parking attendant services to private security staff for lower wages than those of the average police officer. A third and distinct type of privatization is to introduce *charges* for police assistance (Johnston, 1991). In Britain, this policy pushed soccer clubs to set up internal security organizations by employing guards and stewards for delivering crowd management inside their stadiums. Finally, besides their direct privatization policies, governments have fed the growth of private security through *legislation*. For example, following the terrorist attacks in New York and elsewhere, airports, seaports, public transport infrastructures and office towers were obliged to impose premier security standards, which enabled the security industry to grow.

### 4.4.2 Bottom-up privatization

Accompanying the proceeding top-down policies, reconfiguration of public sector activities has also come from the market and society itself (bottom-up privatization). This dynamic is possible because governments allow leeway for self-activating and self-governing organizations to implement security teams to reduce fears, provide services to the public and counter negative perceptions of certain (downtown) urban zones. The police support this nonconfrontational approach and try to define good working relationships to ensure that paid guards can do their jobs properly.[3]

On their part, the business community strongly affects the incentive for privatization because companies feel they can achieve better advertising and earnings from being acquainted with state police services. For example, powerful security corporations lobby for contracts with state institutions to broaden their commercial undertakings and donate physical resources or training to public authorities (Grabosky, 2007). Indeed Bryett (1996: 23) pointed to a 'corporate impact, whereby sources outside of the public domain channel resources into public police systems' with financial advantage as an obvious starting point.

### 4.5 An overburdened police force

Public authorities have faced tremendous criticism about their productivity. Most particularly – as a result of public savings, bureaucratic inertness, rising public expectations and weakened ties between officers and the communities they work for – they are deemed incapable of offering people sufficient protection and reassurance. These factors may motivate the creation of additional private security forms. Nonetheless, theorists have distinguished between a radical and a liberal-democratic interpretation of developments occurring within policing.

---

[3]    See for example Business Improvement Districts (BIDs) across the United States (Vindevogel, 2005).

### 4.5.1 A limited police budget

One frequently suggested explanation for the expansion of private security is the insufficient budget and capacity of police forces. That is, the massive hiring of private security is reasonably taken to be 'an indication that those who hire such protection feel that public police protection is in some way inadequate' (Becker, 1973: 449). Thus, on the whole, police forces are seen as underfinanced, understaffed and overworked. The clear-cut assumption here is that of a government struggling with permanent fiscal crises arising from accelerating budget deficits (J. O'Conner, 1973). Because of these crises, politicians impose *fiscal constraints* on police forces and depend on the private security industry to fill the gap. According to this viewpoint, restrictions in funding form the basic argument for a weakening in the legitimate position of state constabularies. In other words, the police have become merely a partner in the responsibility for safety and security.

A more sophisticated view of the transferal of police duties from the public to the private sector points to the infeasibility of sustaining far-reaching resource reduction – in reality, police funding is on the rise and continues to grow. Thus, there is more at work than simple financial calculations. Indeed, three lines of reasoning are highly relevant to this argument. First, recent policy shifts towards private security have been connected with system failures. From this perspective, the criminal justice system is excessively *bureaucratic* with respect to coordination and responsiveness. Therefore, the state seeks assistance from, among other supportive organizations, private security companies to fulfill the duties of order maintenance and crime prevention (Crawford, 1999: 65-69).

Second, police forces are overloaded, because *public expectations* about what the police can realistically do have risen enormously. In fact, the issue is not so much whether the government should cut the police force budget but that officers are overwhelmed by requests for protection and assistance in response to security concerns. This mammoth burden that society imposes on the police simply outstrips their capabilities (Crawford, 1999: 69-71). Finally, police officers are judged as *too distant* from the communities they should be engaged in. As a result, both people and organizations work out their own security schemes outside the government apparatus, a development that is further vindicated by offensive stances against police brutality and corruption (Bayley and Shearing, 2001: 22).

### 4.5.2 Two schools of thought

The hypothesis of fiscal constraints has been put forward by two dominant schools of thought – the radical and the liberal democratic – which are based on different interpretations of the role and place of private security in widening policing and security networks.[4] The *radical* approach claims that two-tiered, public *and* private, machineries of social control are gradually but comprehensively forming a dispersed web of discipline that penetrates the inner fibers of human associations. At first glance, the government may appear to be losing terrain to civil society and market actors as private security guards and related occupations seemingly switch places with police officers. However, probing beyond the obvious, paid security services are no substitute for the police. Both public and private sectors interweave into an all-seeing or 'panoptical' network (Foucault, 1977) of conspiratorial coalitions between economical and political entities. The existence of such networks 'suggests a development of selective policing biased in favor of wealth and power' (Jones and Newburn, 1998: 104). That is, instead of the toothless government often proposed, radical commentators have observed an extraordinary unfolding of omnipresent hidden controls. Thus, it is not surprising that they have construed the consolidation of public-private partnerships as an unwanted intrusion into the social fabric.

The *liberal-democratic* school, on the other hand, has a more positive attitude toward public-private partnerships. It proposes that, confronted with high crime figures and a loud cry for reassurance, the government pragmatically welcomes paid security guards as allies in safeguarding society. Following this logic, certain peripheral and noncontroversial policing functions are relinquished to the market sector so that police forces can focus on their priorities. For example, security guards often provide extra surveillance for special events and patrol shopping centers. The main consideration here is the encouragement of public-private partnerships as suitable solutions for overstrained police forces. In contemporary political and economic discourses, the liberal-democratic interpretation is clearly the dominant school of thought on sharing police responsibilities. Nonetheless, radical readings should not be dismissed because they give strong warnings of accountability deficits, and raise important questions on civil liberties, human rights and the possible exclusion of (ethnic) minorities. Thus, the privatization of policing has its social and political limits.

### 4.6 Professionalization of private security

In early North-American studies on the private security industry, guards (as well as investigative personnel) are portrayed as aging, marginally paid, poorly educated and barely trained males, some of whom have criminal records (Kakalik and Wildhorn, 1971). This extremely negative profile of private security workers has stuck to the industry ever since. In jurisdictions worldwide, paid guards have been beset with allegations of integrity violations, which

---

[4]     For this distinction, see McManus, (1995: 10–15), Jones and Newburn (1998: 98–104) and Button (2002: 28–31).

painfully illustrates their vulnerability to incompetence, malpractice and abuse (Prenzler, 1998). Nowadays, the market, with assistance from the government, is trying to recover from its dubious image. Leading security companies and industry associations are working desperately to improve the quality and image of their employees in the hope of increasing social trust and acceptance and thereby encouraging the purchase of their services and products. Thus, a distinction can be made between two different processes that arguably have a positive effect on image – external (legal) incentives to professionalize and intrinsic (commercial) motivation.

### 4.6.1 External incentives

The supervision of national private security industries rests on fluid regulation genres of which the most compulsive is 'old-style' state legislation (Zedner, 2006b). This regulation, which encompasses (minimum) standards for training, education, powers, firearms, wages, screening, licensing and democratic supervision, supplies governance that community, market and private security industry cannot (Zedner, 2006b: 278). The implementation of such statutory laws has, commentators have suggested, provided a push towards the professionalization of private security occupations. Moreover, legislation facilitates trust in the market and tends to positively shape consumer mindsets, making critics believe that the state is less a regulator than 'a pimp' of private security (Zedner, 2006b: 279). One way or another, commentators have forecast, stricter regulation and higher quality standards will decrease rather than increase the number of private security firms (Jones, 2005: 15). That is, as ongoing professionalization contributes to higher average client fees, resulting in a price war among competitors, poor quality services will be weeded out. Thus, the trends of professionalization and concentration in private security sectors not only go hand in hand but must be seen as facilitating each other.

### 4.6.2 Intrinsic motivations

Representatives of the private security industry do not necessarily adopt an attitude of refusal toward the introduction of special government legislation and higher quality standards. On the contrary, the larger players particularly turn against an unregulated industry and poor performance. Thus, they are worried about 'cowboys' who vend their low standard services or products at minimum prices and spoil the name of competent practitioners in the field (George and Button, 2000: 36). For the same reason, companies themselves have established skill advancement programs. For example, D. O'Conner et al. (2004: 140) found that such attitudes have raised the current standards of education and training in relation to earlier requirements:

The commodification of security services was largely production-centered, relegated to the mass production of a standardized, low-skilled and minimally trained workforce to a broad range of largely private-sector businesses looking for 'night-watchmen' to manage access and egress points on mass private properties (Shearing and Stenning, 1981). There was little emphasis on the management of security information (e.g. documentation or dissemination of security incidents). While such production-centered regimes still exist, other forms of contract security have an increasing role in the provision of security services. These consumption-oriented security agencies have increased the educational requirements of the workforce they sell. They provide agency-trained security personnel tailored to meet the contractual demands of the clients.

Moreover, in some countries, industry associations have shouldered the responsibility for initiating and enforcing self-regulatory standards. Their lobbying efforts are directed toward the implementation of ethical codes, privacy norms and other guidelines. Yet, given that such standards tend to be voluntary, it remains open to debate whether self-regulation is really a credible and effective measure (Sarre and Prenzler, 1999).

A second type of internal professionalization is the improvement of specialized technologies like detection systems, closed-circuit surveillance cameras (CCTV) and electronic locks as universal remedies for crime and fear. Not surprisingly, the industry continually strives for ever more advanced products to stay one step ahead of smart criminals. Nonetheless, not only is such technology being constantly upgraded, but smart solutions have become widely affordable (George and Button, 2000), which has fueled the buying of new technical devices and further fostered the growth of private security industries.

### 4.7 Conclusion

This chapter has outlined possible explanations for the growth of private security over the past three decades by separately discussing six theoretical factors (see Figure 4.1) Nonetheless, because convincing explanations arising spontaneously from data sources should not be overlooked, this theoretical framework is open to the incorporation of any alternative factors that might explain private security in the Netherlands.

**Figure 4.1: The explanatory model**

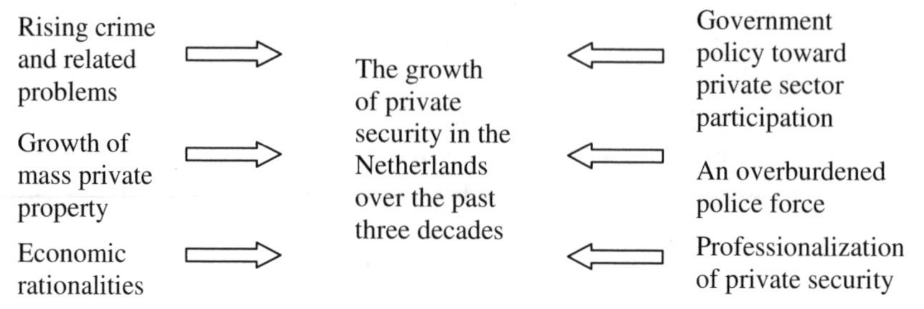

| Rising crime and related problems | ⟹ | The growth of private security in the Netherlands over the past three decades | ⟸ | Government policy toward private sector participation |
| Growth of mass private property | ⟹ | | ⟸ | An overburdened police force |
| Economic rationalities | ⟹ | | ⟸ | Professionalization of private security |

# 5 Studying Private Security: Research Methods

This chapter presents an overview of the research process and the mixed research methodology chosen. Specifically, this latter consisted of an exploration of the overall developments in private security at the national level together with three focused case studies of guarding operations in Dutch examples of mass private property. Accordingly, the first section of the chapter addresses the reasons for the methodological choice and assesses both its strengths and limitations, after which the second section provides a brief description of the selected case studies. The third section then outlines the data collection tools, followed by the fourth section, which specifies the process of reconstructing and analyzing empirical data. The fifth section finally discusses the ethical difficulties of conducting case study research.

## 5.1 Case study research

This research on the reasons for private security's rapid growth in the Netherlands aims to create detailed knowledge about the size and organization of private security, as well as the forces driving its growth. Thus, the research process involves two distinct stages. First, as set out in chapter 4, six potentially influential variables were derived from the literature. Evidently, such *a priori* anticipation does not fit the ideal put forward by some scholars that fieldwork should begin without any propositions (Glaser and Strauss, 1967); however, other researchers have expressed skepticism that such 'a clean theoretical slate' (Eisenhardt, 1989: 536) is even possible. For example Hammersley and Atkinson (2000: 213) raised the following objection:

> [T]he development of analytical ideas rarely takes the purely inductive form implied by Glaser and Strauss (heuristically useful though their approach is). Theoretical ideas, common-sense expectations, and stereotypes often play a key role. Indeed, it is these that allow the analyst to pick out surprising, interesting and important features in the first place.

Thus, there is a good reason to make use of guiding, yet loosely constructed, factors to tentatively explore data.

Such data exploration constituted the next stage of the research. A first objective was to map out the size and organization of Dutch private security sectors nationally; therefore, because detailed information was unavailable, the study drew on general information related to growth figures and possible explanations for the mushrooming industry. Local situations were then assessed using a *case study methodology* (Yin, 2003), chosen because it provides in-depth knowledge about the research topic (private security) and enables refinement of the theoretical assumptions:

> [Q]ualitative data are particularly useful for understanding why or why not emergent relationships hold. When a relationship is supported, the qualitative data often provide a good understanding of the dynamics underlying the relationship, that is, the 'why' of what is happening. [...] This helps to establish the internal validity of findings. (Eisenhardt, 1989: 542)

To verify the relationships between the theoretical constructs and empirical evidence, the methodology adopted a 'multiple case design' (Yin, 2003: 47), a powerful theory building tool in which a large number of observations over time facilitates explanation of considerable variation in the factors and outcomes. If diverse circumstances result in the same conclusions, a persuasive argument can be made for accepting the links between the theoretical explanations and observed shifts in private security. Similarly, under this replication logic, cases that disconfirm relationships signal a need to sharpen the theories or throw out the insufficient explanations.

### 5.1.1 The problem of causality

The goal of explanation building is to stipulate connections or 'causal links' (Yin 2003: 12) between the explanatory factors discussed in chapter 4 and the growth of private security. Nonetheless, proving causal relationships between observed patterns remains problematic. As eighteenth-century Scottish philosopher David Hume pondered, did billiard ball X hitting billiard ball Y really cause Y to move? In this respect, in qualitative studies, identification of causal processes must ultimately be judged by the density of information supporting theoretical notions:

> [T]he demonstration of causation rests heavily on the description of a visualizable sequence of events, each event flowing into the next. [...] At the end of many interviews [and other research strategies] the investigator can offer, with some confidence, a description of how some aspect of the respondent's life or situation came to be. If the same sort of description fits a series of respondents, the investigator can feel justified in proposing a more general statement as a hypothesized mini-theory. [...] All that is necessary to show that a process may be causal

is to make evident how it moves from cause to consequence. (Weiss, 1994: 179–180)

This touchstone may not fully resolve the problem of causality, but, at minimum, *plausible* claims can be made about the most relevant factors setting off certain outcomes, while some insignificant explanations may equally be discarded.

### 5.1.2 The problem of generalization

Besides the problem of causality, use of the case study method also raises the problem of how strong the evidence is for Dutch private security as a whole based on a small number of cases. Overall, statistical generalization from local case studies is bound to be fraught with problems because single examples never provide complete and accurate statements about the entire population. Most important, the concept of generalization assumes a belief in deterministic or conditional laws that lead to similar outcomes under fixed circumstances. However, scholars have raised numerous objections to such assumptions. For example, Hammersley and Atkinson (1995: 236) pointed out that 'while people can behave in a manner that is predictable by law, human life proper involves a transcendence of determining conditions'. In other words, because every single situation is unique in some way, investigating one single case thoroughly does not translate into insight about the entire reality. Consequently, social scientists have advocated the impossibility of drawing conclusions about cases not investigated.

To counteract this problem, this study looks *beyond* the mere distinctiveness of local case studies to interpret the local research findings against the background of national patterns. Nonetheless, qualitative social research does not facilitate natural law-like theories. Rather, as an alternative to statistical generalization – the inference of one sample to a universal population – Yin (2003: 32–33) suggested *analytical generalization*, which he explained as follows:

> A fatal flaw in doing case studies is to conceive of statistical generalization as the method of generalizing the results of the case study. This is because your cases are not 'sampling units' and should not be chosen for this reason. Rather, individual case studies are to be selected as a laboratory investigator selects the topic of a new experiment. Multiple cases, in this sense, should be considered like multiple experiments. Under the circumstances, the mode of generalization is 'analytical generalization', in which a previously developed theory is used as a template to compare the empirical results

of the case study. If two or more cases are to support the same theory, replication may be claimed. The empirical results may be considered yet more potent if two or more cases support the same theory, but do not support an equally plausible, *rival* theory.

These words reflect the critical lesson that scientific progress does not result solely from knowledge confirmation. Rather, there is always a chance of discovering deviant cases. Thus, Yin advised researchers to think about *testing* and *falsifying* their ideas as an elementary step for ongoing scientific inquiry. In this sense, the challenge is not whether results can be generalized to the real world but whether they can be generalized to the explanatory framework. In Yin's (2003: 10) terminology, 'case studies, like experiments, are generalizable to theoretical propositions and not to populations or universes', which suggests that rather than inferring statements from singular cases to reality, researchers should strive to develop and further refine theory.

### 5.2 Case selection

Given the surprising dearth of knowledge about the workings of private security, the fieldwork for this research drew on a combination of national and local investigations carried out between March 2003 and May 2005. At the national level, the dimensions and growth of Dutch manned guarding services had been mapped out over time. However, for a more detailed understanding of what was happening in private security, there remained a clear need for local case studies. Thus, inspired by Wakefield's (2003) fieldwork on the growing role of private security in British society, this research explored three types of leisure facility in which security staff are traditionally active. Wakefield (2003: 87-88) explained her choice of such facilities as follows:

> I felt that the increasing development and usage of large, privately controlled, mixed-use facilities as sites of public life was an interesting and important focus for the research. As leisure environments they could be seen as being more accessible or inviting to the public as a whole in comparison with some other pilot study research sites, such as the university, the transportation terminals or the business parks, which catered for more specific groups of people (such as students, travelers or office workers). I hoped to explore three very different leisure environments so that together, they would serve as broad a cross-section of urban society as possible.

Based on this rationale, the case studies selected for this current research were an amusement park (*Efteling*), a football stadium (*Stadium Feyenoord*) and a shopping mall (*Hoog Catharijne*). These three famous examples of mass private property in the Netherlands (1) are landmarks in the Dutch leisure industry, (2) welcome substantial numbers of visitors, (3) deal with various security risks and (4) have engendered long-running debates about who is responsible for maintaining and restoring order.

*Efteling*, the most famous amusement park in the Netherlands, attracts over three million people per year. Since most visitors are tourists, families and school-aged children, its security staff deals with low profile risks such as antisocial behavior, theft and vandalism. Essentially, Efteling has a *private* status: visitors pay for an admission ticket into the fenced park area where both in-house and contracted security guards have the authority to define and enforce order. The high numbers of visitors flocking into the amusement park places heavy demands on local police resources.

*Stadium Feyenoord*, home of one of the Netherlands' most illustrious professional football teams, currently hosts over a million supporters per year. A commercially owned enterprise that requires Sports Club membership for entry, Feyenoord is nonetheless feared for the serious hooliganism of its inner circle of hard core supporters. Moreover, even though paid security guards, football stewards and event security officers are responsible for rule enforcement and order maintenance *inside* the sports ground, police forces bear all the responsibility *outside* the sports ground. Thus, major soccer events at Stadium Feyenoord (a *private* stadium) have a profound impact on *public* peacekeeping in its immediate vicinity.

Finally, *Hoog Catharijne* is the most visited Dutch shopping mall with at least 40 million visitors yearly. Owing to a concentration of homeless people, drug addicts, psychiatric patients and other displaced persons, the mall has had to cope with huge problems of (petty) crime and (feelings of) insecurity. Moreover, in direct contrast to Efteling and Stadium Feyenoord, the domain of Hoog Catharijne is a privately owned space to which people have *unrestricted admission*. Thus, even though paid security guards, police officers and other supervisors all carry out the safety and security policies of the mall, its ambiguous status as *publicly* accessible yet *privately* owned territory confuses the exact responsibilities of private security versus public police agencies.

### 5.3 Data collection tools
The research method employs a variety of data collection tools, a combination of multiple sources that Yin (2003) referred to as *triangulation*. These multiple data collection strategies, which ensure that converging lines of inquiry provide balanced, accurate and convincing findings, are divided into two phases, the national and the local, explicated in more detail below and outlined in Table 5.1.

### 5.3.1 National level

At the national level, one instrument used to detail the characteristics of Dutch private security was a mail *questionnaire survey* that assessed customer types in percentage of annual turnover and specialized guarding services in percentage of total workforce (see Appendix 1). The survey sample was based on membership in the Dutch Association of Private Security Organisations (VPB) and included 92 security firms, only 13 of which returned the questionnaire. Nonetheless, those companies who responded encompassed 68% of the market's turnover and 64% of the total contract personnel employed in the Netherlands. Therefore, even though the nonresponse rate is likely to have biased the data toward underestimation of the clientele and activities of smaller (non-VPB affiliated) companies, the study does provide useful insights into the Dutch security industry. Additional records such as *statistics* – from census information, security yearbooks, and market research – were consulted for longitudinal trends in public and private policing. Some *documentary sources* were also collected, including policy documents, annual reports and Web sites, in the preparation of desk research. Finally, six *interviews* with leading private security experts and practitioners (i.e., the national and international industry associations' chairmen, security firm directors and a civil servant) were conducted to supplement and enrich the information from the other data sources.

**Table 5.1: Data collection tools**

|  | National level | Local level |
|---|---|---|
| **Survey** | Questionnaire | -- |
| **Statistical records** | Census, market research | -- |
| **Documentary sources** | Web sites, policy documents, annual reports | Web sites, archival records, policy documents, promotional material |
| **Preliminary observations** | -- | Cycling tour through Efteling, attendance at football matches and a pop concert at Stadium Feyenoord, walking tour through Hoog Catharijne |
| **Personal interviews conducted** | 6 | 39 |

## 5.3.2 Local level

At the local level, a number of *documents* were consulted, including Web sites, policy documents, letters, memos and background information about the three case studies were collected, which, besides specific archival records, contained official and openly published resources. Next, the fieldwork included *preliminary observations* made not with the primary goal of full engagement in the research but rather to obtain an overview of the case study environments and familiarity with the local contexts in which private security guards operate. Finally, an essential aspect of case study research was the *interview* because, as Weiss (1994: 1) argued, interviews reveal much about 'the work of occupations', give insights into 'people's interior experiences' and open 'a window on the past'.

The local studies included a total of 39 conversations with 45 respondents (some interviewed simultaneously) representing security managers, security guards, stewards, police officers, public servants, policymakers, politicians and other stakeholders (see Table 5.2). No individual approached refused to be interviewed. The respondents were chosen through snowball sampling (Weiss, 1994) in which the principal respondents – the Head Safety Manager of Efteling, two security managers of Stadium Feyenoord and the (former) area manager of Hoog Catharijne – provided referrals, who in turn suggested further referrals. To systemize the data collection and assure comparability between cases the interview techniques were semi-structured using open-end questions (see Appendix 1). In addition, numerous *informal chats* in cars, offices and at conferences provided a gold mine of information. These unguided conversations were not recorded and transcribed.

**Table 5.2: Interview respondents**

| Efteling (N=7) | Feyenoord (N=23) | Hoog Catharijne (N=9) |
|---|---|---|
| Head safety manager ; (Former) security managers (2); (Former) police officers (2); A politician. | Feyenoord managers (2); Security managers (4); Police officers (2); Policymakers (6); Stewards (2); Manager supporter association; Supporters (5); A hooligan expert. | (Former) area manager; Centre manager; Security manager ; Railway station manager; General manager operations convention centre Jaarbeurs; Police officers (2); Security guards (2). |

## 5.4 Data analysis

The data analysis was divided into three steps. The first was to conduct a (quantifiable) analysis of national level data to derive initial impressions about the extent and nature of Dutch private security and the possible factors driving its growth. The second step was to analyze 'within-case data' for the three mass private property sites 'to become intimately familiar with each case as a stand-alone entity' (Eisenhardt, 1989: 540). The final step was to search for 'cross-case patterns' to gain more sophisticated understanding of similarities and differences between cases (Eisenhardt, 1989: 541). These steps are discussed in turn below.

### 5.4.1 National level analysis

At the national level, drawing on census data, security yearbooks, market research and personal research, the first goal was to construct trends in the number of security guards and annual market turnovers over time and then relate these to trends outlined in the six theoretical approaches. The essential logic here was to compare chronological events in private security with those predicted by the relevant explanatory theories to assess the goodness-of-fit of each theory. In doing so, time periods were reconstructed, which marked 'major shifts' and 'symbolic turning points' in security arrangements arousing from my research findings. When reconstructing the growth of private security, *qualitative data matrices* (Bijlsma-Frankema and Droogleever Fortuijn, 1997) were generated as analytical tools. These charts were construed as textual summaries of findings, which helped to understand the relations between explanatory factors and expanding private security better. Once completed, they commissioned accurate portraits of shifts in private security and showed the content of theoretical dispositions that were presumed to explain these patterns (see Appendix 2). In addition, the mail questionnaire survey was used to gain better insight in the nature of Dutch private security. The data from this survey were entered into Excel software for simple calculations.

### 5.4.2 Within-case analysis

Next, the copious information produced by all three local case studies were sorted and organized as story lines about the practice of private security. Evidence examination began with a thick description (Geertz, 1973) of developments related to manned guarding. Based on interviews and documentary data, time periods were reconstructed that marked major turning points in security arrangements. Various respondents checked the factual accuracy of these story lines and, after some adjustments, gave their approval to the final reports. Once more, using qualitative data matrices, the size and organizational patterns of private security were analyzed through the lens of the six explanatory theories, and the timing and extent of the changes in manned guarding services were noted and compared with the timing and extent of changes in the proposed explanations (see Appendix 2). This strategy enabled all findings to be structured according to the theoretical framework.

### 5.4.3 Cross-case analysis

Finally, in combining all data matrices, the analysis searched for cross-case patterns, a tactic that, according to Eisenhardt (1989: 540-541), 'forces researchers to look for the subtle similarities and differences between local cases. [It] can break simplistic frames [and improves] the likelihood of accurate and reliable theory, that is, a theory with a close fit to the data'. Thus, for an overall understanding of the explanatory patterns across case studies, the analysis again juxtaposed the six theoretical assumptions to produce sharpened conclusions and judgments about the factors that have triggered the growth of Dutch private security over the past three decades.

### 5.5 Ethical considerations

In their dissertations on private security, Wakefield (2003) and Button (2007a) have paid noteworthy attention to their own roles in carrying out field studies. As they pointed out, the central values to be faced are that researchers should be honest and frank about their precise objectives and show sensitivity to issues surrounding, privacy, discretion and courtesy. Thus, the stories about personal struggles and problems that emerged during the interviews are not included in the published report. Not only would reporting such confidentialities be an abuse of the research position but such content is also not relevant to the primary research interest in the growth and practice of manned guarding services.

Participant awareness of the exact nature of the research was ensured through informed consent. Every respondent received a clear explanation of the research plan, was assured of anonymous and voluntary participation and gave permission for the formal conversations to be taped. Subsequently, respondents received a transcript on which they could comment. Some then illuminated the findings or suggested helpful adjustments, based on which corrections were made. Finally, all respondents approved their interviews. Although time-consuming, such guidelines assured trustworthy research and afforded interviewees the opportunity to be more open and articulated in their answers, which evidently benefited the validity and reliability of the findings.

**5.6 Conclusion**

This chapter has covered the methodology used in mapping and explaining the growth of private security in the Netherlands. The discussion has emphasized that causal links are hard to draw, but that plausible claims can be made about relevant explanations for private security growth. It has also stressed that the uniqueness of case study results makes generalization a precarious undertaking. Therefore, here, the research goal has been to update, correct and sharpen general theoretical predictions rather than make real world inferences on the basis of a few empirical studies. Above all, the uniqueness of case studies has a distinct advantage for the provision of detailed knowledge about why things happen and what the practice of private security looks like. Thus, this book's particular strength lies in addressing these questions comprehensively, driven by the concern that, so far, theoretical and empirical information on manned guarding services in the Netherlands has been extremely limited.

**Part 2: A National Case Study**

# 6    Private Security in the Netherlands: A Market in Motion

Over the last three decades, the demand for manned guarding services specifically, and private security more generally, has been on the rise. In terms of personnel and annual expenditures, private security providers now form an indispensable part of the Dutch policing landscape. Yet how large is this industry and what are its exact dimensions? This chapter answers these questions by first discussing the problems encountered in measuring private security and then addressing the history, size and nature of the Dutch security market in an international context. It concludes with a summary of the findings. The sources for this information included a survey questionnaire, statistical records, a document review and six interviews held with the chairman of the Dutch Association of Private Security Organizations (*Vereniging van Particuliere Beveiligingsorganisaties* (VPB) in Dutch), the chairman of the Confederation of European Security Services (CoESS), three directors of leading security companies and a senior staff member of the Ministry of Justice's Legal Affairs and Policy Support Department (*Juridische en Beleidsondersteunende Aangelegenheden, DG Rechtshandhaving*).

## 6.1 Measuring the private security 'industry'[1]

The private security 'industry' is not a clearly defined homogenous group but rather a multitude of sectors, large and small, all related to the provision of security services, investigation, crime prevention, order maintenance, systems planning, technical consulting and security design (George and Button, 2000: 15). Often, these industries differ from each other in structure, authority, function and method, being 'splintered into numerous sub-sectors whose practices and purposes have little in common [...] other than the deceptive unifier of the moniker "security"' (Zedner, 2006b: 270–271). Because this occupational variety makes measuring industry size problematic (Jones and Newburn, 1995: 223–224), experts have used different definitions to describe the industry, which results in the inclusion and exclusion of different security segments. Thus, it is not entirely unambiguous which firms and services should be labeled 'private security' companies. Moreover, because the quality of accessible data varies considerably from source to source, sound information is sometimes difficult to obtain owing to gaps in official registrations: '[w]hat has mostly been available are fragments of information, mixed with speculation and

---

[1]     This section is based on Van Steden and Sarre (2007).

dramatic claims, especially when the media get involved' (Sarre and Prenzler, 2005: 7–8).

In addition, registration systems do not always differentiate between full-time personnel and what appears to be a sizable group of part-time personnel, a lack of clarity that probably leads to *overestimation* of the actual work forces of national security industries. On the other hand, such counts sometimes exclude in-house staff, so it can also be argued that the manpower of private security is in reality *underestimated*. Moreover, because competition is fierce, most private firms prefer not to divulge sensitive information like their earning and personnel numbers to researchers. Finally, the private security industry now encompasses ever more diverse sectors; for example, accountancy firms set up forensic services for their clients and offer private detective work, while private security companies undertake activities like hiring limousines or facility management along with their policing activities. Thus, the private security industry flows into various markets, making counting very difficult. Nonetheless, even though measuring the industry is hedged with caveats, there is consensus amongst observers about its mounting pervasiveness in the Netherlands. Multiple data sources, which are relatively comprehensive and reliable compared to those for other nations (e.g., the United Kingdom), strongly suggest rapid growth during the last quarter century.

### 6.2 The Dutch private security industry[2]

Dutch commercial policing in its contemporary form can be traced back to the early 20th century. First, in 1902, Isaac Beuth established commercial night watches in Amsterdam (Verhoog, 2002: 11–13) whose bicycle-riding, uniformed guards concentrated on the protection of neighborhoods, warehouses and offices. At about the same time, private companies began to employ their own in-house security personnel. For example, in 1905, as the Dutch mining industry flourished, the mining police were founded in the southern province of Limburg. Current research has shown that this semiprivate organization, which had certain police powers and some of whose employees were allowed to carry guns and handcuffs,[3] played a major role in regulating and disciplining workers:

---

[2]    This section is based on Van Steden (2004) and Van Steden and Huberts (2006).

[3]    Today, uniformed private guards have no formal powers over and above those of the ordinary citizen. Moreover, with the exception of dogs, they are not allowed to carry firearms or nonlethal equipment such as a baton, pepper spray and handcuffs. Nonetheless, in practice, guards are trained in controlling mass private properties and derive considerable legal powers from civil laws like property law and contractual law. These powers allow them, for example, to subject people to random body and luggage searches before entering premises.

The Mining Police seemed to be a force that virtually controlled every aspect of the miner's life. The Mining Police supervised the mines and the housing complexes: surveillance was present at all the time. But the social control did not limit itself to a mere guarding of mines. Especially the vast amount of investigations into criminal offences, violations of company rules and 'moral offences' indicate that the presence of the Mining Police must have had a great impact on the lives of miners. (Hoogenboom, 1991b: 93)

During the 1930s, the Dutch security industry entered a difficult episode of its history during which economic depression and social unrest led to the emergence of violent fascist organizations that created the impetus for firmer state regulation of security agencies. In 1936, the Dutch government implemented the Paramilitary Organizations Act (*Wet op de Weerkorpsen*), which laid down a regulation framework for all (vigilante-style) private security organizations. For the period of World War II, when the Netherlands was occupied by Nazi Germany, there is little information about the work of private security firms. Although some studies (e.g., Meershoek, 1999) have documented collaboration between the Dutch police and German *Sicherheitsdiensten* (security forces), there have been no detailed historical investigations on private security organizations under the Third Reich. Nonetheless, Dekkers (1982) observed tight associations between Hitler's Gestapo and the in-house security corps of Philips, better known as the 'Philips police'. The famous electronics giant, he wrote, employed a Pinkerton-style guarding and detective agency that did not hesitate to conclude a pact with the Nazis to maintain and regain authority. One extremely salient detail is that, shortly after its publication in 1982, the Dutch judiciary took the book off the market as a result of these allegations.

Subsequent to the Second World War, the position of the Dutch private security industry changed dramatically. In particular, during the last 30 years, policing tasks have been increasingly carried out by a multitude of commercial organizations. Therefore, despite the problems of definition and diversification outlined above, there is widespread consensus about the mounting pervasiveness of private security, most particularly based on the following four sources: (1) the Dutch National Census, (2) security yearbooks (*Jaarboeken Beveiliging*) (3) Quickscans and (4) personal research. Information from these sources, whose advantages and limitations are briefly discussed below, is used here to measure the size and shape of the industry.

**6.2.1 The census**

Census archives provide detailed information about Dutch private industry; however, because they exclude businesses employing fewer than five people, these records only cover a limited number of security firms. The most obvious points they make are that

- There were 151 security companies in 2001 compared to 104 companies in 1994;
- The gross annual turnover was €959 million in 2001 compared to €429 million in 1994; and
- The number of employees was over 26,000 in 2001compared to 13,000 in 1994.

A closer look also reveals that private security is an extremely labor-intensive industry. In 2001, salaries, pension contributions and social expenses made up 83% of total costs. Moreover, as illustrated in Figures 6.1 and 6.2, the 2001 census data on contributions to annual turnovers for security sectors and activities reveal a highly diversified market. In this respect, although the information does not encompass the entire business spectrum, the private security sector – that is, manned guarding or staffed services, which also entail cash-in-transit (CIT) and access control activities – undoubtedly represents the most significant segment of the industry.

**Figure 6.1: Share of annual turnover generated by private security sectors**
(source: Census database; www.cbs.nl)

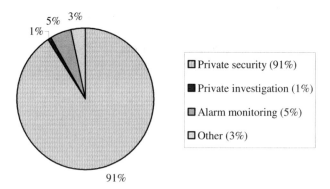

**Figure 6.2: Share of annual turnover generated by private security activities** (source: Census database; www.cbs.nl)

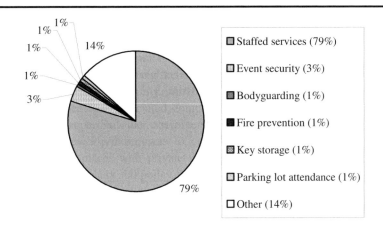

Staffed services (79%)

Event security (3%)

Bodyguarding (1%)

Fire prevention (1%)

Key storage (1%)

Parking lot attendance (1%)

Other (14%)

### 6.2.2 Security yearbooks

Succeeding editions of security yearbooks between 1981 (Heijboer et al., 1983) and 2001 (Tenge et al., 2003), based on compulsory annual reports to the Dutch Ministry of Justice and the head of police for the region in which a private security company operates, offer a longitudinal overview of Dutch private security that reveals the following:

- The total number of private security personnel has increased from 10,227 (1981) to 30,186 (2001); and
- The number of licenses issued (counting contract security, in-house security, central alarm stations and cash-in-transit services) has grown from 462 (1992) to 813 (2001). Once private detective agencies and on-license premises (e.g., hotels, bars, pubs, restaurants, nightclubs and discotheques) are added in, this number reaches 1,535.

As shown in Table 6.1, one particularly interesting finding is that the number of contract guards increases at the expense of in-house guards. That is, in line with a worldwide trend in public and private management philosophy to concentrate on core functions, many commercial organizations have outsourced their supportive in-house staff to specialized security companies. Tenge et al. (2003: 30) estimated that in 2001, about 50% of private guards served on a full-time basis, while 27% had a part-time or on-call contract (23%). Unfortunately, it is not clear exactly how full-time and part-time workers are measured and defined.

**Table 6.1: Private security personnel, 1981–2001** (sources: security yearbooks ranging from Heijboer et al., 1983 to Tenge et al., 2003)

|                          | 1981   | 1991   | 2001   |
|--------------------------|--------|--------|--------|
| Contract security        | 4,348  | 10,443 | 25,412 |
| In-house security        | 5,175  | 5,462  | 2,693  |
| Centralists              | 185    | 586    | 595    |
| Cash-in-transport staff  | 519    | 856    | 1,486  |
| Total                    | 10,277 | 17,347 | 30,186 |

### 6.2.3 Quickscans

Because the Ministry of Justice gave up counting private security in 2001, most up-to-date information comes from annual Quickscans (Donkers, 2003a, 2003b, 2005, 2006), market explorations based on digital surveys of private security companies registered by the VPB. Even though the response rates for these surveys are low (only 10 to 20%), the outcomes are still valid because all large companies (i.e., most of the market) fill in these questionnaires. Moreover, to increase the reliability of measurements, additional data are obtained from SOBB (a foundation offering training and education in the field of private security) and Achmea (a health insurer). The key conclusions of the surveys are as follows (see also Table 6.2):

- The industry's gross annual turnover rose from €1.07 billion in 2002 to €1.16 billion in 2005;
- The number of contract security employees grew from 24,057 (1 January 2002) to 27,950 (1 January 2006); and
- The total contracted workforce converted to FTE employees[4] increased from 21,744 (2002) to 23,630 (2005).

Overall, Quickscan data demonstrate that in 2004, manned guarding services (patrol officers and static guards) produced most (83.9%) of the total annual turnover. In terms of gender, the figures indicate that private security is a male business, with only 27% female security workers in 2005. Moreover, the decrease in FTE employees but increase in the absolute workforce indicates that more people worked fewer hours. Indeed, Quickscan has estimated that

---

[4]      One FTE (full-time equivalency) equals a workweek of 40 hours.

personnel employed by the private security industry now have an average workweek of 4 days. Additionally, attrition data reveal an average personnel turnover of approximately 25% (2005), which is, as the report noted, a 'highly dynamic pattern when set against other industries in the Netherlands' (Donkers, 2004: 6). The reports also make reference to a fleet of corporate patrol vehicles that grew from 1,000 in 2003 to 1,250 in 2005. Indeed, VPB claims that there are currently more corporate patrol vehicles than police cars on duty at night.

**Table 6.2: Private security personnel and annual turnover**
(sources: Donkers, 2003a, 2003b, 2005 and 2006)

|  | 2002 | 2003 | 2004 | 2005 |
|---|---|---|---|---|
| Number of employees (as of January 1) | 24,057 | 25,718 | 26,611 | 26,740 |
| Number of employees (as of December 31) | 25,718 | 26,611 | 26,740 | 27,950 |
| Payroll staff | – | 22,767 | 23,250 | 24,596 |
| Hired staff | – | 2,318 | 1,650 | 1,174 |
| Support staff | – | 1,526 | 1,840 | 2,180 |
| Male | 20,467 | 21,421 | 20,600 | 21,382 |
| Female | 5,251 | 5,190 | 6,140 | 6,568 |
| Employment (FTE) | 21,744 | 21,657 | 21,520 | 23,630 |
| Payroll staff | – | 19,543 | 19,170 | 20,676 |
| Hired staff | – | 852 | 1,280 | 1,016 |
| Support staff | – | 1,262 | 1,070 | 1,938 |
| Absence through illness | 7.9% | 7.3% | 7.0% | 5.9% |
| Annual turnover (in billions of euros) | 1.07 | 1.08 | 1.09 | 1.16 |

### 6.2.4 Personal research[5]
A previous mail survey aimed at exploring the more detailed characteristics of contract private security polled a small number of companies (13 out of 92) that represent most of the market's turnover (68%) and workforce (64%) in the Netherlands. In addition, desk research on published documentary sources

---

[5] This section is based on Van Steden (2004) and Van Steden and Huberts (2006).

provided useful information on distinctive sectors of the private security industry. The results are reported in the following paragraphs.

### 6.2.4.1 Manned guarding

The majority of the approximately 30,000 security guards work as contract personnel for 250 to 400 companies (VPB, 2007: 4).[6] The 2004 survey indicated that of these staff, most (67%) are employed as (static) property protection guards and patrol officers. Other job categories included immigration detention officers (5%), custodial officers (3%), receptionists (7%) and shop supervisors (6%), although companies also offered some specializations (12%) such as aviation security, harbor security, event security, personal protection (bodyguarding), bouncer services and covert security (see Figure 6.3).

### Figure 6.3: Manned guarding services in % of total FTE
(source: Van Steden, 2004)

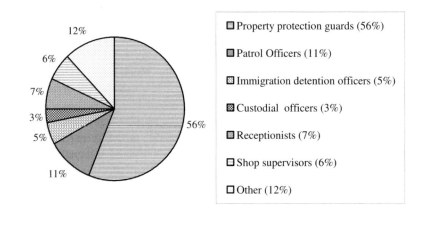

Taken together, the security firms sampled protected approximately 54,000 sites in the Netherlands, over 80% of which were office buildings, industrial complexes, government buildings, shops and shopping centers. Other potential clients included private houses, schools, universities, hotels, bars, discotheques, airports, seaports, leisure parks, holiday resorts, and football stadiums. Not surprisingly, two-thirds (66%) of the customers were private companies operating in the industrial, services and transport sectors. However, the Dutch government (including the criminal justice system) and nonprofit

---

6       An older report estimates the number of private security companies at 875 (2001) (Batelaan en Bos, 2003: 3).

organizations (e.g., schools, universities and housing associations) were also important clients of commercial security companies (Figure 6.4), whereas large corporations tended to employ their own in-house security staff.

**Figure 6.4: Customer type in % of annual turnover**
        (source: Van Steden, 2004)

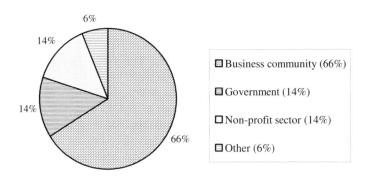

One ongoing trend is for security companies to offer security requirement solutions in the public domain (Stigter, 2000: 27). For example, Parcon, a nonprivate security division of the multinational Group 4 Securicor, hires out supplementary special (sometimes sworn-in) constables (*Buitengewoon OpsporingsAmbtenaren*) to the government. Once sworn in, these officials are vested with limited legal powers to uphold specific laws and operate under the auspices of public authorities; for example, as traffic wardens entitled to impose fines for parking violations. Similarly, private custodial services working with the Dutch Ministry of Justice deliver manpower to detention centers for asylum seekers, illegal immigrants, drug couriers and other prisoners. However, unlike staff in the privately managed prisons and privatized prison sectors in the United States and United Kingdom, Dutch commercial custodial officers only assist public servants with guarding and attending to detainees.

### 6.2.4.2 Central alarm respondents
Even though most major security companies are engaged in alarm-monitoring services, some central alarm respondents have an independent status within the security market. In the Netherlands, around 30 control centers with 600 to 650 employees monitor about 400,000 connected subscribers. In 2001, these centers

detected almost 3 million alarms, of which 95% proved to be false (Tenge et al., 2003). As a result, the government and private alarm respondents entered into an agreement expected to reduce unnecessary demands on police officers.

### 6.2.4.3 Armored couriers

The armored courier sector is really a subdivision of manned guarding services. Only a small number of companies are involved in this business because of strict regulations and the high investment required. At present, about six such companies operate in the Netherlands, employing over 1,500 people (2001). Some foreign firms are also licensed to use their vehicles in the German and Belgium border regions (Tenge et al., 2003). These armored couriers carry out a range of different tasks, but the most well known are the transportation of valuables and the maintenance of automatic teller machines (ATMs).

### 6.2.4.4 Private investigators

Private investigators form a distinct and covert sector within the security industry. When the first Dutch detective agencies were founded in the 1940s, the sector included primarily one-man businesses that made their money from surveillance of unfaithful spouses (evidence of adultery was compulsory for a divorce), missing persons enquiries and the recovery of stolen goods. This first generation of detective agencies was followed during the 1980s by a second generation of better-equipped organizations much more attuned to the business community. As a result, next to their conventional investigations, private detectives began to undertake consultancy work on the security requirements of private companies. During this period, the numbers of former police officers employed in the private investigation sector increased, which sparked further expansion of the sector. Over the last 10 years, third- and fourth-generation agencies have entered the market, employing specialists in complex financial investigations (Hoogenboom, 1999). Such organizations are fairly large and operate in both the Netherlands and abroad to support clients with a range of fraud investigation and related services.

Private interference in financial security operations directed at economic irregularities and white collar crime is taken on by only a very small sector – a mere 2 to 3% of the industry's total employment in the Netherlands. Nonetheless, estimating the exact number of commercial detectives is difficult because some agencies have not registered with the authorities, whereas others refused to send in the obligatory annual report to the Ministry of Justice (Klerks et al., 2001: 24-26). Despite these problems, researchers have suggested that 320 companies are licensed, of which about 200 are active in the market, employing 500 to 600 people, half full-time and the other half part-time or temporary (Tenge et al., 2003: 34).

In addition to traditional detective agencies, the private investigation sector also includes business information bureaus (BIBs), insurance law and claim experts and forensic accountants (Klerks et al., 2001). The BIBs gather data from companies all over the world with the primary aim of informing clients about the potential risks and opportunities associated with, for example, trading partners. The insurance specialists assist customers in lawsuit preparation and investigation into frauds, thefts and suspicious accidents. Finally, the certified forensic accountants conduct investigations on suspected financial malpractice and provide consultation in areas such as prevention plans and risk assessments.

Insurance companies, banks, lawyers, commercial businesses and rich individuals form the primary client base of these private investigators. However, the Dutch government sometimes uses private detectives and forensic accountants to investigate corruption and fraud within the civil service (Klerks et al., 2001). Overall, in 2001, the private investigation sector was engaged in 45,250 cases involving account collection, diverse forms of (economic) embezzlement and creditworthiness checks (Tenge et al., 2003: 34). Nonetheless, besides sometimes using the contract private investigation sector, large corporations like banks, insurance companies and credit card companies also have their own in-house investigators (Klerks et al., 2005).

### 6.2.4.5 Technical equipment services

The manufacturing of technical equipment like locks, burglar alarms and fences is an often overlooked segment of private security segment, because 'the use of these goods is both too episodic and too widespread throughout society to be contained within a discrete definition of policing, let alone private policing' (Joh, 2004: 57). Nonetheless, technical equipment services represent an important economic dimension of the Dutch security market. Indeed, according to the professional trade association UNETO-VNI, in the Netherlands, this sector consists of an estimated 335 companies, 205 small firms (1–9 FTE employees) and 130 large companies (10 or more FTE employees). The employment figures for technical equipment services suggest at least 6,500 people in a market that in 2004 was worth over €810 million.

Taking into account the breadth of its products, this sector is difficult to define, although most manufacturers sell intruder alarms, CCTVs, access control systems and fire protection systems. The core business of technical equipment services is the protection of entities like office buildings, shops and shopping centers, industrial complexes, government buildings and (exclusive) private houses (Van der Graaff and Pleijster, 2004). One noticeable development in this sector is that technical equipment services are increasingly offered in conjunction with manned guarding services. Moreover, the trade associations for the two sectors have lately amalgamated into the Union of Private Security Organizations (VvBO in Dutch). According the VBO, on the basis of 210 survey questionnaires (response rate = 38%), the annual turnover of the private security industry at large reached around €2.45 billion by the end of 2004. This turnover was generated by a workforce of almost 37,000 FTE employees active in both the manned guarding and technical equipment sectors (Van der Graaff and Melchior, 2005).

## 6.3 An international perspective[7]

Dutch private security does not flourish in a social vacuum but in a globalizing environment of ever-expanding international markets. Indeed, the resurgence of security industries is a worldwide phenomenon in both Western and developing countries. A snapshot of these processes in the European Union (EU) is presented in Table 6.3, although the information is admittedly subject to the same classification limitations and counting problems mentioned previously. For the public and private policing sector employment figures that are its focus, the table draws on CoESS (Morré, 2004) and SEESAC (SEESAC, 2005) reports, which update the first comprehensive comparative study on private security (De Waard, 1999).

Although the EU is tending to move toward an integrated guarantee of safety and security, the size of private security industries varies drastically from country to country. Nonetheless, even though data must be treated with caution, recent figures indicate a growth from around 600,000 security employees in 1999 to well over a million today. The indisputable leader in Europe is Poland, with a security force of 200,000, followed closely by the United Kingdom, Germany and France. In addition, Hungary has an exceptionally high security/police ratio of 2.00, meaning there are twice as many private guards as public police officers active in the country. Scandinavian and south European countries such as Denmark and Italy traditionally employ low proportions of security personnel, with 97 and 95 guards per 100,000 inhabitants, respectively. The Netherlands takes a moderate position, with 184/100,000, which is below the EU average of 253. From a global perspective, as shown in the Table 6.4 overview of available data for private security industries outside the European Union, this greater provision of commercial policing and security is unexceptional. Thus, in indicative terms only, it suggests that the influence of these industries has generally been more extensive around the world than within most EU-affiliated countries, including the Netherlands.

---

[7]        This section is based on Van Steden and Sarre (2007).

**Table 6.3: Private security in the European Union**
(sources: Morré, 2005; SEESAC, 2005)

| Country | Total police | Total private security | Police per 100,000 inhabitants | Private security per 100,000 inhabitants | Private security/ police ratio |
|---|---|---|---|---|---|
| Austria | 30,000 | 6,790 | 366 | 83 | 0.23 |
| Belgium | 39,000 | 18,320 | 379 | 178 | 0.47 |
| Bulgaria | 28,000 | 130,000 | 374 | 1,724 | 4.6 |
| Cyprus | 3,000 | 1,500 | 386 | 193 | 0.50 |
| Czech Republic | 47,400 | 28,100 | 465 | 275 | 0.59 |
| Denmark | 14,000 | 5,250 | 259 | 97 | 0.38 |
| Estonia | 3,600 | 4,900 | 257 | 350 | 1.36 |
| Finland | 7,500 | 6,000 | 144 | 115 | 0.80 |
| France | 145,000 | 117,000 | 240 | 194 | 0.81 |
| Germany | 250,000 | 170,000 | 303 | 206 | 0.68 |
| Greece | 49,900 | 25,000 | 468 | 234 | 0.50 |
| Hungary | 40,000 | 80,000 | 400 | 800 | 2.00 |
| Ireland | 12,000 | 20,000 | 308 | 513 | 1.67 |
| Italy | 280,000[8] | 55,000 | 482 | 95 | 0.20 |
| Latvia | 10,600 | 5,000 | 461 | 217 | 0.47 |
| Lithuania | 20,000 | 10,000 | 556 | 278 | 0.50 |
| Luxembourg | 1,573 | 2,200 | 340 | 476 | 1.40 |
| Malta | 1,800 | 700 | 455 | 176 | 0.39 |
| Netherlands | 49,000 | 30,000 | 301 | 184 | 0.61 |
| Poland | 103,309 | 200,000 | 267 | 518 | 1.94 |
| Portugal | 46,000 | 28,000 | 439 | 267 | 0.61 |
| Romania | 45,830 | 37,291 | 207 | 168 | 0.81 |
| Slovakia | 21,500 | 20,840 | 398 | 386 | 0.97 |
| Slovenia | 7,500 | 4,500 | 375 | 225 | 0.60 |
| Spain | 193,450 | 89,450 | 481 | 215 | 0.46 |
| Sweden | 18,000 | 10,000 | 200 | 111 | 0.56 |
| United Kingdom | 141,398 | 150,000 | 235 | 249 | 1.06 |
| **Total** | **1,609,360** | **1,255,841** | **324** | **253** | **0.78** |

[8]     This number is based on De Waard's (1999) estimate of the Italian police force numbers, because of missing data in the CoESS report.

**Table 6.4: Private security outside the European Union**[9]

| Region | Security force | Region | Security force |
|---|---|---|---|
| **South Eastern Europe** | | **Africa** | |
| Albania | 4,100 | Nigeria | +100,000 |
| Bosnia - Herzegovina | ±2,000 | Kenya | 48,800 |
| Croatia | ±15,000 | Sierra Leone | +3,000 |
| Kosovo | 2,580 | South Africa | +250,000 |
| Macedonia | 3,000 | | |
| Moldova | +3,000 | **Pacific** | |
| Montenegro | +1,900 | Australia | +49,400 |
| Serbia | ±30,000 | | |
| Russia | +850,000 | **Latin America** | |
| Ukraine | 33,000 | Colombia | 190,000 |
| | | Mexico | 150,000–450,000 |
| **Asia** | | Brazil | 400,000–570,000 |
| Japan | 459,305 | Venezuela | 75,000 |
| South Korea | 115,845 | Chile | 45,000 |
| | | Argentina | 75,000 |
| **Middle East** | | Peru | 50,000 |
| Saudi Arabia | 16,000 | Central America | 105,000 |
| | | Other countries | 70,000 |
| **North America** | | | |
| USA | +1,500,000 | | |
| Canada | 82,000 | | |

One important issue related to international trends in private security is the ascendancy of multinational firms as happened recently in the Netherlands. Giant and stock exchange-listed multinationals such as the Securitas Group and Group 4 Securicor (G4S) now represent a globalization or transnationalization of commercialized security provision. Such expansion has produced massive security conglomerates that, taking the example of G4S, employ an astonishing

[9] These numbers are derived from miscellaneous sources, including the Law Commission of Canada (2002), Volkov (2002), Abrahamsen and Williams (2005a,b,c), Prenzler (2005), Reames (2005), SEESAC (2005), Abelson (2006), Button et al. (2006), Cardia and Wood (2006), De Jong (2006), Hiscock (2006), Manning (2006) and Yoshida and Leishman (2006).

405,000 staff, working in over 100 countries and generating a yearly turnover of €6.10 billion.[10] In addition, a diversity of commercial security activities is penetrating national and subnational institutions like fire departments, ambulance services, car assistance services, custodial services and even markets of violence (Eppler, 2002) such as military operations and mercenaries (Singer, 2003). It is therefore safe to predict that transnational private security will increasingly expand their functions in securing local (urban) domains across every continent.

### 6.4 Summary

The expansion of private security companies and manned guarding services has generated increasing discussion over the last 30 years. However, many of these debates and concerns rest on rather wobbly foundations because information on the size and nature of the Dutch industry is fragmented and speculative. Therefore, by combining several sources, including prior personal research, this chapter has strived, through summary and commentary, to give a more accurate picture of developments.

As regards actual *private security companies*, according to the security yearbooks, there are at least 1,500 licenses issued in the Netherlands. It must, however, not be forgotten that some such licenses remain unused, that some security companies hold multiple licenses (e.g., a permit for both guarding and CIT services) and a substantial number of licenses (around 400) are granted not to specialized security companies but to facilities like bars and discotheques that employ door supervisors. Taking these factors into account, current estimates vary between 250 and 400 operational companies in the Netherlands.

Nonetheless, census estimates are much lower because the census counts only firms employing more than five people. Apparently, as Stigter (2000) pointed out, the industry consists for the most part of single 'mom and dad' companies. That is, private security firms are frequently very small businesses. In fact, Dutch private security is an oligarchic industry dominated by two multinational conglomerates and a merged national company – Group 4 Securicor, Securitas and Trigion (formally PreNed and Falck) – with a collective annual turnover of €735 million (Dessing, 2006a: 4), which represents 63% of the market share.

In terms of *annual turnover*, it is evident that Dutch private security has expanded rapidly in past decades. Combined census and Quickscan data reveals an increase in turnovers from €429 in 1994 to €1.16 billion in 2005. Moreover, these figures are exclusive of the overall market growth of security equipment like intruder alarms, CCTV and fire prevention systems, whose production and

---

[10]     For more information, see: www.G4S.com.

installation was worth an estimated €1.36 billion plus in 2004, for a total private security turnover of €2.45 billion (Van der Graaff and Melchior, 2005: 9).

As regards *personnel*, the security yearbook data indicates that in-house staff are concomitantly replaced by contract staff, but, on the whole, they suggest a personnel growth from 10,227 guards in 1981 to 30,000 in 2001. Other research is more moderate. For example, Quickscan counted a total of about 27,950 (23,630 FTE) employees, not counting in-house personnel, in 2005. Nonetheless, once the in-house sector is included, the total number of guards can still be estimated at some 30,000, which, in relative numbers, is below the EU average.

# 7 Private Security Growth: Exploring Explanatory Factors

Whereas the previous chapter sought to map out the growth of the Dutch private security industry, this chapter asks how this growth can be explained. As outlined earlier, academic publications have presented several explanatory factors that can be summarized under the headings rising crime and related problems, growth of mass private property, economic rationalities, government policy toward private sector participation, an overburdened police force and the professionalization of private security. The following discussion analyses each category in turn, then the final section offers preliminary conclusions about the constellation of factors argued to give rise to the industry. These conclusions form the foundation for a more in-depth understanding of mounting private security, which is developed in the third part of the book.

## 7.1 Rising crime and related problems

The rise of private security is often associated with growth in recorded crime rates that, according to official police statistics, increased more than tenfold (sixfold, if corrected for population growth) between 1960 and 2004. As Figure 7.1 demonstrates, after an explosion in the 1960s, 1970s and early 1980s, registered crime rates have been flattening out:[1] except for a few upturns in the 1990s, the line for prior years drops slightly. However, the data presented here contain only the most serious offences: many (minor) incidents remain unreported, which inherently implies an additional huge 'dark number' of cases. These latter can be measured by crime victimization surveys designed to assess the number of hidden crimes and the consequences of such offences (Eggen, 2005). According to these surveys, as of 2004, 3.4 million people annually become victims of one or another type of criminal assault. Moreover, some individuals are victimized more than once, producing a total estimate in excess of 4.5 million offences per year.

---

[1] Wittebrood and Nieuwbeerta (2006) questioned the idea of rising crime during the prior quarter century, arguing that higher crime levels in the 1980–2004 period can be mostly explained by improved police registration and a generally increased citizen willingness to report offences.

**Figure 7.1: Registered crime rates (x 1,000), 1960–2004**
(source: Census database; www.cbs.nl)

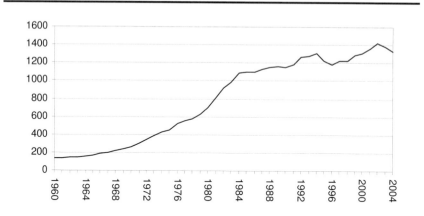

### 7.1.1 Crime and business losses

Researchers and policymakers alike have lately begun to record the huge direct and indirect business losses incurred from crime. One report, the Businesses and Organizations Monitor (abbreviated MBI in Dutch), set the total costs for criminal victimization in 2001 at €1.3 billion (Visser et al., 2002; random sample of 5,000 businesses). Another more recent project, the Trade and Industry Crime Monitor (abbreviated MCB in Dutch) estimated that businesses lost approximately €700 million in revenues in 2004 (Oomen et al., 2004; 37,831 surveyed companies, response rate = 53%), primarily from theft, fraud, devastation and burglary, frequently carried out by the business's own employees (i.e., insider crimes). The catering, retail and transport sectors were the most vulnerable for crime and disorder problems with between 40% and 50% falling victim. Both these publications indicated that businesses' cumulative investment in crime prevention strategies, while predominantly in the form of technical solutions (e.g., locks, fences, alarms), also includes human supervision (e.g., security guards, receptionists, janitors) among the top 10 precautions.

### 7.1.2 Crime and fear

In addition to crime and victimization studies, both the census and the Police Population Monitor (Intomart, 2005) have carried out national surveys on feelings of insecurity (also termed 'subjective insecurity') using items related to scary neighborhood places, changes in outdoor leisure activities, the perceived chance of a burglary and fear of being home alone. The latest figures indicate that 21.8% to 24% of the respondents (a random sample of 52,560 citizens) occasionally felt insecure, which represented a slight decline from previous years. Nonetheless, in the context of a world risk society obsessed with protecting itself against invisible threats, crime and fear still rank high on the political, social and media agendas. This is particularly true since the terrorist acts of September 11, 2001, which pose new dangers to national security. However, there seems no evidence that Al-Quaeda was a decisive factor in the growth of private security: apart from small waves after the attacks, terrorism appears not to have had a long-lasting impact on the industry as a whole,[2] although the technical sector producing security equipment like x-ray machines, CCTV, identity card systems and bomb-detectors has probably benefited most from the hysteria.

### 7.2 Growth of mass private property

Changes in post-industrial landscapes have attracted rising attention from urban sociologists. For example, Burgers (1999) outlined developments in the ordering, use and experience of (quasi-)public spaces, including mass private property, that are greatly affecting the geographic layout of modern cities. He focused, distinctively, on trends in business accommodations and office spaces, retail sectors and leisure markets and residential areas; trends, briefly examined below, that have emerged as a central issue in contemporary, US-dominated, discussions about burgeoning private security.

### 7.2.1 Business, retail and leisure facilities

Market research has identified in excess of 4,000 types of business accommodations (e.g., factories, storage facilities and distribution centers) and office spaces in the Netherlands (Mensen and Rijt-Veltman, 2005; desk research, 1,800 surveys among entrepreneurs and a few expert interviews). Many of these corporate premises are 'motorway locations' built near major highways and intersections and only reachable by car, a trend occurring largely since the 1980s. From 1993 to 2000, the supply of business accommodation remained stable at 3 to 4 million m[2] in, but since 2003, this number has rapidly increased to 6.5 million m$^2$. The market for office buildings has followed the same pattern: growth percentages have doubled over the last few years.

A second, and perhaps largest, motivator of mass private property growth is the expanding retail sector. Mensen and Rijt-Veltman (2005: 13)

---

[2]     It may even be possible to expect an impact in the opposite, public, direction. Following the 9/11 attacks, private security staff guarding airports in the US were accused of incompetence, which meant that their posts were returned to state hands (Seidensat, 2004).

counted circa 2,500 shopping locations, of which 2,100 contain five shops or
more. Moreover, as indicated by the Dutch Council of Shopping Centers, the
number of systematically developed shopping centers (i.e., larger neighborhood
and community centers within a two or three mile radius, as well as various
regional malls) has grown rapidly upwards from 1957 (see Figure 7.2). Yet the
oldest existing Dutch example of a shopping center, in the Hague, dates back to
1885.

As a final example of mass private property, it is worth noting that the
Netherlands, like other European countries, has copied the North American
practice of spending much spare time in commercially exploited leisure
facilities.[3] This development is mirrored in holiday, sports and entertainment
sites, many of which have a fairly long history. For example, Stadium
Feyenoord was opened in 1936 and Efteling in 1952. The former has
progressively been reshaped into a citadel-like 'security bubble' (Bottoms and
Wiles, 1997: 351) open to members or supporters with club cards.

**Figure 7.2: Number of shopping centers, 1950–2004**
(source: Dutch Council of Shopping Centers)[4]

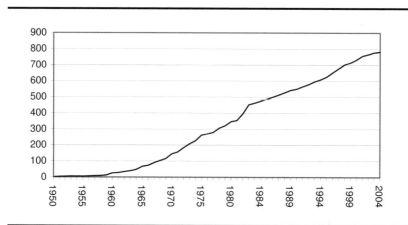

Taken together, the above observations do not suggest that North
American examples of mass private property can uncritically be duplicated in
the Netherlands. The Dutch are, for example, unfamiliar with so-called edge
cities (Garreau, 1992) containing shiny office towers and suburban mega malls.

---

[3]    Mommaas et al. (2000) and Harms (2006).
[4]    This graph draws on a database provided by the Council. The total number of
systematically developed shopping centers is currently estimated at nearly 920 in
the Netherlands. Owing to missing information for construction years, it was
impossible to include all centers in the graph.

Thus, despite the newly developed and distinctive commercial areas at the outskirts of larger municipalities, which in no way resemble the large urban perimeter zones in the US, inner cities have continued to attract many people. Moreover, Dutch politicians and policymakers have put in great effort to maintain and revitalize town centers (Mommaas et al., 2000).

### 7.2.2 Communal spaces: Residential areas

The Social and Cultural Planning Office of the Netherlands reported a growing inequality in living conditions between residential areas, one that often runs along the lines of ethnicity (Gijsbrechts, 2004). Specifically, young, highly educated and dual earning native residents have left town, which directly affects the accumulating proportion of ethnic non-Western minorities, most of whom live in the four major cities of Amsterdam, Rotterdam, Utrecht and the Hague. Such segregation dynamics have been evident from the 1970s and are widely anticipated to continue into the future.

Nonetheless, visible communal polarization, while detectable, is much less marked in the Netherlands than in the US and elsewhere. Thus, even though recent reports of the construction of Haverleij, an exclusive castle-like residence near Den Bosch,[5] a housing association's ambitious plans for a 'senior city' near Nagele,[6] and designs for expensive new buildings tend to follow the logic of enclavization, there is no indication that this 'clubbing of security'[7] will be commonplace in the near future. Rather, a combination of scarce space, urban planning policies and an overall social safety net seems to forestall far-reaching impoverishment, insidious ghettoization and widespread advancement of closed estates.

### 7.3 Economic rationalities

Changes in spatial ordering are firmly empowered by transitions to capitalism – and consequently, by growing wealth and prosperity. In this regard, the Dutch economy has enjoyed major expansion over the past quarter century, which has promoted protective and preventative measures (see Figure 7.3). Given the magnitude of the interests at stake, organizational *raison d'être* tends to reduce crime risks in and around properties (although other risk factors like fires or natural disasters may also contribute). The number of subscribers to alarm monitoring stations serves as a good example: according to the security yearbook, in 2001, there were 401,000 connections compared to the 13,170 of 20 years earlier, which represents an immense boost of around 3,000%.[8]

---

[5]     www.haverleij.nl.

[6]     www.seniorenstad.nl

[7]     Hope (2000) and Crawford (2006c).

[8]     Tenge et al. (2003: 33) and Heijboer et al. (1983: 49).

**Figure 7.3: Economic growth in the gross domestic product (GDP) at market prices (in millions of euros), 1950–2004**
(source: Census database; www.cbs.nl)

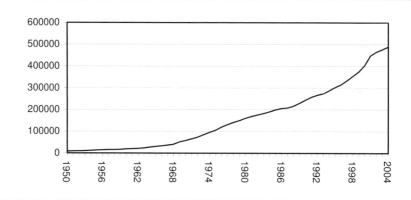

### 7.3.1 Public-private partnerships

In contrast to Pastor's (2003) finding for the US, the Dutch culture does not follow the 'carrot and stick approaches' of liability exposure, lawsuits and privatization policies. Rather, it has tried to achieve consensus on the handling of crime and disorder problems through dialogue among state and nonstate stakeholders. On both the national and regional level, platforms for crime control (*Nationale en Regionale Platforms Criminaliteitsbeheersing*) assemble police and criminal justice agencies, insurance companies, business representatives, the private security industry and others to form public-private partnerships. These platforms are committed to the Dutch Center for Crime Prevention and Safety,[9] which is the central contact point for a host of steering groups and networks on tackling crime.

Through such networks, the government and corporate sectors are poised to work together by means of instruments like quality marks and local initiatives for enhanced security of, among other areas, shopping centers, business parks, residential areas and entertainment quarters. One major step was taken in this direction in 1992 when the VPB and the Board of Chief Constables of Police (*Raad van Hoofdcommissarissen*) signed a cooperation agreement. Nonetheless, solid cooperation between the police and security guards remains captive to ideological dogmas on private surveillance in the public sphere (Hoogenboom and Muller, 2002). Specifically, according to (left-wing) political opinion, police officers must be and remain the sole protectors of public order. However, this insistence has not prevented the increasing visibility of

---

[9]      For more information, see www.ccv.nu

commercial patrols in busy city centers, tourist-oriented yacht basins and wealthy neighborhoods. Rather, private guards have spread around the country and are widely recognized as an integral part of safety and security management.

### 7.3.2 Spillover effects?

Hypothetically, the omnipresence of paid private security creates spillover effects. That is, if one organization decides to employ guards for commercial reasons, others may soon follow. Nonetheless, there is good reason for reservations against viewing such practices as self-enforcement successes. First, in the context of mass private property, an average 35% of business and shop owners act as free riders (Decisio, 2004; 21 expert interviews) who, rather than paying for commercial patrols, benefit from private security at the expense of local business communities. This practice makes the cost of hired guards fairly high and diminishes the support for collectively organized and financed programs. As a result, security staff become so expensive that, eventually, participants are forced to leave the scheme. Second, private security growth appears cyclically sensitive. That is, in periods of economic recession, customers tend to first seek savings by cutting funds for such services as private guarding and cleaning. Finally, the traditional mass private property market for contract guards is likely to be saturated in the long term. Therefore, leading security firms try to penetrate new markets like state detention services, environmental inspectorates and traffic wardening. Most particularly, because of political sensitivities about the quality and commercial objectives of private security, this is not an easy job.

### 7.4 Government policy toward private sector participation

Since the last half of the 1970s, Dutch public authorities have continuously acknowledged citizens and private (civil and commercial) organizations as active and responsible associates in safeguarding civil society. This historical development is outlined below, beginning first with the recognition of private organizations like security companies as crime prevention associates and ending with the stricter law enforcement tactics that have tended to replace the tolerant attitude for which the Dutch police are known.

### 7.4.1 A working group on private security

A first milestone in private security management politics was government attention diverted onto the growing presence and significance of contract and in-house guards. This attention constituted a pragmatic step to coming to grips with the initiatives already emerging in the industry. In effect, the Working Group on Guarding and Protection (*Werkgroep Bewaking en Beveiliging*) pressed for refurbishment of the outdated Paramilitary Organizations Act that had regulated the manned guarding sector since 1936 (the act made no allusion to detective agencies). This working group urged haste on the basis that 'the established contacts between the private security industry and the police could bring about useful combined actions of both sectors' (Ministerie van Justitie, 1977: 2). At the same time, it declared a fear of the 'morbid growth of technically less equipped companies and loss of quality for the industry when special legislation takes too long' (Ministerie van Justitie, 1977: 2). However, realizing that the design of a new law would take many years, the working group formulated temporary addendums to the outdated legislation. In addition, in 1979, it created a permanent Advisory Board for Guarding and Protection (*Adviescollege Bewaking en Beveiliging*) to render the government assistance in policy issues surrounding private security. Nonetheless, a new private security law (*Wet Particuliere Beveiligingsorganisaties en Recherchebureau; WPBR*), was not implemented until 1999, which illustrates the difficulty of reaching agreement about private security regulation.

### 7.4.2 Crime prevention and integral safety policy

In 1985, the policy plan *Society and Crime* (*Samenleving en Criminaliteit*), based on the recommendations of Member of Parliament Hein Roethof, gave the first strong push to preventive and proactive schemes (Ministerie van Justitie, 1985). Primarily, the ministry regarded petty crime as an administrative problem for a range of state and nonstate organizations. Thus, public authorities found opportunities for physical upgrades like 'vandalism-proof' bus stops, while, equally important, private institutions and citizens also had to 'do their bit' for a safer society.

Some years later, in 1990, the policy program *Law in Motion* (*Recht in Beweging*) made the first explicit mention of the desirability of strengthened private security in and around quasi-public spaces like shopping centers and industrial complexes (Tweede Kamer 1990/1991). This allusion resulted in the government leaving room for profit-seeking companies to carry out low level order maintenance functions, with private auspices like business communities increasingly undertaking the authorization of policing.

Finally, in 1993, a next firm step was taken when the Ministry of the Interior, along with other ministries, introduced integral safety strategies for instituting broad public-private partnerships, including the police, fire departments, health care services, youth work and many more outside the traditional field of government   (Ministerie van Binnenlandse Zaken en Koninkrijksrelaties, 1993). In line with this, police elites have taken a conspicuously positive stance on the expansion of citizen and private security involvement in combating crime and insecurity. Their views are drawn from a survey among chief constables (response rate, 36%), mayors (response rate,

44%) and chief public prosecutors (response rate, 44%) (Huberts et al., 2004; see Table 7.1).

**Table 7.1: Elite views on private policing** (% that agrees/strongly agrees)
(source: Huberts et al., 2004)

|  | **Police** | **Government** | **Judiciary** | **All** |
|---|---|---|---|---|
| The private security industry is indispensable in combating insecurity in society. | 89% | 91% | 100% | 93% |
| Citizen involvement, as in neighborhood watches, is indispensable to combating insecurity in society. | 67% | 46% | 82% | 65% |

### 7.4.3 Direct privatization

In close connection with governing crime, a more narrow privatization policy – one focused on ways of 'loading-off' and 'contracting-out' ancillary policing services – has recently topped the government's agenda. Specifically, as previously mentioned, multinational security companies progressively succeeded in gaining access to governmental occupations like traffic warden and custodial supervisor. Subsequently, such trends have also raised the relevant political question of whether police services can be sold to generate income from private sources. For example, the tremendous cost of policing high risk football matches has fueled much debate about who, ultimately, should provide the necessary funding. Nonetheless, the Dutch government remains cautious about such proposals (e.g., Mans, 1999): its official stance is that, because police officers have a fundamental responsibility for protecting all Dutch citizens, their services should not be influenced by private financial interests, which could violate this principle.[10]

### 7.4.4 Stricter law enforcement

Simultaneous with privatization policies, politicians have turned toward enforcing police tactics within a rigorous performance framework. Most notably after 9/11, the 2002 assassination of politician Pim Fortuyn, and the 2004 murder of film maker Theo van Gogh, the traditional image of a mild Dutch penal climate (Downes, 1988) changed dramatically (Van Swaaningen, 2005). Today, strong emotional arousal dominates citizen opinions on (possible)

---

[10]     Nonetheless, see Chapter 10 for an example of a private organization purchasing public police services in the Netherlands.

lawbreakers and wrongdoers, attuning public authorities to forceful and penalty-directed anticrime programs (Pakes, 2006). The title of the government memorandum *Controlling Crime: Investing in a Visible Government (Criminaliteitsbeheersing: Investeren in een Zichtbare Overheid)*[11] speaks for itself, and other publications have followed the same logic. As outlined in the report *Toward a Safer Society (Naar een Veiliger Samenleving)*,[12] current government objectives are stringent maintenance of public norms and values by both state and nonstate policing bodies, crime fighting and the banishment of (habitual) offenders from society. In addition, regional police covenants have been signed in the form of result-based agreements that, besides setting forth targets for more fines, dictate handing over more criminals to the Public Prosecution Service (*Openbaar Ministerie*). All such efforts are continuously evaluated as a starting point for more efficient and effective goal achievement, a trend in line with the rise of contractual governance (Crawford, 2003b). Thus, formalized obligations and compliances loom large in regulating individual and organizational behavior.

## 7.5 An overburdened police force

A persistent explanation for the growth of private security is the 'demand-gap' argument (Jones, 2005: 12) that police forces, while not necessarily suffering diminishing expenditure in absolute terms, suffer under a burden that continues to outstrip their available personnel and financial resources and leads to complaints about low police performance levels. The accepted solution to this dilemma is to use private policing to provide sufficient protection. However, exploring this line of thought first requires some explanation of the Dutch police system.

### 7.5.1 The Dutch police in brief

Historically, public policing in the Netherlands has been highly decentralized (Jones, 1995). Following the 1957 Police Act (*Politiewet*), which basically confirmed the principles established in 1851, the police administration consisted of 148 municipal forces and a state police force (*Rijkspolitie*). However, in 1993, a new Police Act engendered a radical reorganization of the fragmented and localized policing landscape into 25 regional forces supplemented by a National Police Agency (*Korps Landelijke Politiediensten*; KLPD), with several supporting divisions like traffic, railway and water police (Wintle, 1996). In addition, the Royal Military Constabulary (*Koninklijke Marechaussee*; KMAR)

---

[11]     Ministerie van Justitie en Ministerie van Binnenlandse Zaken en Koninkrijksrelaties (2001).

[12]     Ministerie van Justitie en Ministerie van Binnenlandse Zaken en Koninkrijksrelaties (2002).

represents a military police force carrying out both civil and military tasks. For example, the KMAR, in close cooperation with the KLPD, guards the Members of the Royal House and is the primary police agency at Schiphol International Airport, but it also performs law enforcement duties for the Dutch army.

One crucial distinction defined in the 1993 Police Act is the division of responsibilities for actual police action (authority or *gezag*) versus finance and personnel (administration or *beheer*). As a result, the Dutch police organization is subject to a dual system of control. Issues of police policy and management are determined by 25 regional boards (*regionale colleges*) consisting of the mayors (or burgomasters: *burgemeesters*) of all municipalities within the force area. The mayor of the largest regional municipality acts as police force manager (*korpsbeheerder*), participating with the regional chief constable and chief public prosecutor in a system of triangular consultation and decision-making (*driehoeksoverleg*). These officials meet with all mayors in the region and establish policy on the distribution of finance, personnel, vehicles and buildings. Once general decisions have been made, mayors, police chiefs and public prosecutors implement the policies at the municipal level.

In essence, this system guarantees democratic governance by separating various powers over the police between different branches. However, in terms of transparency and government supervision, it may be argued that the Dutch police system tussles with diverse problems. First, the rather vague theoretical difference between 'administration' and 'authority' is hard to maintain and second, supervision over regional boards is inadequate (Muller, 2002). Specifically, municipal councilors can only apply *indirect* influence via respective mayors (who are not elected but appointed by the Queen), which suggests that regional boards have a fairly autonomous position within the police service. Thus, in terms of accountability, public policing in the Netherlands arguably suffers from a structural democratic deficit.

### 7.5.2 Mounting criticism

According to staff numbers, compared to EU member states, the numbers of the Netherland police have lagged behind other countries for many years (Van Dijk and De Waard, 2001), although recent statistics indicate sizeable investments in public policing over the last decade or so (see Figures 7.4 and 7.5). Nonetheless, Dutch beat officers are often trapped in a scapegoat position because of rising endemic disapproval of police officers' overall performance. The origins of such criticism are detailed in the following paragraphs.

**Figure 7.4: Expenditures on police regions (in millions of euros), 1994–2005**
(source: Census database; www.cbs.nl)

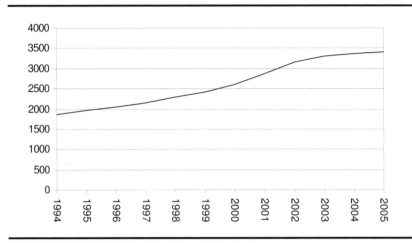

**Figure 7.5: Number of police officers at regional forces and KLPD
(in FTE), 1994–2005** (source: Ministry of Justice) [13]

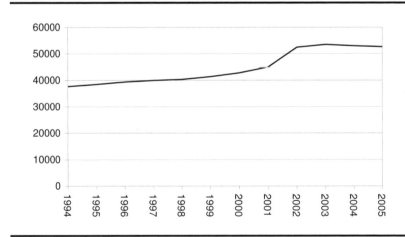

[13]     This graph draws on data provided by the Ministry. The swift growth after 2002 is
         due to a new counting system that includes police trainees in total staff numbers.

### 7.5.2.1 Bureaucratic obstacles

A first line of criticism concerns the allocation of police resources. As Table 7.2 shows, the category 'management and office work' encompasses an enormous amount. Indeed, for four selected regional forces with approximately the same working conditions and assignments, the Dutch Court of Audit (*Algemene Rekenkamer*) found that 43% to 51% of their time and finances go to filling out forms, policy-making, communication, education, logistics, illness, absence and other factors not directly contributing to executive police work (Tweede Kamer, 2002/2003). Thus, the Dutch police are inherently subject to bureaucratic inertia, which decreases their visibility in neighborhoods and streets

**Table 7.2: Police capacity in the Netherlands, 2001**
(source: Dutch Court of Audit; Tweede Kamer, 2002/2003)

|                                | Force 1 | Force 2 | Force 3 | Force 4 |
|--------------------------------|---------|---------|---------|---------|
| Management and office work[14] | 43%     | 51%     | 48%     | 45%     |
| Criminal investigation         | 9%      | 12%     | 10%     | 10%     |
| Community policing             | 39%     | 31%     | 27%     | 24%     |
| Operational support            | 6%      | 5%      | 8%      | 10%     |
| Emergency calls                | 3%      | \*\*[15]| 7%      | 10%     |
| Other work                     | <0.5%   | 1%      | <0.5%   | 1%      |

### 7.5.2.2 Public pressure on criminal justice

The very low (15% to 20%) clear-up rate (Eggen et al., 2005: 89) and minimal conviction level in the Netherlands have further negative implications for the (perceived) performance of Dutch police forces. Indeed, Boutellier sketched the criminal justice chain connecting total number of offences (input) with actual imprisonment (output) as an upside down pyramid or 'safety delta' to illustrate that out of 4.5 million (but probably much more) offences, only 52,000 offenders ended up in prison (see Figure 7.6),[16] Of course, this picture is somewhat tentative because first, a moderately small group of notorious recidivists (*draaideurcriminelen*) is responsible for a huge amount of (petty) crime and second, the public prosecution service inflicts punishments other than prison sentences. For example, offences can also be punishable by fines and alternative deterrents. Juveniles taken into custody for so-called minor offences

---

| [14] | These numbers include the absence of police officers owing to, for example, illness training or work outside their own jurisdiction. |
|------|------|
| [15] | Emergency calls are embedded in other categories. |
| [16] | This idea is based on Boutellier (2004). |

such as vandalism are often not sent to jail but rather must participate in projects that include damage compensation. These objections compress the gap between number of offences and number of imprisonments. Nonetheless, the core message is that criminal justice and police alike – flooded by criminal cases – feel colossal, and rapidly increasing, pressure to perform. Thus, intense public longing for reassurance and law enforcement has resulted in an apparently overstrained system, which authorities try to relieve through a combination of crime-fighting and crime-prevention strategies.

**Figure 7.6: The 'safety delta'**

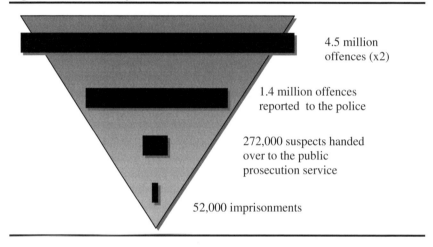

4.5 million offences (x2)

1.4 million offences reported to the police

272,000 suspects handed over to the public prosecution service

52,000 imprisonments

Huberts et al. (2004), drawing on a survey of chief constables (response rate, 36%), mayors (response rate, 44%) and chief public prosecutors (response rate, 44%), made roughly the same diagnoses. As illustrated in Table 7.2, an overwhelming majority (81%) of these respondents agreed that the government is ostensibly not capable of controlling crime in society. Thus, politicians felt trapped between problems of police and public service capacity, on the one hand, and citizen's security desires, on the other. Accordingly, in line with policy developments, 87% of survey respondents thought that crime policies have become harsher over the past years, whereas 58% agreed with the statement that 'a lot of the assistance police officers render to citizens is "welfare work", which the police should abandon'. In contrast, 42% of all respondents supported the idea of community policing in the belief that police assistance to citizens should have higher priority.

**Table 7.3: Elite views on crime, policing and public expectations**
(% that agrees/strongly agrees) (source: Huberts et al., 2004)

|  | Police | Government | Judiciary | All |
|---|---|---|---|---|
| Crime policies have become harsher over the past years. | 89% | 73% | 100% | 87% |
| Harsher crime policies are the result of: | | | | |
| 1) Increasing crime and (feelings of) insecurity. | 44% | 36% | 64% | 48% |
| 2) Disappointing results of previous policies. | 67% | 55% | 64% | 62% |
| 3) Increasing unrest among citizens and in the media. | 100% | 82% | 82% | 88% |
| Much of the assistance police officers render to citizens is 'welfare work', which the police should abandon. | 56% | 55% | 64% | 58% |
| Community policing and police assistance to citizens deserves higher priority. | 25% | 91% | 9% | 42% |
| Today's politics are trapped between citizen's calls for safety and the realization that the government is not capable of guaranteeing this safety. | 78% | 82% | 82% | 81% |

### 7.5.2.3 Dissatisfied citizens

In a democratic and emancipated country like the Netherlands, assertive citizens view themselves as no longer submissive to public authorities. Rather, they deem themselves 'clients' who deserve recognition and proper treatment. As the 2005 Police Population Monitor stated, the number of survey respondents (a random sample of 52,560 citizens) who reported being '(very) satisfied with the overall police performance in the neighborhood' has dropped from 62% to 54% over the last twelve years (Intomart, 2005: 82). Despite a more recent report suggesting that these satisfaction rates are slowly improving (Intomart, 2006), citizens have become more critical of the police. Many complain that officers fail to act vigorously enough and criticize the discouraging outcomes after reporting crime to the police. Interestingly, in chorus with complaints about a failing police force that is too soft, qualitative perception research has revealed that many individuals react negatively to the police putting more energy into order maintenance and rule enforcement. They find it 'terribly unfair' that they are fined for minor traffic offences like speeding while hard crime and disorder are, in their eyes, not handled appropriately (Van den Berg and Soffer, 2005: 112).

### 7.5.2.4 A business perspective

From a business perspective, opinion research among top business executives has demonstrated that the satisfaction level for police effectiveness is unswervingly low: 'the Netherlands is among the nethermost regions, just above countries like Greece, Belgium and Italy' (Van Dijk and De Waard, 2001: 13). Moreover, according to the 2002 Businesses and Organizations Monitor, half (51%) of the companies they surveyed were dissatisfied with police conduct following a crime report (cited in Visser et al., 2002). Indeed, the primary reason for never reporting criminal offences, besides choosing private solutions to deal with damage and losses, was mistrust of the police. For example, in line with research from 2002, the 2004 Trade and Industry Crime Monitor (Oomen et al., 2004) found that, on average, 52% of the firms surveyed had a negative opinion about the police, with respondents pointing mainly to disappointing results.

### 7.5.2.5 Recent developments in police policy

In November 2005, the Steering Group Evaluation of the Police Organization (Stuurgroep Evaluatie Politieorganisatie, 2005) reacted to general discontent with police functioning by proposing police reform. Their point of departure was a 'concern model' to improve the national cooperation and coordination between regional forces, the National Police Agency and other police units. According to this proposal, the locally embedded authority over the police forces stayed intact, municipal councils strengthened their accountability powers, stricter performance measurements had to assure higher police output and regional councils were admitted to regional safety administrations (*regionale veiligheidsbesturen*), which oversee fire departments, ambulance services and additional emergency services.

This latter, termed an 'integral safety' approach, is also currently in vogue among the Board of Chief Constables of Police. Their 2005 memorandum *Police in Evolution* (*Politie in Ontwikkeling*) on the future of Dutch policing emphasized the mushrooming of state and nonstate supervisors in the public domain (Projectgroep Visie op de Politiefunctie, 2005). In fact, because such fragmentation of police providers and auspices is an actuality that can no longer be denied in the Netherlands, the board suggested joint programs ('program management') as an adequate means for coherent and effective task sharing, within which, at the local level, the municipality would serve an essential coordinating function. Nonetheless, surprisingly, to date there has been little or no discussion about such proposals, even though the elevated position of private organizations in local security networks necessitates assiduous reflection on quintessential governance functions like management, democratic control and accountability.

### 7.6 Professionalization of private security
Academic commentators have spilled much ink bemoaning the unprofessional practices of paid security personnel. In crudest terms, private guards are asserted to be incompetent workers who challenge, if not destabilize, one of the most imperative police functions – domestic security. Although this view is overly exaggerated, leading private security companies do indeed work hard to overcome their negative image. The sections below first detail their struggles and then describe broader efforts to improve legislation and training.

### 7.6.1 A struggling industry
On November 22, 2004, the 65th anniversary of the Dutch Association of Private Security Organizations (VPB), its chairman declared the industry 'mature' and 'ready for a promising future'. About one year later, the multinational company Group 4 Securicor used the same jubilant tone when discussing the congress Growth and Change in the Practice of Private Security (*Groei en Verandering in de Praktijk van Particuliere Beveiliging*) inspired by my own research project (Zeist, May 26, 2005):

> Remarkably, scholars at VU University, who have conducted intensive research on 'hard' numerical evidence of, and interrelations between, private security, crime levels and public order maintenance, organized the congress. This is a significant development. Scholarly attention for

> private security namely [sic] implies that private security has conquered
> a fully-fledged role in the Dutch policing landscape. Private security
> has reached certain maturity. (Group 4 Securicor, 2005: 2)

However, in spite of such self-confidence, private security appears to be an
industry struggling with itself. One sweeping critique is that the industry has a
tremendously demand-driven focus on low prices, which impedes advancements
in staff proficiency. For example, in 2005 market research on professionalization
as a function of customer satisfaction  – including the price/quality ratio of
services, the accessibility and proactiveness of office workers and the accuracy
and knowledge of guards employed by multinationals (Dessing, 2005; 250
completed surveys) – the Dutch private security industry scored 6.9 on a 1 to 10
scale. When assessed against the benchmark of 'facility services' (7.4), this
score is mediocre. Intriguingly, clients are more positive about smaller private
security organizations than about the leading ones (Dessing, 2005: 14). Follow-
up market research from 2006 (Dessing, 2006b) indicated that satisfaction with
private security, with a score of 7.4, was rising. However, respondents insisted
that smaller (family-run) enterprises were doing a finer job than their
multinational competitors, with the eminence of security work a point of
ongoing contention.

     In addition, from both outside and inside the industry, critics have noted
that the personal skills of executive personnel are unconvincing. Seen
negatively, this 'type of chap' does not always inspire confidence. Thus,
according to Terpstra (2007), those in new policing occupations like contract
guarding, even after they have passed the prescribed courses, may lack the
indispensable professional resources and statutory authority necessary for their
work. As a result, scholars have argued, private security work is depicted as
unappealing and so marginally paid that it fails to attract the cleverest workers
(Livingstone and Hart, 2003). This vicious circle of low pay and low quality is
hard to break because customers, who can barely differentiate between look-
alike companies competing in the same market, see cheap guards as the best
value for money. Realistically, the security industry still strives to overcome its
deeply engrained stereotype of a 'grudge purchase'.

### 7.6.2 Legislation and training
On a national level, since the reports of the Working Group Guarding and
Protection (1975, 1977) and the 1999 implementation of the Private Security
Providers and Detective Agencies Act (WPBR in Dutch), the government has
worked hard to gradually improve regulatory systems for private security and
bestow professionalism upon employees. The WPBR strengthened, among other
things, legislation on the licensing, training, uniforms, complaint procedures and

day-to-day activities of both the guarding and investigative sectors of private security. Today, such companies must be licensed by (and registered with) the Ministry of Justice in The Hague. Before granting them a permit, the ministry runs a criminal background check and requests the obligatory Basic Diploma for Security Employees. This diploma involves completion of a maximum 12-month (on-the-job) training program that covers both theoretical and practical aspects of security work. Some larger security companies offer extra courses on specific security functions and first aid.

Obligatory basic training programs have been evaluated positively in terms of professionalization, although improvements, including better design of course materials and practical applications, have also been strongly recommended (De Ruijter, 2006; 13 expert interviews and 137 completed surveys). One exception to the regular education requirements is the stewarding sector. Stewards at sports events only receive very limited training delivered by the Royal Dutch Football Association. To fill this void, the football world has recently introduced event security officers (ESOs), a type of more highly qualified steward.

### 7.6.3 An international perspective

From an international perspective, in assessing the formal content of such legislation, Button (2007b) rated the Netherlands among the top three of a European Champions League in term of private security regulation in 15 member states (see Table 7.3). He judged the quality and comprehensiveness of national legislation and regulation based on the following criteria:

- A licensing system for contract private security staff is in place (2 points) or not in place (0 points);
- Mandatory training for unarmed security guards; no compulsive training = 0 points; up to 40 hours = 1 point; 41 to 80 hours training = 2 points; 81 to 120 hours = 3 points and 120 hours plus = 4 points;
- A minimum level of training and skill is a requisite for security managers (yes – 1 point; no = 0 points);
- A licensing system for in-house private security staff is in place (2 points) or not in place (0 points); and
- Explicit licensing regulations for security firms (2 points) or not (0 points). (Adapted from Button, 2007b: 121–122)

In practice, problematically, the clarity and enforcement of legislation in the Netherlands is weak. Practitioners complain that rules are imprecise, ambiguous and not always adequate. Moreover, as evaluation research has revealed, the supervision of the industry differs considerably between police regions, leading to unequal treatment of private security companies (Batelaan and Bos, 2003; various expert interviews). One undesired and potentially harmful side effect is that companies whose licensing application is rejected try to get a working permit in any other, more willing jurisdiction. Even worse, because the industry does not like 'bell-ringers' and because, contrary to WPBR standards, the police and public prosecution service barely uphold the law, the effectiveness of accountability mechanisms is unsatisfactory. Thus, faced with many more pressing worries, local and regional government officials give obviously low priority to the statutory regulation of private security. Overall, the WPBR has arguably not slowed down the unfettered growth of licenses in the Netherlands, especially as requirements with regard to, for example, criminal background checks, compulsory diplomas and certified equipment have not much increased (or even lowered) start-up costs, thus making it relatively easy for newcomers to enter the market.

**Table 7.4: Champion league of EU regulation** (source: Button, 2007b)

| State | Licensing security guards | Training unarmed guards | Managerial competence/ training standards | Licensing in-house guards | Special licensing security firms | Total points |
|---|---|---|---|---|---|---|
| Spain | 2 | 4 | 2 | 2 | 2 | 12 |
| Belgium | 2 | 4 | 2 | 2 | 2 | 12 |
| Netherlands | 2 | 3 | 2 | 2 | 2 | 11 |
| Portugal | 2 | 2 | 2 | 2 | 2 | 10 |
| Sweden | 2 | 4 | 2 | 0 | 2 | 10 |
| Denmark | 2 | 3 | 2 | 0 | 2 | 9 |
| Finland | 2 | 3 | 2 | 0 | 2 | 9 |
| France | 2 | 1 | 2 | 2 | 2 | 9 |
| Ireland | 2 | 1 | 2 | 2 | 2 | 9 |
| Austria | 2 | 0 | 2 | 0 | 2 | 6 |
| Germany | 2 | 1 | 2 | 0 | 0 | 5 |
| Greece | 2 | 0 | 0 | 2 | 0 | 4 |
| Italy | 2 | 0 | 0 | 0 | 2 | 4 |
| England & Wales | 2 | 1 | 0 | 0 | 0 | 3 |
| Luxembourg | 0 | 0 | 0 | 0 | 2 | 2 |

The foregoing argument is especially noteworthy in light of the European Commission's pronouncement that the comparatively strict Dutch legislation contravenes a January 2004 draft directive aimed at encouraging freedom to transport goods, capital and services within the EU. This judgment opened the doors for stern self-regulation, guidelines and benchmarking within the market. In reaction, the Dutch industry association VPB recently introduced a code of conduct and quality label for its members to propagate their reliability and integrity nationwide. Similarly, in the supranational arena, CoESS (an European umbrella organization for national private security associations) is exploring ways of harmonizing the requirements of different legal systems as it attempts to set the minimum norms and rules that are arguably important to public assurance that associated companies are professional and trustworthy throughout Europe. However, the practical implications of these policies have, until now, been works in progress.

## 7.7 Analysis
The following paragraphs evaluate the 'goodness of fit' between privatizing policing and the explanations for this privatization. After first mapping out trends in the security industry, the discussion focuses on major shifts in size and organization. These shifts are then evaluated separately as determinants of the timing and extent of changes in the explanatory factors. This tying together of patterns culminates in a preliminary explanation for the growth of private security in the Netherlands.

### 7.7.1 Shifts in the size and organization of private security
Over the last thirty years, security employment rates in the Netherlands have experienced a series of growth spurts, particularly between 1985 and 1990 and 1995 and 2001 (see Figure 7.7). As a result, the Dutch private security industry has enjoyed rapid turnover growth (see Figure 7.8). The market now employs some 30,000 guards.

### 7.7.2 Rising crime and related problems
The expansion of private security has habitually been linked to skyrocketing crime problems and terrorist attacks. Yet, while this explanation sounds logically attractive, empirically, it is not very persuasive. First, the industry began growing the moment that recorded crime rates became relatively stabilized (see also Van der Vijver, 2001: 31), albeit at high level and at the expense of high (business) losses. Second, fear of crime is in decline, while private security is still growing. Third, the recent terrorist attacks in New York (2001), Madrid (2004) and London (2005) did not stimulate overall industry growth; rather, its total workforce remained stable over that period. Admittedly, there may be 'suspended effects', but several other factors, outlined below, are more likely contributors.

**Figure 7.7: Total workforce of contract private security guards, 1981–2006**
(sources: Census database (www.cbs.nl); Donkers, 2003a, 2003b, 2005 and 2006)[17]

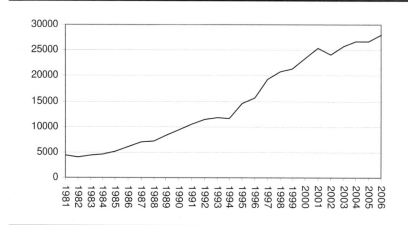

**Figure 7.8: Total turnover of the private security industry (in millions of euros), 1987–2005** (sources: Census database (www.cbs.nl); Donkers, 2003a, 2003b, 2005 and 2006)

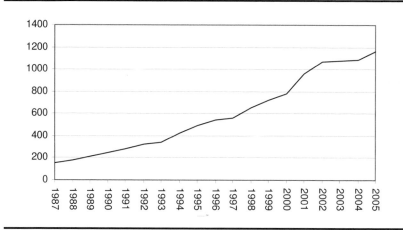

---

[17]     The dip between 2001 and 2002 results from combining two different data sources: it does not necessarily represent a fallback in private security.

### 7.7.3 Growth of mass private property

At first glance, there is support for the prevalent idea that changes in spatial ordering have fueled the necessity for security guards. The construction of business accommodations, office complexes, shopping centers/malls, leisure facilities and other quasi-public spaces has indeed intensified since the 1980s. That said, however, the influential mass private property gives no pervasive answer to private security growth, most particularly given that occurrence of mass private property pre-dates the boosts in contract guards have always been, and increasingly are, active in nonprivate spaces like neighborhoods. Thus, more precise elucidation of the rapid increases in private security is needed

### 7.7.4 Economic rationalities

Relations between economic development and a booming security market are plausible, because wealth breeds both opportunities for criminal behavior and income to install extra protection. On the other hand, since economic growth has slowed down perceptibly over the last few years, private security's workforce and annual turnovers have been sliding too. This decline may justify the conclusion that the industry is cyclically sensitive. Another drawback is that free riders refuse to contribute to the guarding services, rendering private security schemes at, for example, office complexes unattractive for paying participants. Private security is thus a precarious enterprise whose growth cannot be trivially extrapolated into the future.

### 7.7.5 Government policy toward private sector participation

Over the years, the Dutch government has redistributed responsibilities like parking warden services and custodial services to commercial organizations, but even so, direct privatization (i.e., the loading-off and contracting-out of government tasks) cannot single-handedly explain the industry's growth. The upsurge of, among other occupations, parking wardens and detention officers has actually not been extensive enough. Yet public authorities have continually propagated within society the urgency of preventing and detecting crime. In other words, there is good reason to claim that the government, mainly through its 1980's crime prevention policy and its 1990's integral safety policy, has created a social environment in which the private industry could flourish (see also Van der Vijver, 2001: 32). As Joh (2004: 68) pointed out, '[p]rivate police today find themselves the beneficiaries in the debate over the responsibility and capability of government to control crime'.

### 7.7.6 An overburdened police force

The theory of fiscal constraints, downsizing police departments and a resultant security vacuum hold no ground in the Netherlands. Rather, statistics indicate that public funding of the police has been intensifying considerably to accommodate extra personnel. For example, in the thirteen years since the 1993 reorganization, expenditures have increased from just below 2,000 to around 3,500 million euros. Correspondingly, the employment level in public policing has risen from around 38,000 to almost 53,000 FTE. These figures bring to the forefront the dramatic dilemma of an 'impossible police mandate' (Manning, 1977: 13) in which the police are unable to pledge full reassurance to citizens, businesses and organizations. Indeed, police forces must carry out elementary social control functions in the face of ongoing frictions between towering public expectations and the weight officers can realistically bear given their administrative burden, scarce time and policy priorities. The pursuit for safety outstripping police resources thus seems a background condition for the government's entrusting secondary policing responsibilities to the security industry.

### 7.7.7 Professionalization of private security

The success of contract security companies has paid off moderately well in professionalization advances and know-how. Nonetheless, even with progress in training and quality standards, private security is, above all, an extremely competitive industry, which has limited interest in spending too much on innovation and improvement. It is the lowest price, not the excellence of the work, that is the prime factor in most customers' selection of a company – a situation that is evidently hampering evolution in the quality of manned guarding services. One exception is the technical equipment sector, which probably invests most in research and development.

### 7.8 Preliminary conclusions

The above analysis makes possible the drawing of some preliminary conclusions about the factors driving private security. First, *rising rime and related problems* have not corresponded to shifts in private security. That is, crime rates have flattened and declined as the industry began its rise in the Netherlands. Moreover, terrorist attacks have had no strong impact on private security. On the contrary, the overall number of guards has shown no extraordinary growth since 9/11.

Second, trends in *mass private property* have had no decisive effect on private security growth. Although rises in contract guards to some extent coincide with growing numbers of, for example, shopping centers, the industry has also expanded in other directions (e.g., residential communities). Equally important, many Dutch examples of mass private property pre-date recent increases in private security personnel.

Third, *economic rationalities* and *waves* have appeared that match patterns in private security. For example, after the industry encountered head winds following the economic slowdown of 2000, its security market plummeted somewhat. Moreover, free riders are challenging private security growth. Customers prefer to buy guarding services at the lowest costs and refuse to pay for joint arrangements when prices run too high. In other words, economic rationalities seem important in explaining shifts in private security.

Fourth, the *government policy* of concomitantly spreading responsibility for crime prevention to individuals, communities and nonstate organizations has turned out to be an influential factor. Most particularly, it has resulted in the Dutch industry being drawn into multiple public-private partnerships aimed at crime prevention in (semi)public spaces.

Fifth, government policy toward responsibilization and privatization has meant pragmatic solutions to an *overstrained criminal justice apparatus*; large investments in police manpower have clearly not been sufficient to compensate for the everyday burden laid upon police officers. Thus, the idea of an overburdened police force serves as a background factor for today's politics directed to private security.

Finally, the *professionalization of manned guarding services* cannot by itself illuminate the industry's accomplishments. Rather, such steps are an effect not a cause of growing private security. Thus, the professionalization thesis must be rejected.

# Part 3: Local Case Studies

# 8    Efteling: World of Wonders

Efteling, the most famous amusement park in the Netherlands,[1] is located in the rural town of Kaatsheuvel (municipality of Loon op Zand; population, 23,000). Even though most of the three million yearly visitors who enjoy the picturesque fairy tales and dazzling attractions are law abiding families, an intelligent security approach is needed to deal with the huge streams of people. Therefore, in 1985, Efteling established an in-house private security force inside the park premises to take over the protective duties formerly carried out by park keepers.

This current chapter outlines the history of Efteling (Van den Diepstraten, 2002) and its security guards from 1952 to 2005. After an introductory section, the discussion addresses four time periods that epitomize changes in the size and organization of private security. Data collection, beyond the preliminary direct observations and review of relevant literature, consisted of six interviews with seven respondents (two interviewed together) – Efteling's head safety manager, three (former) security managers, two (former) police officers and a politician.

## 8.1 The forerunner of Efteling (1933-1952)

Kaatsheuvel, a small village in central Brabant, had once thrived on an industry of tanners and shoemakers but during the 1930's worldwide depression, it was facing hard times. Therefore, in 1933, when two Roman Catholic clergymen, Father Klein and Father Rietra, put forward the idea of building a sports park for the town's children, the initiative was warmly embraced as a socioeconomic incentive, and the sports park – consisting of a football pitch, two training pitches and a playing field – opened its doors on May 19, 1935. Even though the initiative proved to be an instant success, it was not until after World War II that the premises were expanded, from 12 to 65 hectares, after the municipal council sold Efteling a large tract of land. In 1950, the premises became the property of the Efteling Nature Park Foundation, 'providing physical development and relaxation for the residents of Loon op Zand, within the spirit of Roman Catholicism' (Van den Diepstraten, 2002: 8). As a result, Efteling was granted permission to dig a lake and develop extra facilities like tennis courts, walking paths, parking areas and a small forest to shelter ten life-like animated fairy tales to attract a larger public from beyond the surrounding villages.

---

[1]    For more information, see www.efteling.nl.

## 8.2 Period 1: Anton Pieck's dream (1952–1980)

In 1952, the year of its official opening, the Fairy Tale Forest enjoyed enormous popularity as almost 230,000 visitors came to see Sleeping Beauty's castle, Snow White and the Seven Dwarfs, Longneck and other fairy tale characters. Curiosity probably contributed to this surprisingly large amount of visitors as much as entertainment because Efteling was a pioneer in the Dutch leisure market and the fairy tales, skillfully designed by artist Anton Pieck and brought to life through the technical ingenuity of Peter Reijnders, were unique and innovative.

The park's attractiveness assured a steady revenue stream, making new land purchases possible. In 1955, Mayor Van der Heijden, who also chaired the park's board, agreed to further expansion of the park from 65 to 150 hectares, approximately 8 hectares of which were added to Efteling itself (enlarged to 72 hectares), while the rest were used for investment ventures like the holiday resort Het Kraanven (opened in 1960, but closed in 1985) or remained vacant. Again, Efteling had a good sense for opportunity: the total number of visitors continued to show steady growth (see Figure 8.1).

**Figure 8.1: Number of visitors to Efteling, 1952–2004** (source: Efteling)[2]

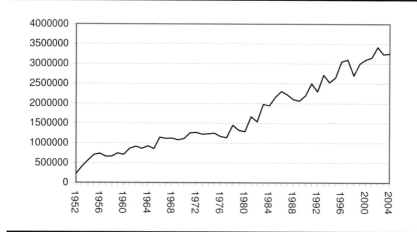

During the 1960s and 1970s, Efteling invested further in its Fairy Tale Forest, introducing, among other things, a steam train, souvenir shops, coffee corners and a restaurant. This gradual expansion went hand in hand with

---

[2]      Numbers include paying visitors at the entrance gate plus non-paying visitors (e.g. children under three years of age), visitors having an annual season ticket and visitors attending special events such as parties.

strengthened internal safety and security structures. A first aid station was founded in 1962, followed by an internal fire service in 1973. As daily earnings (and thus the risk of a hold-up) rose, other upgrading included the installation of bulletproof windows and alarm systems at cash desks and the purchase of an armored cash transport vehicle for carrying assets.

However, no noteworthy modifications in surveillance and control practices took place. Rather, policing duties like regulating large crowds fell largely to the park keepers, often aging employees who carried out general maintenance duties (e.g., litter collection) while monitoring visitor behavior. The park keepers retained this role of overseeing the park as a secondary task to their housekeeping role until the late 1970s. As the head safety manager explained, 'surveillance and control were very loosely organized. You should not forget, though, that families with children hardly caused any serious problems'.

## 8.3 Period 2: The Fairy Tale Forest and beyond (1980–1985)

The peaceful picture sketched above changed somewhat throughout the 1980s. Because business results were disappointing and visitor growth was in decline, Efteling decided to alter its policy objectives. In addition to traditional families, the park tried to reach a new, younger target group of adolescents in the 14 to 25 age bracket by presenting itself as more than just a Fairy Tale Forest. To this end, a steel roller coaster was built (Python, 1981), which, like the Fairy Tale Forest, turned out to be extremely popular from its first day of operation. Teenagers were attracted to the sensational experience of a wild ride and flocked to the park. From then on, the character of Efteling changed drastically. While Efteling's management still saw its Fairy Tale Forest as important, the general emphasis shifted to attractions that brought thrilling adventures to life – for example, the swinging pirate ship Half Moon (1982), the Piraña water slide (1983) and a breathtaking bobsled run (1985).

Nonetheless, groups of young people created more trouble than traditional families had ever done: they were increasingly involved in altercations, vandalism, petty crime and trespassing, forcing the park management to take stricter preventive measures. Because park keepers were no longer able to cope with the new situation alone, Efteling frequently called upon 10 to 15 army reservists to informally render part-time assistance. The personnel manager, who had served as a volunteer with the Dutch land forces, simply mobilized some colleagues without thinking much about the issues of training and legislation. As one security manager put it, 'the question was: do you want a part-time job? No problem. Put on a uniform, pick up a cap, and help to patrol Efteling during a busy day'.

In the years after 1981, Efteling sought a more strategic approach to its corporate security. Not only had the number of potential troublemakers been rising, but, as the park expanded, insurance companies and public authorities were also placing higher demands on the park in terms of liability, fire prevention and crime prevention. Initially, contract guards replaced the reservists to prevent nuisance and preserve social order; however, management soon decided to establish an internal security team. Without denying the advantages of flexible contract security, there was a clear need for a core group of guards. First, because they worked for more than one client, contract personnel had insufficient knowledge of specific circumstances and security risks in the park. Second, it was financially unattractive to invest in personnel that came and went. Rather, the management felt that quality standards could best be improved and a high level of commitment and skillfulness ensured by employing domestic security staff.

## 8.4 Period 3: 'We sell memories and emotions' (1985–1990)

In 1985, Efteling formed a private security team of 12 guards (4 full-time staff and 8 seasonal workers), who were sometimes supplemented during the high season with hired contract staff to assist with daily routines. As outlined in Box 8.1, these routines, which include a range of tasks, can be categorized into five security functions within the park: (1) order maintenance, (2) medical care, (3) customer-related services, (4) housekeeping and (5) information management.

Evidently, the security staff's order maintenance function was most rigorous: although the guards had no special status within public police laws, they derived this function and affiliated powers from the fact that, on entering private facilities like Efteling, paying visitors agree *de facto* with the house rules displayed at the entrance gate. These rules forbade smoking, excessive noise, drunkeness and/or use of drugs, trading alcohol and drugs, carrying weapons and displaying verbal and/or physical aggressive behavior. When people posed a threat to others by disobeying one or more of the house rules, they risked (long-term) exclusion because, dependant on the offence's significance, the Efteling management retained the right to impose a banning order against one or more persons, enforced by the security team, or when necessary, by the police. In practice, people were rarely removed from the park, because the average visitor had no intention of making trouble on a family day out.

Even so, as far back as 1985, private security involvement in upholding house rules went beyond merely reacting to antisocial behavior and crime prevention. Another major reason for establishing the in-house operation was related to commercialization processes, marked by the management's decision to convert Efteling's legal status from a foundation to a private limited company. The park's management explicitly endorsed 'selling memories and emotions' (Van den Diepstraten, 2002: 167) so, against this background, it needed a strong but low-profile private security force. As one interviewee informally argued:

> Fairy tales always have a happy ending, although, I must say, there are never private security guards present in the story. What I mean is: we are keen on preserving a pleasant atmosphere through the efforts of an unobtrusive, but present security force. There is no reason to bother visitors with conspicuously dressed 'police-style' guards.

## Box 8.1: Core tasks of in-house and contract private security guards

**Order maintenance:** access control, CCTV monitoring, foot patrols and bike patrols, overseeing visitor behavior, preserving the public peace, preventing nuisance and crime(-related) incidents, warning people to desist from such offences as antisocial behavior, making citizens' arrests and, ultimately, excluding offenders from the premises.

**Medical care:** responding to emergencies and providing first aid (in collaboration with nurses and medics working at Efteling).

**Customer-related services**: responding to visitors' requests, returning lost children, providing information.

**Housekeeping:** managing the car park, storing and transporting keys and payments, overseeing buildings and roads, detecting and reporting inconveniences such as a broken pavement.

**Information management:** filling out forms; (informal) information sharing with ambulance services, (internal) fire services, local police forces (often unidirectionally) and others.

Interestingly, after private security was implemented at Efteling, the *Rijkspolitie* (the former Dutch national state police force) developed closer relationships with the park. In fact, police officers partly trained and educated the newly formed team, advised Efteling about technopreventive measures for protecting property and, the most far-reaching, started to render assistance by taking up a more or less permanent position within the park. Their motivation was simple: Efteling was already absorbing a large share of available police resources from time to time, so, for pragmatic reasons, officers had a clear interest in the guards' competencies and working methods.

During this strengthened relationship between police officers and private security staff, the number of in-house guards declined from 12 to 8 (2 full-time workers and 6 seasonal employees). However, the daily workload for both police officers and security guards increased, mainly because since 1985, Efteling has opened for extended hours during the summer. At that time, there were even complaints from the local trilateral consultancy (*driehoeksoverleg*) of the mayor, chief constable and public prosecutor that too few police were available to patrol both the amusement park and the municipality (meeting, March 14, 1985). Policy-makers therefore questioned whether, in light of future security risks, Efteling could go ahead unhindered (meeting, October 11, 1986). Yet, somewhat counterintuitive to such worries, the police decided to retreat from Efteling, a decision about which a retired police sergeant formerly based in Loon op Zand offered the following retrospective:

> Sometime in the late 1980s, it became fashionable to set priorities and give up duties. Buzzwords were 'core tasks', 'reducing costs', 'efficiency' and 'effectives'. The very close relationship we had with the park was, all of a sudden, gone.

The small police station at Efteling from which officers were deployed to support the private security guards was closed down. For Efteling, this was a clear sign that local authorities had started to set clear priorities for public order maintenance objectives. Guards could no longer fall back on self-evident police assistance and were expected to bear greater responsibility themselves. The time had come for autonomy and no special favors from the police.

### 8.5 Period 4: A jester's dance (1990–2005)

In the early 1990s, the private security team expanded rapidly from 8 to 17 guards (see Figure 8.2) working 24/7 shifts to protect property from such risks as night intruders. The work floor was also improved by construction of a bombproof command and control room from which guards could oversee the park (1990). The head safety manager interviewed explicitly linked such developments with the ongoing retreat of the police officers. In particular, after the regionalization of the Dutch police forces in 1993, the amusement park received diminishing priority and many officers were reallocated away from Efteling toward other spots in the wider area:

> I think that especially since the 1993 police reform things have irreversibly changed. The old crew of police officers and private security guards who knew each other pretty well fell apart, because police officers were stationed elsewhere in the region. There were, of course, still contacts between the police and Efteling, but not as much as before.

**Figure 8.2: Number of in-house security guards, 1985–2004**
(source: Efteling)

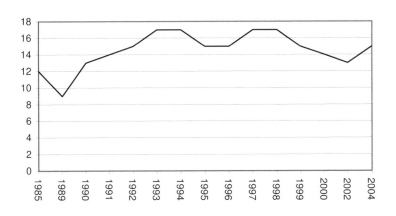

Between 1993 and 2003, the police strength in the Loon op Zand municipality remained roughly the same – somewhere between 25 and 28 FTE employees According to the mayor, this level was normally sufficient but limited during the stressful holiday season, which gave credence to the need for stricter provision of assistance. For its part, the private security team felt the police force was far more distant. The multiple agreements that officers made about the amount of support and assistance they could provide increasingly encouraged Efteling to take primary responsibility for its own order maintenance. As two interviewees explained,

> the primary responsibility for safety and security was delegated from police officers to Efteling guards. We picked up more and more signals to take care of our own business and evaluate results with the local authorities. This has led to a better structured and more professional security policy (the head safety manager).

> The security staff grew more mature as the police retreated. Their increasingly distant attitude was definitely felt and led us to organize our domestic security better (a security manager).

In addition, respondents alluded to an ongoing commercialization process that influenced the transitions in private security. While still focusing on day-trippers' fascination with fairy tales and attractions, the management began exploring broader markets of business and entertainment. Laying the foundation for a hotel, including luxurious tourist accommodation and thematic meeting rooms for business events (1992), constituted a new chapter in the history of Efteling. Specifically, it prepared the way for other initiatives like an eighteen-hole golf course (1995) and, somewhat later, the Efteling Theatre (2002) suitable for both large theatre productions and indoor business gatherings. Sporting a new logo, the magical jester Pardoes, Efteling entered the market for parties and dinners as well as product presentations and festivities. The park had become, as its brochure claimed, 'a world of wonders'.

Beginning in 1996, Efteling started treating its guests to even longer opening hours during the summer time and, in 1999, for the first time in its existence, also welcomed them in the winter. This intensified use of the facilities fuelled the risk for incidents and order problems at Efteling. Moreover, the visitors tended to cause more trouble. For example, during the 1990s, Efteling experienced a slight rise in violence, theft and vandalism for which the police were sometimes called as reinforcements for the private security team. As a result, although their number dropped by four people, the remaining guards agreed to work full time, meaning that fewer people had to take on a greater workload. One security manager clarified the situation as follows:

> Once in a while, there was discussion about what a 'reasonable' security level might be. We could have established a stronger permanent staffing, but for economic and financial reasons it was decided otherwise. The management opted for a smaller and more robust in-house team, supplemented with hired guards. Private security is always a compromise between usefulness and costs.

Together with extended opening times in summer and winter, changes in labor relations also contributed to a restructuring of the in-house security team. The immediate cause was the implementation of the so-called Flexi-Law (*Wet Flexibiliteit en Zekerheid*, 1999), which strengthened the legal position of flexible workers (especially those with on-call contracts) in regard to salaries. This law meant, in essence, that seasonal personnel who did not work over the off-season were becoming more expensive as Efteling had to keep paying them. In addition, according to the Flexi-Law, employers could only renew a temporary contract twice: once a contract was renewed for the third time (or an individual was contracted for more than three years), it became permanent. As a result, some seasonal workers were offered alternative employment at Efteling; others stayed as full-time security guards. At present, the staff consists of 15 people assisted by a maximum of 6 guards from a contracted private security firm.

## 8.6 Recent developments: Toward an integral safety policy

Shortly after the new millennium, the municipality of Loon op Zand formulated its Integral Safety Plan 2003–2007, which emphasized that 'citizens, and organizations should be closely associated with supporting crime prevention and community safety for they are all part of the same community'. This report was compliant with a national policy aimed at better cooperation between public authorities and civil society through the formation of public-private partnerships. In practice, Efteling approved draft agreements with the local police and other emergency agencies that laid down a 'safe realm' protocol (*Veiligrijk*) of scenarios to specify support in the case of acute safety problems like looting (public order), bacterial infections (health), extreme weather conditions (physical calamities) or collapsing constructions (accidents).

In so doing, this philosophy of integral safety also affected the position and tasks of Efteling's internal guarding team, which became further incorporated into the wider safety and security structures (see Figure 8.3). Today, the private guards all possess diplomas for first aid (*Eerste Hulp* and *Bedrijfshulpverlening*) and, in crisis situations, some form all-round rapid response teams (*Snel-Inzet-Teams*; SITs) designated as skilled rescue squads. Thus, the trend at Efteling is seemingly multitasking.

## Figure 8.3: The organizational structure of Efteling's safety and security

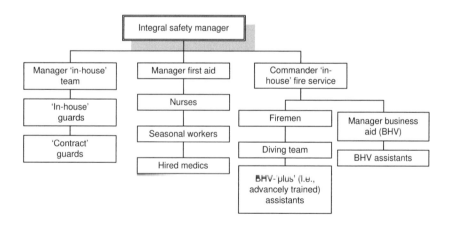

This integration of private guards with other domestic security agencies serves two principal goals. First, it better adapts private guards to caring duties: rather than seeming like distant 'policemen' they have been progressively framed as customer-oriented employees who are simultaneously sympathetic and strict. Second, in terms of the calamities, incidents and other serious disruptions that could severely damage park amiability, it is in line with Efteling's persistent efforts toward integrating and maximizing risk reduction management. The park has, after all, extensive commercial interest in continuing to be a safe and family-friendly destination packed with exciting attractions and impressive shows.

## 8.7 Analysis

The following paragraphs evaluate the goodness of fit between privatizing policing and the explanations for this privatization. First, it maps out trends in the Efteling's in-house security team with a focus on major shifts in extent and nature. Second, it evaluates these shifts as explanations for the changes in private security by tying together patterns to produce an explanation for the growth of private security at Efteling.

### 8.7.1 Shifts in the extent and nature of private security

Until the 1980s, park keepers, whose primary tasks were to sustain and maintain Efteling, also exerted some low level social control like surveillance and peacekeeping. That year, voluntary army reservists took over order maintenance activities to ensure security at the park. In 1985, the reservists were replaced by in-house security guards, who formed a core group of 4 full-time and 8 seasonal workers. In 1989, this in-house staff reduced to 9 but increased shortly afterwards (1992–1998) to a maximum of 17. Subsequent years (1999 to 2005) were marked by a sudden decrease of personnel: four people left the group, while the others were offered full-time contracts. In 2007, the in-house team consisted of 15 guards whose daily work was multifaceted, involving service-oriented customer care and housekeeping services as well as the more police-like duties of foot-patrol, rule enforcement and risk management. In addition to its own staff, during peak periods, Efteling employed flexible contract guards as extra eyes and ears.

Over the years, the relationship between Efteling security and the police has altered from cooperation to coexistence. Today, the agencies maintain good contact and sometimes meet on an informal basis to discuss problems. However, police officers are rarely visible in the park, except in the case of serious calamity. Moreover, following the implementation of the integral safety policy, the in-house security team, the police, the municipality, ambulances services and fire services negotiated a formal covenant befitting the complexity of responsibilities, tasks and competencies involved. This covenant must guarantee coordinated public-private responses to unforeseen crisis situations.

### 8.7.2 Rising crime and related problems

The institution of a private security team at Efteling was originally motivated by problems with disobedient youth. Yet further developments in antisocial behavior and petty crime did not correspond to an absolute expansion of private security, although, as the number of guards fell between 1999 and 2002, small increases in theft and vandalism led to fewer people working longer hours. Thus, shifts in private security can be explained by crime-related incidents.

### 8.7.3 Growth of mass private property

Changes in the spatial ordering, narrowed to changes in actual park size, occurred long before the foundation of the private security team. In fact, Efteling reached its definitive form by the early 1950s. Moreover, throughout its history, the park has invested heavily in new attractions to welcome ever more visitors, yet none of these trends has coincided with shifts in manned guarding. In other words, changes in mass private property can be dropped as an explanatory factor.

### 8.7.4 Economic rationalities

The suggestion of economic rationalities – redefined as growing, or at least altering, commercial interests – as an explanation struck a chord with respondents. In their view, Efteling has been constantly improving the in-house force's equipment and organizational structure for reasons of insurance constraints, longer opening hours and customer care. One recent example of such upgrading is the integration into private security of a broader integral safety structure that combines enforcement with emergency care and crisis intervention. Thus, economic rationalities were important in explaining shifts in private security.

### 8.7.5 Government policy toward private sector participation

During the mid-1980s, Efteling established close police contacts, which loosened after the government-initiated withdrawal of the late 1980s, early 1990s. Thus, Efteling became primarily responsible for policing its own premises, a shift that shaped the park's decision to amplify the size of its in-house team to a permanent security staff of around 17 guards. The 1993 police reorganization represented a definite breaking point in police officers' accommodating attitude, as 'mixed' teams who knew each other well split up and their precedence moderated A further step in government policy was the 2003 integral safety approach that placed crime on a par with disasters such as blazes, rollercoaster crashes and health epidemics. This policy resulted in a draft protocol that set standards for public/private cooperation during any emergency and brought the private security team under a broad umbrella of specialized subfields including ambulance and fire services. Thus, government policy that assigned more responsibilities to Efteling was important in explaining shifts in private security.

### 8.7.6 An overburdened police force
It is hard to say whether, as the overburdening thesis proposes, the local police force of 25 to 28 FTE employees was or was not congested with work. However, given the expanding workload generated by Efteling, there is support for the idea that, primarily since 1981, the increase in visitors to Efteling has laid exponentially increasing weight on police resources. This increase has in turn led to increasing resistance on the police's part. Thus, around the beginning of the 1990s, a period characterized by heightened government support for communal crime prevention, officers left the park, a decision that led to private security guards being given the first responsibility for problems and emergencies.

### 8.7.7 Professionalization of private security
The professionalization of in-house guards was most visible under the integral safety policy, when, for reasons of government policy and commercial interest surrounding public relations, there was a tendency to better prepare guards for crisis solving and first aid emergencies. Nonetheless, because professionalization seemed more a consequence of, rather than a contribution to, private security involvement, it can be dismissed as an influential factor.

### 8.7.8 Changes in labor law: A new factor
Unexpectedly, the thorough reorganization of Efteling's security team resulted from the 1999 Flexi-Law aimed at improving the employment rights of in-house seasonal workers. Instead, the law negatively affected the entire in-house security workforce at Efteling, where, because of their declining financial attractiveness, seasonal guards were discharged and replaced with full timers. As a result, the team shrunk to 13 guards.

### 8.8 Summary
Based on the case study results, this section has summarized the explanatory power of each factor assumed to drive shifts in private security at Efteling. Specifically it found that that changes in spatial ordering and use of mass private property, an overburdened, or at least more critical, police and professionalization of in-house security staff did not directly account for shifts in private security; while crime and disorder problems, economic rationalities, government policy toward private sector participation and changes in labor law did.

# 9    Stadium Feyenoord: 'Hand in Hand, Comrades!'

Stadium Feyenoord, nicknamed De Kuip[1] (the Tub), is the home ground of Football Club Feyenoord, one of the Netherland's top football teams. More than one million visitors per year attend the exciting football matches at the stadium,[2] some of whom take their love for the club to the extreme, causing problems not merely in Feyenoord's home city of Rotterdam (600,000 inhabitants) but throughout the Netherlands and even abroad. These hard-nosed supporters form relatively small groups of hooligans (or 'ultras'), whose collective violent behavior is the cause of both social and political concern. In 1991, Stadium Feyenoord established an in-house private security team. Until then, a loosely organized system of football attendants (*suppoosten*) and private guards, together with police officers, provided safety and security inside the stadium.

This chapter outlines the history of Stadium Feyenoord (De Wolff, 1997) and its security personnel from 1945 to 2005. After an introductory section, the discussion addresses four time periods that represent changes in the organization and size of private security. Again, information was gleaned not only from the preliminary direct observations and relevant literature but from 19 interviews with the following 23 respondents: Club Feyenoord's director of finance and operations, the director of Stadium Feyenoord, two security managers of De Kuip Safety and Security (Feyenoord's security team), two managers of Bijl Security (a private security firm), two police officers, six policymakers,[3] two former attendants (both now stewards), the manager of the Feyenoord Supporter Association, five dedicated supporters and an independent expert on hooliganism.

## 9.1 The early history of Feyenoord (1908–1945)
In 1908, a group of friends started a football team for the working classes populating the Rotterdam's southern district. This team, initially called Wilhelmina but later renamed Feyenoord for the neighborhood in which it was located, achieved much success in the 1930s, winning several local and national championships. Partly because of these victories and partly because of the absence of other sports and entertainment facilities in the area, the games attracted a rapidly growing crowd of fans. The thousands of people flocking to

---

[1]    For more information, see www.dekuip.nl.
[2]    In addition, Stadium Feyenoord regularly organized large-scale pop concerts.
[3]    These policymakers worked for the municipality of Rotterdam (two respondents), the public prosecution service of Rotterdam, the Royal Dutch Football Association and Stadium Feyenoord, respectively.

the matches motivated Feyenoord to plan a brand new stadium. Between 1931 and 1934, Leen van Zandvliet, chairman of the club's board, presented visionary concepts on what he considered an ideal football arena. On the basis of his proposals, architects designed an impressive functionalist stadium (600m²) offering space for roughly 60,000 visitors. A few years later, in March 1937, Van Zandvliet's dream came to fruition as Feyenoord won the first match played on the new pitch. This match (Feyenoord vs. Beerschot: 5–2) attracted an estimated 38,000 people, while the average number per event reached 40,000 that year (see Figure 9.1). Despite the impending Second World War, Stadium Feyenoord could face the future with confidence.

**Figure 9.1: Number of visitors to De Kuip, 1937–2004**
          (source: Stadium Feyenoord)

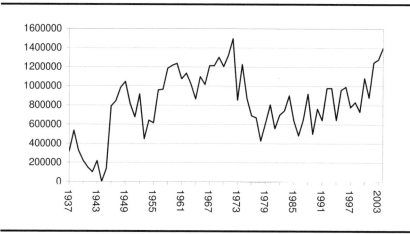

## 9.2 Period 1: A stadium for the working class (1945–1974)

Shortly after World War II, during which the German occupiers almost dismantled the stadium, Feyenoord again succeeded in attracting crowds of enthusiastic fans. Since 1958, particularly, the year that the Royal Dutch Football Association (KNVB in Dutch) introduced professional football into the Netherlands, Feyenoord has celebrated major sporting achievements. For example, in the 1960s and '70s, the team won several national championships (1961, 1962, 1965, 1969) and even conquered the Euro Cup, the World Cup (both in 1970) and the UEFA Cup (1974) titles.

One elderly supporter looked back at this period as a time of relative peace. Of course, he pointed out, Stadium Feyenoord was an arena for the working classes, the dockworkers and factory laborers, who, culturally, were eager for 'a good fight' from time to time. Their violence was, however, incidental and spontaneous rather than organized, but the nature of such violence altered throughout the 1970s as youngsters (white males aged 15 to 35) began to attend matches for the sole purpose of brawling. As the respondent put it,

> I sat next to Ajax supporters coming from Amsterdam. These supporters were (as they still are) the biggest rivals of Feyenoord. We bought each other beer and had a friendly chat. For many this is unthinkable nowadays. The hatred goes so deep. I cannot believe what has happened. It is absolutely incredible and disgraceful.

In the old days, football attendants, often described as 'aging blokes wearing a hat', were still capable of taking responsibility for social order. Feyenoord took them from a pool of volunteers who, in exchange for 'a cigar and a drink', punched tickets, pointed people to their seats and kept an alert eye on the crowd. This friendly (perhaps somewhat overly romanticized) situation slowly changed when supporters became increasingly unwilling to accept any type of authority. In the words of a fanatic Feyenoord fan, 'we don't have respect for authority; we defy authority!'

Trying to cope with the new situation, Feyenoord improved its domestic security structures. On May 31, 1972, the day of the European Championship final (Ajax versus Inter-Milan), a radio and control room came into use, and by 1973, the stadium had begun to hire specialized personnel from Bijl Security, a small contract security firm whose uniformed guards arrived with dogs to restore peace and order. The cost of such services had to be paid by Feyenoord itself, because the insurance companies saw football-related violence as an inexorable natural disaster.

In terms of football-related group violence, security staff perceived the UEFA Cup final between Feyenoord and Tottenham Hotspur (May 29, 1974) as a symbolic turning point in the Netherlands. For the first time in history, Dutch television broadcast hooligan riots nationwide as British ultras attacked Feyenoord fans and destroyed the stadium's interior. Approximately 100 people were wounded. From here, the phenomenon of hooliganism spread across the country. Hard-core supporters became more organized and mobile, while the media increasingly sensationalized their hostilities against rival fans. How and why such violence became so manifold is still open for debate (e.g., Frosdick and Marsh, 2005), but while intriguing, answering these questions goes beyond the scope of this research.

### 9.3 Period 2: Football hooliganism (1974–1990)

From the 1970s onwards, a growing number of loyal fans regularly made their way to De Kuip, where some devotees found a sense of kinship in which honor, brotherhood and loyalty were (allegedly) essential values. Citing the club song, Feyenoord allowed them to stand 'hand in hand' so that a supporter could distinguish 'spectators' from 'real supporters'. From this perspective, spectators represented those who were not closely involved with the 'ups' and 'downs' of the club. That is, they only followed Feynoord in good times. Real supporters, however, came to all matches and felt immensely loyal to the club, promoting an intense solidarity among them. As one respondent explained, 'the dumbest mistake people make is that they consider football a game. Wrong! Football is religion'.

Thus, a select companionship of hundreds of passionate 'believers' started to dedicate their entire lives to Feyenoord. Some of them, recognizable by the symbols tattooed on their right forearms, formed hooligan gangs that did not hesitate to use massive violence against 'provocative outsiders', including the police. In this regard, former attendants remember very hectic situations. For example, one recalled that

> it was not uncommon that home and away supporters were herded like cattle at the nearby train station. Surrounded by dogs, security guards, mounted police and riot squads, they were then forced to rush as quickly as possible into and out of the stadium. I can tell you that looked quite bizarre.

Nonetheless, measuring the exact extent of football hooliganism during the 1970s and 1980s is impossible because there are no reliable data sources. Therefore, it was also impossible to gage the number of confrontations involving Feyenoord hooligans (and hangers-on). In addition, statistically sound information on the scope of verbal abuses like anti-Semitic hate speech ('Hamas, Hamas, all Jews on the gas!') are nonexistent, so, there is no record of serious insults and chants that fans must have frequently yelled, at Ajax supporters in particular.[4]

What is certain is that football matches often deteriorated into chaotic (and sometimes brutal) clashes between hooligans. For example, in 1983, one Feyenoord hooligan stabbed a British Tottenham Hotspur supporter with a knife in front of the television cameras. In 1987, during an international match, the Cyprus goalkeeper was hit by a smoke bomb and some years later, in 1989, Feyenoord supports threw two fragmentation bombs containing metal splinters into a group of Ajax fans injuring four people. Such serious violence shocked

---

[4]    Ajax hooligans identify themselves as 'Jews' because the city of Amsterdam in which Stadium Ajax is located has a long Jewish heritage. This epithet therefore serves as the inspiration for Feyenoord hooligans vitriol against their 'natural enemies'.

the Netherlands, turning football hooliganism into a social and political problem. Recognizing the problem, Dutch public authorities, predominantly the police, became increasingly involved in controlling exuberant supporter behavior. From 1980, so-called combi-arrangements (combining a football ticket with a reduced train fare) made it necessary for dozens of police officers to escort visiting fans traveling to and from the stadium. The main police tasks were overseeing coaches and keeping supporters from wrecking public transportation property.

Then in 1986, the police took an important step in combating football hooliganism by founding the Dutch Central Unit for Hooliganism (*Centraal Informatiepunt Voetbalvandalisme*; CIV),[5] which specializes in collecting, analyzing and distributing information to a variety of actors including national authorities, municipal authorities, football clubs and the KNVB. The police also made efforts to contain escalating football hooliganism at the local level. For example, in 1987, the Rotterdam-Rijnmond force established its own football unit, employing approximately 7 full-time and 40 part-time staff.[6] These people served as uniformed or plain-clothes officers exercising preventive and repressive controls inside and outside the sports ground. Most often, they conducted body searchers at the turnstiles, enforced banning orders, monitored antisocial behavior and responded to hooligan rampages. However, this policing of (high risk) matches became extremely costly, especially because, despite continuing political debate, police forces are legally forbidden to charge clubs for their presence inside and outside the football ground.

In addition, despite Stadium Feyenoord's improvements to its domestic safety and communication structures (e.g., they purchased modern walkie-talkies), the old system of attendants was never completely reformed. Throughout the 1980s, Feyenoord still randomly drew people from a group of around 600 volunteers willing to maintain social order at De Kuip. According to one former attendant, 'we called a list of people and whoever happened to come to the match was given a shirt and a small tip in exchange for their services. It was like recruiting some men for unloading a ship at the dock'. As a result, the quality of the attendants, who were barely trained and sometimes even bribable, was far from the highest standards. Consequently, a fan enthusiastically recalled that

> the old-fashioned attendants were fantastic. You gave them a *knaak* [approximately 1.25 euro] and you had free entrance to the stadium. There were no silly safety measures that prevented supporters from spontaneously visiting a match.

---

[5]    For more information, see www.civ-voetbal.com.
[6]    This unit was dismantled during the reorganization in 1993 but later restored for Euro 2000.

By the mid-1980s, Stadium Feyenoord had slightly stiffened its personnel policy, which encouraged poorly functioning attendants to leave. Moreover, guards and attendants relieved the police of preventative body search duties at the stadium's turnstile entry gates (1986) not only because such duties did not fit with primary police tasks, but because stadium-employed personnel had greater authority to ban unwanted persons from attendance. Specifically, private security had the civil power, on the basis of house rules, to punish people with exclusion for behaviors such as throwing firecrackers, public drunkenness, drug use, indecent chanting and physical assaults. The police, in contrast, could only eject individuals who were breaking criminal laws. Thus, in terms of efficiency and effectiveness, private security staff offered important advantages over police officers.

### 9.4 Period 3: Reducing hooliganism (1990-1997)

By early 1990, persistent hooligan violence had made De Kuip very unpopular among fans, who practically boycotted the stadium. Together with disappointing results and a key sponsor facing liquidity problems, Feyenoord was driven to the verge of bankruptcy. In this period, the stadium appointed Jorien van den Herik, a Dutch entrepreneur, as the new chairman (1991), and under his leadership, the stadium began following a more commercial course. One of Van den Herik's first ambitious actions was to demand a complete renovation of Feyenoord to create a more positive image, with the aim of attracting new visitors, investors and sponsors.

At around the same time, in 1990, the KNVB issued new safety and security guidelines for professional football clubs with a major goal of diminishing heavy police presence at matches. With these guidelines, the KNVB was responding to government insistence on lowering excessive costs and getting the stadium's ground management to accept more responsibility for controlling unruly supporters. As an internal police report stated:

> The time has come for a preventive and pro-active approach. A new division of roles (and costs) between the government and the football world is needed. [...] Within the context of Rotterdam, this means that Feyenoord is primarily responsible for maintaining order at the stadium. From its monopoly of violence springs supplementary police responsibility for safeguarding the surrounding public domain, especially in the case of 'high-risk' matches.

This fusion of financial crises and political urgency served as a unique catalyst for rapid changes in the old system of attendants. First, in 1991, the management set up De Kuip Safety and Security (KSS), an in-house stewarding agency (see

Figure 9.2) that employed 5 people (3 full-time and 2 part-time) to manage frontline personnel including football stewards, medical stewards, contract private security and a facility assistant responsible for the storage of keys, clothing and portable communication devices. This security team started with 100 people selected from among the 600 volunteers who applied for football steward training courses. However, many new stewards were advised to leave because, even though the training courses were relatively easy and compacted into only a few days, these individuals simply lacked the personal qualities for long-term employment in De Kuip now that skill demands had been elevated. To fill this void, KSS took over personnel from Bijl Security and hired new personnel (see Figure 9.3).

**Figure 9.2: The organizational structure of De Kuip Safety and Security**

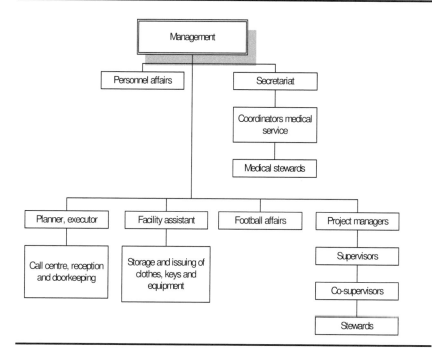

Finally, in 1994, De Kuip underwent a complete makeover including complete restoration of the stadium's toilet and catering facilities together with many other improvements like full-seat accommodations (which reduced visitor capacity from 60,000 to 50,000) and an eye-catching glass entrance building (*Maasgebouw*). This latter served not only as a fashionable gateway to the stadium but also housed a brasserie, a large hall of fame, luxurious suites (sky boxes) and rooms for weddings and business meetings. In short, De Kuip expanded into a multipurpose complex designed to profit from its commercial potential. As well as refurbishing the grounds, Feyenoord made additional advancements such as upgrading its surveillance camera system, introducing electronic tourniquets and installing solid partitions to separate rival supporter groups. This isolationist tactic, in conjunction with techno-preventive solutions, seemed successful in tackling hooliganism inside the stadium. Nonetheless, as future years proved, the perverse effect of the security measures was that the football-related violence spread to places further away.

**Figure 9.3: Number of in-house stewards, 1993–2005** (source: Feyenoord)

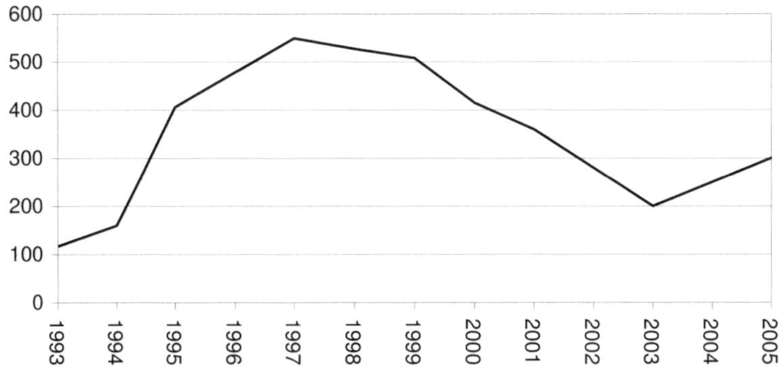

### 9.5 Period 4: Carlo Picornie and beyond (1997–2005)

During the 1990s, there had been numerous aggressive supporter encounters but barely any incident caused national commotion. One exception was a prearranged confrontation between more than 300 Feyenoord and Ajax hooligans near the A-9 motorway from Haarlem to Alkmaar. On March 23, 1997, the Feyenoord team was due to play AZ in its home stadium in Alkmaar as incoming hooligans from Rotterdam, notably escorted by the police, abandoned their cars near the town of Beverwijk. Taking the astonished police officers by surprise, they stopped in the middle of the road, climbed over some crash barriers and ran towards a group of Ajax (F-side) hooligans who were waiting for them. In the massive fight that followed, Carlo Picornie, an ex-hooligan leader of Ajax, was stabbed to death and others were seriously injured. The police arrested dozens of people and found about 200 weapons ranging from chains and knives to steel poles and hammers (Kerr and De Kock, 2002).

Shortly after this lethal incident, Dutch public authorities decided to reschedule high-risk football matches from the evening to the afternoon, and police investigation into hooligan gangs intensified. In addition, Feyenoord introduced personal club cards (*gold cards* and *silver cards*) for away matches. This initiative served two purposes: it guaranteed cardholders a seat in the other team's stadium and, by making it easy to trace offenders, rescind their card and exclude them from the football grounds in case of mischief, it furthered Feyenoord's goal of moderating disorderly behavior.

Nonetheless, such strategies were no panacea. Although the older generations backed down after the murder in Beverwijk, 16 to 21-year-old youngsters formed new hooligan groups that, owing to excessive use of drugs like XTC, caused even greater problems. It was thus inevitable that Rotterdam would suffer even more violence. For example, on April 25, 1999, when Feyenoord won the national football cup, hooligans and affiliated rioters disrupted the inaugural ceremony. Following large-scale brawls and lootings, the police took 87 people into custody. However, after an investigative report concluded that the fracas resulted from a combination of alcohol, drugs and anti-police sentiments, the detainees declared that police provocation had sparked the new outburst of violence (COT, 1999).

### 9.5.1 Integral safety policy

Meanwhile, as a consequence of the 'Beverwijk battle', further strategies were being developed for reducing football hooliganism. Along the lines of the conditions laid down by the 1997 policy document *Football Vandalism and Football Violence* (*Beleidskader Voetbalvandalisme en -Geweld*), Feyenoord, the municipality of Rotterdam, the Rotterdam-Rijnmond police force and the public prosecutor's service signed a local covenant on reducing hooliganism (this covenant was reconfirmed and tightened in 2003). Their goal was to develop enhanced cooperation between a set of 'integral safety partners' to whom specific responsibilities would be formally assigned. Local governments and clubs were mandated to be primary responsible for order maintenance, meaning that police officers controlled fans outside the ground, while clubs increasingly relied on stewards and private security guards inside. Ironically, however, the number of police officers deployed to Feyenoord has more than doubled over the last decade (see Figure 9.4). Obviously, reducing police costs is easier said than done. As several respondents argued, the different interests of diverse organizations made the policy process complicated and time-consuming. It took years before all parties involved came to a common position on what constituted the type of 'good' cooperation that would allow fewer police to be on hand at the stadium. Several of these viewpoints are outlined below.

**Figure 9.4: Number of police officers deployed to Feyenoord, 1995–2006**
(source: CIV; www.civ-voetbal.com)

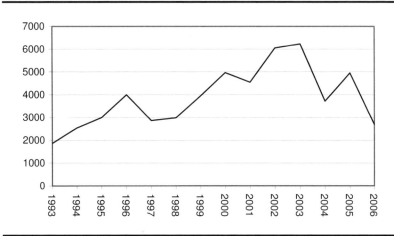

### 9.5.1.1 Stadium Feyenoord

The government increasingly expected private guards and stewards to take responsibility for safety and security inside the stadium. Simultaneously, Stadium Feyenoord felt commercial pressures to optimize the comfort of its venue. To attract 'regular' visitors (i.e., families or fathers with their sons), football enjoyment must occur within a regulated setting. However, improvements in crowd management cost money, so that making the right choices on a limited budget became a key concern. At the same time, entrance fees had to remain affordable to ensure that supporters – not least, the most dedicated – would attend.

### 9.5.1.2 Municipality of Rotterdam

While demanding safe and secure matches, local government also realized that Feyenoord was profitable 'city marketing' that assured product sales all over the world. Safety and security were thus balanced against competing commercial interests. As the deputy head of the public order office openly admitted, 'politically and economically speaking, it is not wise to twist the neck of Feyenoord, which serves as a renowned football temple'.

### 9.5.1.3 Rotterdam-Rijnmond police force

The police force took a crystal clear stand on the control of hooligan violence, insisting that, football being a 'private party', Stadium Feyenoord must, at least within its grounds, take the primary responsibility for order maintenance.

Nonetheless, Feyenoord continued to place a heavy burden on police personnel and resources. As one police officer complained,

> Rotterdam is a football-loving city that has no interest in serious disorder. If assessments make clear that risks are too high, the 'triangle' [of mayor, public prosecutor and chief constable] easily calls in extra riot police to ensure that a match passes peacefully.

### 9.5.1.4 Public prosecution service

The public prosecutor favored the introduction of civil stadium bans for severe misbehavior because, as the police had made clear, football clubs had to exercise their own authority to suspend football offenders from the sports ground, and criminal law should only be a last resort.

### 9.5.2 Commercialization of in-house security

Since 1997, Stadium Feyenoord has substantially strengthened the quality of its security personnel, which has stimulated a new exodus of stewards. After 1999, the number of employees dropped considerably from around 500 to 200 people. Probably contributing to this trend was the strengthened legal and financial position of flexible workers. As outlined in chapter 8, the 1999 Flexi-Law (*Wet Flexibiliteit en Zekerheid*) granted nonpermanent employees more rights in terms of salaries and labor contracts, which suddenly made on-call stewards (in particular the underqualified and underskilled) far less attractive. Hence, KSS began searching for appropriate alternatives.

Eventually, after positive experiences during EURO 2000, De Kuip contracted The Security Company (TSC) to control football matches, a decision that meant a drastic increase in the security budget, from €805,000 (1996) to €1,680,000 (2003). To compensate for the financial costs of hired professional guards, Feyenoord, striving to optimize the return on its personnel policy, creatively transformed its own stewarding agency KSS into a profitable organization renamed Sport and Event Security (S&ES). During the 2004/2005 football season, S&ES was made fully operational as a private security company.

In daily practice, the S&ES staff fulfilled three basic functions of 'safety', 'security' and 'service' (Box 9.1), designed to assure 'friendly but firm policing' (Adang, 2001) that encouraged supporter enjoyment in a welcoming but controlled atmosphere within which violence was, as much as possible, prevented and, eventually, repressed. To achieve this goal, S&ES began training its own personnel, together with novices, as Event Security Officers (ESOs), a brand new certified private security function in the Netherlands. The football world introduced this form of 'higher-profile stewarding' (Frosdick and March,

2005: 180) for several reasons. First, the theoretical and practical education (3 months) of these officers, who fall somewhere between guards and stewards, is limited compared to full private security guard training (6 to 12 months) but much more elaborate than the training packages for stewards (only a few days). Second, ESOs specialize in securing sports events, Feyenoord's 'core business', whereas traditional private guards' training is not directly related to football matches. Finally, and perhaps most important, ESOs, unlike stewards, can be hired out to external customers, making them far more commercially viable than had previously been the case.

### Box 9.1: Core tasks of in-house and contract private security personnel

**Safety:** Preventing and signaling troubles (searching people at the entrance gates, proactive action to forestall violence, anticipating technical inconveniences like broken chairs, responding to (mid-sized) emergencies, storing keys).

**Security:** Maintaining order inside the stadium (overseeing the crowd, making citizen arrests, taking detainees into custody, limited information sharing with the police, excluding unwanted visitors).

**Service:** Customer care (welcoming visitors, showing visitors their seats, providing various types of information to visitors).

### 9.6 Recent developments: Toward repression and prevention

The aforementioned 'friendly but firm' approach was visible in diverse facets of policing hooligans. Inside the ground, so-called flexi-teams of three competent stewards carried out both policing and assistance tasks, bolstered by cooperation from three police colleagues that provided backup when necessary. Thus, stewards were the first to take preventive measures against outbursts of violence and other calamities, with police officers standing by to assist them with repressive force. What gradually evolved was an active crossover between public and private crowd management.

Outside the grounds, the municipality of Rotterdam, in close collaboration with Feyenoord, implemented a social policy in which two 'fan coaches' were assigned to potentially troublesome adolescents. These coaches served as intermediaries between youth care and welfare work on the one hand and De Kuip on the other. Most particularly, they focused on first offenders with the specific aim of knowing and being known and preventing them from engaging in worse mischief. For example, the fan coaches, along with S&ES, offered delinquent juveniles sanctions other than long-term exclusion from the stadium; for example, 'penalties' that benefited Feyenoord (like distributing brochures, sweeping the stadium) but were also assumed to have a pedagogic effect on the offender. A security manager explained the strategy as follows:

> High-risk groups have to be kept on the road inside as well outside De Kuip. We therefore persist in a double-edged policy of sanctioning and care. Wrongdoers must, of course, be corrected, but we also want to charm them. They need to feel taken care of, resulting in good customer relations and, hopefully, normal behavior.

The motivation behind the convergence of enforcing (zero tolerance) and preventive (social) policies was to curtail hooliganism while letting police officers change places with private security staff. So far, this strategy looks promising. Researchers and policy-makers now wait to see whether these trends will be prolonged into the future.

### 9.7 Analysis
The following paragraphs evaluate the goodness of fit between privatizing policing and the explanations for such privatization. After mapping out trends in De Kuip's in-house team, the discussion focuses on major shifts related to the extent and nature of football stewarding services and then evaluates these shifts as explanations for changes in private security. Combining the patterns culminates in a preliminary explanation of why private security has grown at Stadium Feyenoord.

### 9.7.1 Shifts in the extent and nature of private security
Until 1991, Stadium Feyenoord drew mostly on 600 voluntary football attendants and a small group of Bijl Security guards for its domestic security functions. However, in that year, the stadium management created an in-house stewarding organization, De Kuip Safety and Security (KSS), which employed 100 of the most trusted and capable attendants as part-time stewards. Throughout the 1990s, after KSS brought in staff from Bijl Security, this number amplified to over 500. Yet, since 1997, and particularly since 1999, KSS has seen a spectacular decrease in in-house personnel. Subsequently, at the time of the EURO 2000 championships, flexible contract guards supplied by The Security Company (TSC) replaced around 300 in-house personnel who had left. In 2004, with 200 staff remaining, KSS (recently renamed Sport and Event Security or SE&S) reinvented itself as a commercialized private security company. Its stewards were transformed into Event Security Officers (ESOs) engaged in safety, security and service duties, who, unlike their predecessors, can be brought into action outside the stadium. Although the main role of guards and stewards was to prevent troubles (safety) and look after customers (service),

their presence also reflected order maintenance and rule enforcement (security) to control antisocial and criminal behavior.

The representatives interviewed from both Feyenoord and the police force were positive about their relationship. They reported on joint operations, sharing facilities, attending the same briefings, swapping know-how and forming combined teams. However, cooperation was not restricted to the policing sphere. Besides fire and ambulance services, SE&S has recently (2003) begun working with fan coaches, government-subsidized liaisons between Stadium Feyenoord and the youth workers involved in preventing adolescent hooliganism. This project is part of a larger program combining hard and soft tactics to restore a more pleasant ambiance to football matches.

### 9.7.2 Rising crime and related problems

Changes in football hooliganism seem of little or no direct importance to alterations in the size and organization of private security. For example, it was not until 1991 – more than 15 years after the first outburst of violence and vandalism at De Kuip (in 1974) – that Stadium Feyenoord set up its own in-house stewarding team (the KSS). Further brutal football-related incidents also had little effect on Feyenoord's security policy. For example, the killing of Ajax-hooligan Carlo Picorni (1997) produced a wave of national indignation and criticism but did not immediately lead to structural reforms in the stewarding process. Rather, the conversion of KSS to a professional private security company (S&ES) was only completed in 2004.

### 9.7.3 Growth of mass private property

Transfigurations in De Kuip's security infrastructure are also unrelated to spatial ordering and visitor numbers. Not only has the physical size of the stadium complex barely increased except for small extensions (in 1994), but alterations in the stadium's private security have never corresponded with supporter influxes. As a result, it can not be validly argued that changes in (the use of) mass private property impacted on stewarding and guarding services at Stadium Feyenoord.

### 9.7.4 Economic rationalities

Commercial motives for shifts in the size and organization of private security became perceptible with three critical events in Feyenoord's history. First, at the beginning of 1990s, De Kuip experienced a profound financial crisis when its football team became unglamourous, visitors avoided the stadium and sponsor funds dried up. The installation of a new chairman meant a breakthrough for Feyenoord, which, under his leadership, instituted its own in-house security team (KSS, in 1991) and renovated its stadium complex (in 1994) to make football matches safer and more appealing for well-mannered fans. Subsequently, aiming for a more competent stewarding team, KSS slowly removed inept personnel and, following EURO 2000, replaced them with TSC guards. Nonetheless, this step doubled the overall spending on domestic security from €805,000 in 1996 to €1,680,000 in 2003. Finally, in 2004, management commercialized the KSS so that De Kuip could begin to recoup rising investments by selling external security services. This development was marked by the introduction of ESOs, a type of 'higher profile' steward. Thus, financial and economic rationalities were important to understand shifts in private security at Stadium Feyenoord.

### 9.7.5 Government policy toward private sector participation

Even though police officers had already transferred body search duties at the turnstile entry gates to private staff (1986), the national government's hard work to responsibilize the football world for hooliganism did not impact Feyenoord prior to 1991. At that time, public authorities pressed the stadium management (via KNVB) to raise security standards, which, in tandem with commercial interests, led to the provision of a stewarding team inside the sports ground. Subsequently, the 1997 and 2003 covenants between Feyenoord, the municipality of Rotterdam, the Rotterdam-Rijnmond police force and the public prosecutor provided incentive for a more intelligent public-private policing arrangement. Specifically, these protocols demanded a clearer division of respective roles, duties and expectations. At the same time, private security staff was increasingly considered to have the first responsible for the safety and security of matches. Hence, government policy toward the responsibilization of Feyenoord impacted on shifts in the extent and organization of its in-house security team.

### 9.7.6 An overburdened police force

Clearly, the Rotterdam-Rijnmond police force felt excessively overburdened by the workload involved in regulating football matches. Yet despite the police's own recognition that demands on staff outstripped their capacity, local government overruled their protests on the grounds that general safety and public order during intense game schedules should take highest priority. As a result, the number of officers sent out to Stadium Feyenoord spiraled upwards, although the stewarding team steadily improved at the same time. This trend was broken in 2003 because of improved public-private arrangements. Thus, concerns about heavy police presence at the stadium did not coincide with the upgrading of private security.

### 9.7.7 Professionalization of private security

Substantial evolutions in the professionality of security personnel have come about in three stages. After 1991, stewards slowly took the place of voluntary football attendants, assisting Feyenoord in exchange for 'a drink and a cigar'. Later (EURO 2000 and afterwards), these were in turn partially substituted by TSC guards specialized in event security. Most recently, since 2004, KSS (renamed SE&S) has begun to train its stewards as specialized ESOs working for multiple event organizers, including Stadium Feyenoord. However, this professionalization process was an effect, not a cause, of management decisions directed toward an appropriate balance between improved quality standards and commercial considerations. As a consequence, the professionalization thesis must be rejected.

### 9.7.8 Changes in labor law: A new factor

The 1999 Flexi-Law (a labor law) bolstered the employment rights of on-call in-house employees and, accordingly, accelerated the discharge of those unsuitable for their work. In reality, it was in KSS's interests to dismiss these latter anyway simply because they had became financially less attractive. The legislation provided an extra impetus for its management to do so.

### 9.8 Summary

Based on the case study results, this section has summarized the explanatory power of each factor assumed to drive shifts in private security at Stadium Feyenoord. Specifically, it found that crime and disorder problems, changes in spatial ordering and use of mass private property, police complaints about excessive allocation of resources to football matches and professionalization of in-house security staff did not directly account for shifts in private security; while economic rationalities, government policy toward private sector participation and changes in labor law did.

# 10    Hoog Catharijne: Retail Heart of the Netherlands

Hoog Catharijne, known as the 'retail heart of the Netherlands', is situated in the old city centre of Utrecht (275,000 inhabitants) with direct access to the central railway station.[1] Welcoming an estimated 40 million visitors per year[2] and covering 60,800m², Hoog Catharijne is the busiest shopping mall in the Netherlands. Many come to visit the 180 different stores, but there is also leisure in the form of a cinema, a music hall (*Vredenburg*), a theater (*Beatrix Theather*), restaurants, pubs, snack corners and a large exhibition/convention centre (*Jaarbeurs Utrecht*). Overall, Hoog Catharijne is a multifunctional complex that, despite its commercial potential, does not look back on an entirely successful past. The homeless and drug addicts have caused much trouble to the contract security team, who have faced a tough job in keeping up a pleasant atmosphere. Cooperation efforts between private guards and police officers underwent various ups and downs before consensus was reached in 2001 on a workable integral safety plan.

This chapter explores the history of Hoog Catharijne and its plurality of policing personnel from 1973 to 2005. After an introductory section, the discussion addresses four time periods that represent changes in the size and organization of both public and private forces. As before, information from preliminary direct observations and a document review was supplemented by data from eight interviews with nine respondents (two interviewed together): the (former) area manager, the centre manager, the security manager, the railway station manager, the general manager of operations of Jaarbeurs Utrecht, two (former) police officers and two security guards.

## 10.1 Hoog Catharijne's early history (1962–1973)

After World War II, Utrecht enjoyed a period of prosperity when neighboring municipalities consolidated to form one city. This enlargement presented the city with enormous economic opportunity. Located at the central axes of the Netherlands, within reach of many other cities, Utrecht was a splendid location in which to build a huge shopping mall in conjunction with office buildings, apartments, conference facilities and public transport facilities. However, the Hoog Catharijne project, initiated in 1962, met strong opposition from local protest groups. Nonetheless, despite such objections, construction work proceeded, resulting in an official opening ceremony on September 24, 1973.

---

[1]    For more information, see www.corio-eu.com and www.utrecht.nl.
[2]    Including passers-by, this number can reach as high as 60 million; however, there are no detailed statistics available on visitor growth.

One significant feature of Hoog Catharijne is the branched system of roofed quarters divided into pedestrian corridors and squares, which connect the shopping areas and public transport platforms with downtown Utrecht. In contrast to its massive concrete exterior, these pedestrian walkways, as the original plans advertised, breathe luxury and style so that visitors can experience a relaxing day of shopping fun. However, although inviting, the problem with such an open space soon became apparent: not only ordinary families but also unwanted intruders like homeless addicts and psychiatric patients felt free to spend time at the mall.

### 10.2 Period 1: A magnet for the homeless (1973–1982)

Shortly after the 1973 opening, Hoog Catharijne began serving as a magnet for growing numbers of homeless. For them, the shopping mall was a natural end point because intercity trains from all directions arrived at the nearby railway station. Not only did Hoog Catharijne offer excellent shelter – warm and dry, it also provided sufficient resources for getting food, water and other supplies. In addition, the mall's interior of corridors, squares, elevators, hidden corners and an underground parking lot made it an even a more attractive place to hide. Yet neither the city council nor the real estate developer, in their focused effort to build an alluring shopping center, had ever contemplated the potentially negative safety and security aspects of the architectural design. As a result, mostly after dark, the mall's corridors could look gloomy enough to make average visitors uncomfortable.

Therefore, as Hoog Catharijne became established, the police brought in an HC (Hoog Catharijne) team of 12 officers, while the shopping mall appointed 40 full-time contract guards, which number and organizational structure (see Figure 10.1) remained generally the same over the years. As an agent of the property company pointed out,

> a staff of 40 full timers is the optimal number for the shopping mall. Economically speaking, we cannot afford to put more guards under contract. The increased expense of such a mandate would be simply too costly for the retailers, who, in the end, pay the bill.

At the time, this mixed provision of visible patrols represented a unique policing arrangement in the Netherlands. However, from the beginning, conflicting interests arose between representatives of the police, the municipality and the property owner. All faced serious problems of crime and disorder, but none agreed on close cooperation through partnerships. Thus, despite a signed agreement assuring activities geared toward cleaning, maintenance and security issues (*beheersovereenkomst*, 1982), because of Hoog Catharijne was a hybrid –

privately exploited but publicly accessible – safety and security remained open for discussion. Moreover, as a local ordinance emphasized, visitors and passers-by had to be allowed unrestricted right of entry to the railway station after closing time, yet pedestrian corridors inside the mall were not public roads according to the admission criteria laid down in road laws. Essentially therefore, nobody fully accepted the blame for this public-private 'no-mans land' and all refused to undertake appropriate action.

**Figure 10.1: The organizational structure of private security at Hoog Catharijne**

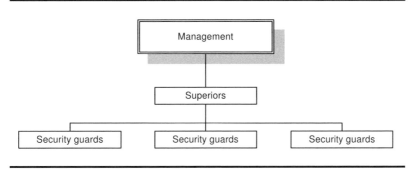

## 10.3 Period 2: Rising tensions (1982–1987)

Over the years, increasing numbers of (addicted) homeless produced intensely disturbing criminal and disorder problems, yet exact crime figures remained unavailable. First, because of lack of confidence in police abilities, a presumably large number of crimes were never reported. Most notably, retailers did not see police officers (and with them, security guards) as influential enough to create a safer shopping mall. Second, police statistics on local crime had to remain classified and so closed to the general public, including researchers. Third, there was no complete picture of trends, because two distinct police departments (district Paardeveld and district Marco Polo) registered their own data for different branches of the mall. Fourth, these aggregated data were polluted with crime figures from the mall's immediate neighborhoods, so even if there had been sound information available, it would have been virtually impossible to identify precise problems because of too much 'noise' in the statistics.

Nonetheless, regardless of such difficulties, interview respondents seemed to agree that drug-related crime (and related anxieties) got out of hand during the 1980s, creating tensions that, as indicated previously, erupted in disagreements over the care and control of marginalized groups. Whereas the private operator argued that disorder arising from social deprivation was a problem for local authorities, the municipality, pointing to the mall's open and chaotic design, accused the property owner of public nuisance caused by the homeless. These disagreements constantly hampered further public-private cooperation. Not that the interviewees reported major tensions over the years: there was little contact between guards and police officers, who met irregularly and had little confidence in joint activities. As one police officer explained, 'we endlessly discussed "who does what" in patrolling Hoog Catharijne, but this could not be worked out to the satisfaction of all'.

The security manager underscored this division by describing security provision as long split into 'two separate worlds' (see also Klein Theeselink, 2003). Only when activities matched – for example, police examination of private CCTV recordings to identify a suspect – did officers and guards operate in tandem. Under normal circumstances, they went their separate ways with competing interests (see Table 10.1) and different tasks (Table 10.2).

**Table 10.1: Competing interests of the police and private security team**

| Police | Private security |
|---|---|
| Emphasis on **public interest** (tax-payer funded) of safety and security. | **Client-driven** (customer funded) approach to antisocial behavior, disorder and crime. |
| Focus on **keeping public order** and **crime control**. | Focus on **commercial interests** (i.e., keeping the mall safe and pleasant). |
| **Patrolling a wide area:** Hoog Catharijc and other parts of Utrecht. | **Patrolling a small area:** Hoog Catharijne and its immediate. surroundings |
| **Limited information sharing** with security guards (because of privacy laws). | **One-way information sharing** with the police (urging for more 'all-round' information sharing). |

## 10.4 Period 3: Policy experiments (1987–2001)

Little by little, Hoog Catharijne gained a bad reputation as the mall deteriorated considerably. Most specifically, the Guild Quarter (*Gildenkwartier*), a somewhat forgotten mall area leading off the main passageway, became trapped in downward spirals. As the homeless started to wander around and litter accumulated, other visitors began to avoid the area. This abandonment, in turn, stimulated the entry of more obstreperous people, which increased the mall's vulnerability to decay. At a certain point, shopkeepers in the Guild Quarter went bankrupt and left, which prompted the worried city council of Utrecht to intervene with a 1987 policy experiment aimed primarily at revitalizing Hoog Catherijne and recovering control. To this end, a specially formed Hoog

Catharijne working group (*Werkgroep Hoog Catharijne*) – made up of representatives from local and national government, the property company, the police and public prosecution service, the business community, the Dutch railways, the neighborhood committee and several researchers – set out practical guidelines to reduce the following:

- Feelings of insecurity among visitors, residents and shop workers;
- Violence against visitors, residents and shop workers;
- Shoplifting;
- Vandalism and dirt;
- Nuisance from drug addicts and other unruly individuals;
- Bike and moped theft; and
- Wrong parking of bikes and mopeds.

The group's central goal was to make visitors feel secure at Hoog Catharijne, because, as surveys had indicated, even though factual crime figures seemed more or less identical for both the mall and downtown Utrecht, the shopping public expressed more anxiety about crime in the mall. This inconsistency may have stemmed from the signs of disorder in Hoog Catharijne such as graffiti, street litter, messy cycle sheds and frequent encounters with disreputable, albeit not necessarily dangerous, drunks, drug addicts and psychiatric patients. In sum, the inhospitable, worn-out shopping environment very much fed people's fears.

Making inferences from these findings, the working group chose situational crime prevention strategies to channel deviant behavior. A first pragmatic step was the closure from 11:00 PM to 6:00 AM of two quarters (the Guild Quarter and the Radboud Quarter). The rationale was to concentrate streams of visitors for more efficient police oversight and better face-to-face contact. Additionally, in terms of prevention, policies concentrated on the employment of supplementary uniformed foot-patrols, technological solutions (e.g., improved surveillance cameras, security gates at stores), public information campaigns and security training for shopkeepers, while the criminal justice apparatus sharpened repressive measures against vandalism, petty crime, drug dealing and antisocial parking by bicycle and moped riders. Such a law and order approach was deemed necessary for fear reduction.

However, by 1990, these policy experiments were, for the most part, being negatively evaluated because they had failed to achieve most goals of (subjective) insecurity reduction. Initiatives to fight crime and disorder through information campaigns, training, techno-prevention and smoother public-private working relationships had proved disappointing, as had attempts to reduce damage from bicycle theft, litter, graffiti, and so on. Nonetheless, closing off some branches of Hoog Catharijne, as well as the introduction of foot-patrols, proved adequate in dealing with public incivility and feelings of insecurity.

**Table 10.2: Core tasks of the police and the private security team**

| Police | Private security |
|---|---|
| **Surveillance and order maintenance** in 'public' space (i.e. pedestrian corridors). | **Surveillance and order maintenance** in 'public' and 'private' spaces (i.e. pedestrian corridors, car park, loading docks). |
| Emphasis on **enforcing approach** to anti-social behavior, disorder and crime. | Emphasis on **preventive approach** to anti-social behavior, disorder and crime. |
| Gathering information from CCTV cameras in case of disruptions and calamities. | CCTV monitoring, filling forms, sharing information. |
| Providing backup if necessary, excluding unwanted visitors from the shopping mall. | Responding to alarm activations, excluding unwanted visitors from the shopping mall. |
| Imposing fines upon people, arresting (notorious) wrongdoers | Making citizen arrests, taking detainees to custody, calling the police. |
| **Assistance of the public** by responding to emergencies, giving people a helping hand, providing them with information. | **Customer-related functions** such as responding to emergencies, giving visitors a helping hand, providing them with information. |
| n/a | **Housekeeping functions** such as overseeing pedestrian corridors and escalators, reporting on breakages and defects. |

### 10.4.1 Private funding of pubic police patrollers

In the wake of these policy experiments, the municipality chose not to recruit security guards for the foot-patrol roles, a remarkable decision given the overall trend toward allotting responsibility for policing and security to private enterprises. However, as the city council wrote in its proposal of July 16, 1988, 'there are serious disadvantages attached to private guards operating on public [sic] roads'. Supporting arguments for this viewpoint boiled down to two issues. First, because security guards officially had no more power than any other citizen, they could not offer the public much in terms of protection and reassurance. Second, given regulations and democratic accountability, the council was suspicious of guarantees against misconduct and violence, especially because muddled addicts were difficult to deal with so guards sometimes strained the legal limits.

Hence, the council launched a new form of executive police rank at Hoog Catharijne, the police patroller (*politiesurveillant*), who held limited powers and, unlike fully armed colleagues, was only equipped with handcuffs and a baton (which also made them cheaper than fully fledged policemen). Compared to private security guards, these police patrollers had a broader mandate and, equally important, they were part of the local constabulary force. This affiliation bypassed the legal complexities of information exchange, democratic control and personnel steering inherent in fluid networks and, by granting the new supervisors public status, ensured consolidation of state sovereignty over policing.

To facilitate ancillary manpower, all parties came to an exceptional solution. The property company agreed to provide private funds for 5 to 7 additional police patrollers to walk the beat at Hoog Catharijne, although it should be emphasized that the mall owner had no voice in the steering of patrollers. Rather, according to the 'police contract' formally signed in 1990, private money flowed *indirectly* via the council budget so that the local triangle (i.e., the mayor, public prosecutor and chief constable) was ensured ultimate authority over all foot-patrols. Nonetheless, the Hoog Catharijne ownership went along with the contract. As one manager explained,

> for effective public order maintenance, financing police patrollers is a better choice than contracting a new group of security guards. Police patrollers can serve as a backbone to guards, giving them indispensable authority.

### 10.4.2 Ongoing struggles

Meanwhile, pressures had built up for a structural cooperative venture whose alliances involved more than the previous, easily transferable, short-term promises. Interviewees hinted at three important developments. First, owing to the 1993 regionalization, police teams involved in keeping order at Hoog Catharijne had gained a stronger position: relegation of financial and personnel decision to a higher, regional level made the police relatively more independent from the municipality of Utrecht. Such increased autonomy made the police increasingly aware and critical about the allocation of manpower, leading to discussions of what officers should and should not do. For instance, police officers felt that care for the homeless addicts was not their primary concern.

Second, after security staff had been strongly criticized for their unorthodox working methods, particularly fights between guards and offenders, the municipality called for greater interaction between security and police personnel. The homeless, in particular, displayed progressively more critical opinions about private security personnel, refusing to unquestionably accept guards overstepping the mark. However, on their part, guards needed a certain legitimate authority to function properly, which required good teamwork with public authorities, including police patrollers, who would endorse them in case of emergency. Finally, the city council and the property company were becoming increasingly concerned about the degeneration of Hoog Catharijne – particularly, the indigent Guild Quarter and the addict-infested loading dock known as the 'junk tunnel' (junkentunnel) – and the (potentially) negative consequences for their public image.

In 1997, a new collaborative experiment in safety and security management began but once again failed. Relationships between the municipality of Utrecht, the police and the property company had become so bad that ongoing disputes and conflicts virtually needed to be settled in court. The municipality of Utrecht tried to repair this situation by beginning negotiations for the placement of three homeless shelters, containing user facilities and drug rehabilitation programs, in and around Hoog Catharijne. According to the plan, not only would these shelters relieve the mall by giving displaced persons an opportunity to freshen up and relax, but the homeless could then gradually be ferried out to eight newly constructed hostels on the outskirts of the city. The treatment and spreading out of the offenders, policy-makers had realized, was the best option for tackling the inconvenience caused by drug addicts. Moreover, because building trust was evidently a critical condition for greater success than had previously been achieved, in 1999, the HC team opened a permanent police desk in the shopping mall to provide proper communication between patrollers and shopkeepers.

## 10.5 Period 4: An integral safety approach (2001–2005)

The above initiatives marked a turning point in the uneasy status quo between struggling factions. Under the mayor's supervision, the municipality, the property company and the police force signed a declaration of intent to improve safety and security of what was named the 'station area', comprising Hoog Catharijne, the railway station and its wider vicinity. This agreement marked the beginning of a period of détente. In 2001, shortly after consensus had been reached, the city council appointed an area manager to initiate, coordinate and evaluate integral partnerships between the police and public prosecution services, the security company, social workers, residents and others. These partnerships were formally laid down in a Station Area Safety and Livability Plan (Veiligheids- en Leefbaarheidsplan) published in June 2003.

Subsequently, under the supervision of the manager, several project groups formulated compassionate but strict approaches to the homeless, drug addicts, panhandlers and other undesirables. Social workers improved these individuals' living conditions, offering round-the-clock medical services, basic necessities and regulated government provision of needles, methadone and heroin. The mall also underwent a thorough cleanup, and the property owner convinced popular chains like Media Markt (a consumer electronics superstore) and Hennes and Mauritz (a large fashion store) to open shops at Hoog Catherijne in the hope that they would attract a fresh stream of visitors to bring life to the unprofitable areas like the Guild Quarter.

Police patrollers unanimously 'adopted' various shops (*Winkeladoptieplan*) to establish good contacts with the retailers, discuss security problems and forestall (criminal) nuisance. However, their in-mall desk shut down after three years of operation because, in practice, people rarely came to visit. Nonetheless, in exchange, the police brought in four bike officers to enhance their visibility and reduce response times. In addition, closing down the so-called junk tunnel and other inhospitable corridors made it even more impossible for undesirables to sleep inside the shopping mall – one of several house rules that security guards, assisted by police patrollers, successfully enforced together with drug dealing and drug use prevention. Individuals who overtly breached these regulations were immediately barred from Hoog Catharijne, facing long-term exclusion and even a prison sentence in the case of repeated norm violations. Care *and* repression, a carrot *and* a stick, were the key to such actions.

Nonetheless, despite intensified cooperation, the security team and police force entered into no formal agreements. Rather, with the exception of special events like late night shopping, the sole common ground for stronger cooperation seemed mutual assistance in crises situations. Thus, even though the area manager interviewed expressed the desirability of letting private security and police operate from one safety centre (*Veiligheidscentrum*) to improve mutual task and information sharing, to date, agencies have not moved toward joint tasking because of minimal confidence, dissimilar interests and legal obstacles. However, these attitudes may change in the upcoming years.

## 10.6 Recent developments: A drastic facelift for Hoog Catharijne

The latest efforts in fighting crime and disorder at Hoog Catherijne have proven successful. In 2005, the Station Area Safety and Livability Project even won two prestigious awards – the Hein Roethof Award (a national award for best practices in crime prevention) and the European Crime Prevention Award. Reflecting on the lessons from collaborative efforts, in October 2005, public and private bodies signed a supervision arrangement (*Toezichtsarrangement*) that today forms the basis for future goal setting, mutual cooperation and priority safety issues. A recently compiled Station Area Master Plan (*Masterplan*

*Stationsgebied Utrecht*) set additional guidelines for reconstructing the town centre beginning in 2006. Once completed, this construction will constitute a drastic facelift for Hoog Catharijne and its immediate environs.

## 10.7 Analysis
The following paragraphs evaluate the goodness of fit between privatizing policing and the explanations for it. After mapping out the trends in the Hoog Catharijne security and police teams, the discussion focuses, as before, on major shifts in the extent and characteristics of public and private policing. Such shifts are then evaluated to produce preliminary conclusions about the growth of paid public policing at the shopping mall.

### 10.7.1 Shifts in the extent and nature of policing
After its founding in 1973, shopping mall Hoog Catharije employed 40 full-time contract guards and the police established a 12-strong HC team to patrol and safeguard the mall. Even so, contrary to theoretical expectations, the privatization processes were not significantly related to changes in contract security operations. Rather, these latter can be associated with the formation in 1990 of a handful of privately funded police patrollers to reinforce the HC team. Such a formation was uncommon because of the government ban on charging for police services in the Netherlands for reasons of undesired private involvement in the steering and allocation of patrol officers. However, Hoog Catherijne *indirectly* subsidized the patrollers through a municipal fund, which assured their independence under local constabulary authority.

Nonetheless, interviewees repeatedly portrayed relations between the police and private security guards as troubled and twisted. Even though their patrolling and order maintenance duties strongly overlapped, real collaboration remained elusive. Instead, both agencies formed their own domains, which hindered cooperation. At the heart of this controversy lay divergent interests, general suspicion, mutual misperceptions and laborious communication. The 2001 integral safety plan did engender an improved working climate, but even today a solid public-private partnership is still in its infancy. Exploring further possibilities for greater routine collaboration will perhaps yield stronger alliances in future years.

### 10.7.2 Rising crime and related problems
Owing to a lack of reliable statistics on Hoog Catharijne, measuring the magnitude of crime problems over the years proved difficult, although interview data suggested that, with the arrival of the (addicted) homeless, crime rates rose sharply at the mall. On the other hand, the same can be argued for central Utrecht as a whole. More important was the heightened public perception of the

risks and dangers stemming from beggars strolling around in the chaotically designed mall. Nonetheless, supplementary, privately-financed foot patrols were not put into action until 1990, over 15 years after the first observable signs of deterioration. It could thus be reasonably argued that crime, disorder and fear did not unduly influence the privatization of policing in this case study.

### 10.7.3 Growth of mass private property

The size of Hoog Catharijne has remained the same since it opened in 1973. Except for the rearrangement of the Guild Quarter in 2003, no noteworthy changes have been made to the complex's layout. Admittedly, visitor numbers have climbed over the years, but there is no evidence that this development influenced the 1990 privatization of the public police services. In other words, this factor can be rendered inapplicable.

### 10.7.4 Economic rationalities

Economic considerations – especially the owner's wish to invigorate the mall and reverse its tarnished reputation – were arguably a prelude to Hoog Catharijne's agreement to the 1990 police contract, which favored police patrollers with the appropriate legal powers to effectively intervene and restore public order over security guards. Thus, this factor was significant for understanding developments in policing at the mall.

### 10.7.5 Government policy toward private sector participation

The city council's approval of the 1990 police contract was crucial in the appointment of auxiliary police patrollers. The two key reasons for the council's advocacy of public foot-patrols to ensure effective and democratic policing related to Hoog Catharijne's public-private nature: first, such patrols enjoyed a greater legal mandate than security guards and second, they resided under the Utrecht constabulary force. At the same time, in an agreement that rests on the notion of granting special favors to retailers, policy-makers voiced the desirability of levying charges. Hence, government decision-making influenced changes in policing at the mall.

### 10.7.6 An overburdened police force

No cogent evidence exists that police resources have inadequately kept pace with public demands; however, police officials have continually emphasized Hoog Catharijne's obligation to help safeguard its venue. Thus, the 1990 decision to fund public patrollers privately represented not so much the overburdening of police resources but a reciprocal responsibility for the security situation. In other words, this factor turned out minimally important in accounting for shifts in policing.

### 10.7.7 Professionalization of private security

For this case study, the professionalization of private security staff was not an issue: rather, the municipality preferred police patrollers to contract guards because they met higher quality standards. This factor can hence be dismissed as irrelevant.

### 10.8 Summary

Based on the case study results, this section has summarized the explanatory power of each factor assumed to contribute to the privatization of public policing at Hoog Catharijne. Specifically, it found that crime and disorder problems, changes in the spatial ordering and use of mass private property, the overburdening of police resources and the professionalization of in-house security staff did not directly account for privately funded public police patrollers being allowed to operate in the mall; while economic rationalities and, most particularly, government policy did.

# Part 4: Analysis, Conclusions and Discussion

# 11    Dutch Private Security: An Analysis

This chapter pulls together loose ends and addresses the explanation for growing private security in the Netherlands. Subsequent to the within-case analysis carried out in the previous chapters, the search here is for cross-case patterns that enable the building of a theory from the case study research. Thus, to enhance the visibility of explanations 'beyond initial impressions' (Eisenhardt, 1989: 541) the chapter juxtaposes the differences and similarities between the cases investigated. The first section begins by summarizing shifts in the extent and nature of Dutch private security, after which the second section revisits the theoretical model developed earlier and analyzes the relevancy of the preliminary assumptions. Finally, the chapter presents a summary about the factors that have determined private security growth in the Netherlands.

## 11.1 Shifts in the extent and nature of private security

The Dutch manned guarding services market has undergone great expansion over the last three decades. After an 80-year period of relative obscurity, private security guards have stepped into the spotlight, growing from around 10,000 in 1980 to 30,000 today. The guarding sector showed fastest growth between 1985–1990 and 1995–2002, but this trend has since flattened out. In general, the Dutch security industry is widely recognized as highly oligarchic, with only three (multinational) companies dominating the market.

At the local level, the *Efteling* in-house security team, after its establishment in 1985, decreased from 12 employees to 9 in 1989 but grew again in 2004 to 15, which number excludes the additional guards hired on a flexible contract basis. More recently, to advance all-round risk management and offer higher quality care to customers, Efteling's in-house team was incorporated into a larger integral safety organization that includes ambulance and fire services.

*Stadium Feyenoord,* after instituting the De Kuip Safety and Security (KSS) team, began in 1991 with 100 in-house stewards, which number climbed to over 500 by 1997 but fell back to 200 in 2005 (again, these figures exclude external contract staff that fill any void). The remaining stewards have been retrained as event security officers (ESOs), higher profile crowd managers. In both cases, private guarding grew out of typically secondary social control occupations like park-keepers and football attendants for whom security provision is an important but not a central part of the job. The rise of private security guards can thus be related to a decline of more informal or indirect sources of social control; in other words, social control has been formalized.

One notable exception to the above trend is the public-private arrangement instituted at *Hoog Catherijne*. Here, privatization refers to shifts not in private security but in the way public police – specifically, police patrollers –are funded. The turning point for this shift was the 1990 police contract that transformed approximately 5 *publicly* employed but *privately* paid auxiliary police officers into a 12-strong operational team. This contract represented an extraordinary tax construction in which Hoog Catharijne financed the foot-patrols *indirectly* via the council budget. Nonetheless, even though the logic for privatization was supposedly dissimilar from that of the other cases, it still remains to determine the reasons for such a remarkable solution.

As regards the duties of paid guards in mass private properties, it is obvious that their profit-maximizing mandate has always been central to their delivering multifarious services, resulting in a juggling of soft client-oriented approaches with hard order maintenance and exclusion. Within this context, in terms of security governance, private guards primarily served as defense lines around police officers, particularly when both parties shared the same goals of surveillance, targeting (repeat) offenders and deploying interagency teams. Nonetheless, optimism about tight cooperative endeavors must be tempered. The Hoog Catharijne case plainly indicates that workable relationships between security guards and police officers can be very difficult, if not impossible, to achieve unless interests and objectives match really well.

Thus, possibilities for greater interaction must be found in major events, (potential) accidents and direct emergencies (see also Sarre and Prenzler, 2005: 195). For example, at so-called 'high risk' matches at Stadium Feyenoord, security guards and police officers join together in mixed teams to spot hooligans and protect the crowd from violence. In addition, at Efteling, police officers only enter the park to assist guards with calamities. Overall, despite calls from the police and security sectors alike for better confidence and more routine practices, public-private partnerships often go no farther than good intentions and shallow contacts.

## 11.2 The original model

As outlined earlier, academic literature on private security growth has provided a fairly complex list of explanations clustered around rising crime and related problems, growth of mass private property, economic rationalities, government policy toward private sector participation, an overburdened police force and professionalization of private security. The question is which of these factors offers the most pervasive explanation of the rise in private security.

## 11.2.1 Rising crime and related problems

One first, intuitively attractive, explanation is that rising crime has triggered the demand for private security. However, surprisingly, there is little support for this suggestion in the case of the Netherlands. Rather, statistics for the national level show considerable delays between seriously increasing crime figures and the renaissance of private guarding services. In fact, crime rates stabilized when private security enjoyed its heyday during the mid-1980s and mid-1990s. Moreover, despite popular expectations to the contrary, terrorism appears to have had no lasting overall effect in the Netherlands: rather, private security growth has flattened since 2001.

Cross-comparison of the *Stadium Feyenoord* and *Hoog Catharijne* data reveals time lags between spreading deviancy and private security initiatives. Initially confronted with hooliganism in 1974, Feyenoord did not set up an in-house stewarding organization until 1991. Similarly, Hoog Catharijne, faced since the 1970s with increasing misbehavior like public drunkenness, vagrancy and drug possession, still did not implement the police contract until 1990. At *Efteling* amusement park, the private security-crime nexus was more visible: its management reacted to rebellious youngsters by starting an in-house security team in 1985, which it reinforced in the late 1990s following modest rises in theft and vandalism. These measures were designed to protect Efteling's charming family-oriented image so necessary to the park's 'core business' activity of enchanting its visitors with peaceful fairy-tale surroundings.

## 11.2.2 Growth of mass private property

The assumption that transformations in urban life – mostly the spreading of mass private property – have contributed to the proliferation of private security is an influential and enduring thesis. Yet, as this research has indicated, although the number of properties like shopping centers has indeed grown over the past thirty years, the spreading of many other accommodations has not been occurring at the same time as the mushrooming of manned guarding services. Rather, leisure facilities like *Stadium Feyenoord* (1936) and *Efteling* (1952) were built long before private security came to the forefront in the Netherlands.

Moreover, paid guarding services have always been, and increasingly are, bound up with spaces like neighborhoods and town centers that, because they fall outside the mass private property category, weaken these properties' distinctive relationship with corporate interests. In addition, compared to, for example, North America, the spreading and size of mass private property in the Netherlands are relatively modest, and the three case studies suggest that at the local level, enlargement of such premises and growth in visitor numbers has little or no impact on private security. It may even be argued that increased visitor inflows provide more informal social control that requires the presence of fewer paid guards.

### 11.2.3 Economic rationalities

The economic development factor has robust explanatory power for private security growth. Even though, admittedly, the Dutch economy clearly showed positive trends before the renaissance of paid guarding, the security market's booming success and recent stabilization fits fairly well with economic waves over the past 30 years. It must be recognized, however, that many customers do not pay for the guarding services they enjoy, but parasitically depend on others. As a result, private security companies have had to struggle with many free riders, an estimated 35% of all participants in collective protection arrangements for business parks, shopping venues and other mass private properties (2004).

At the local level, more than once, corporate crises have resulted in alterations in the size and organization of private security. Thus, as previously mentioned, the *Efteling* management established a 12 strong in-house private security team the moment that boisterous youths began undermining the park's fairy-tale flavor (in 1985). Similarly, the chairman of *Stadium Feyenoord* agreed to an in-house stewarding team at a time of profound financial instability (1991). Finally, major public image problems compelled *Hoog Catharijne* to agree to the private funding of police patrollers (1990) in a police contract that was part of wider policy experiments aimed to counter the upward spiraling of drug nuisance, theft, deterioration and decay.

### 11.2.4 Government policy toward private sector participation

The privatization of policing occurs either directly through the loading-off or contracting-out of peripheral occupations like parking wardens and custodial guards to the market or indirectly as government leaves room for spontaneous or bottom up initiatives. However, the former support services account for too small a segment of the private security industry for that development to persuasively explain the spreading of private security throughout the Netherlands. Rather, the latter, associated with policies on crime prevention network formation (1985) and integral safety chains (1992) by public and private policing and security bodies, seems to hold more ground.

As the case study on *Efteling* demonstrates, the shifts in policing of these properties resulted from public-private partnerships transferring the responsibility for security toward private services. When the police withdrew from the park in the late 1980s/early 1990s, they explicitly transferred tasks like prevention and surveillance to the in-house security force. Likewise, the Rotterdam police force relegated preventative tasks like body searches to *Feyenoord* security staff (1986), but, for politically motivated reasons, the officers did not withdraw from the stadium. At the same time, tightened safety and security policy (1991) and formalized public-private covenants (1997, 2003) marked slow but steady steps towards improved solutions, both technological and manned. In recent years, improved cooperation between Feyenoord and the government has had an encouraging effect on the desired swing away from police presence inside the ground.

*Hoog Catharijne*, however, represents a different situation altogether. As already noted, rather than a rise in private guards, in 1990, this property saw the introduction of public police patrollers. The political justification for a contract allowing the police to levy payments for their services was that retailers were receiving special favors from the government. Since Dutch police forces formally have no special legal rights to charge for any of their services, this arrangement constitutes an unusual, highly localized municipal experiment.

### 11.2.5 An overburdened police force
This study's findings refute the hypothesis that constrained police budgets lead to security firms filling some sort of security gap. In fact, over the past decade, the Dutch police have received substantial financial reinforcement – 1500 million euros and 15,000 FTE in manpower. However, despite large government investment, public demands on police forces have outstripped police performance, denoting that, in very broad terms only, it is not absolute but relative restrictions on police resources that have been central to government agendas aimed at the responsibilization of citizens, organizations and communities.

In addition, results of the case studies on *Stadium Feyenoord* and *Efteling* also undermine the widely held theory of persistently underfunded and undermanned police forces. Rather, police reluctance to bear progressively more weight on their resources stemmed not from insufficient budget but from widespread public perceptions of inadequacy. This finding is insightful in that such perceptions have arguably contributed to the passing of responsibilities from police officers to private security guards and stewards. Nonetheless, the *Hoog Catharijne* case is less clear cut in that it was not the police's desire to step back but a public-private agreement to pay a fair share for additional police patrollers that motivated shifts in security provision.

### 11.2.6 Professionalization of private security
Overall, the professionalization of private security has seemingly had no positive self-enforcing effect on reputation and growth. Therefore, modest and incipient moves to higher rated services can most probably be interpreted as a *result* rather than a *cause* of broader trends in private security. Apart from stricter legislation and self-regulation, an important contributor to the

professionalization of guarding personnel, as the local case studies suggest, is economics. For example, it was clearly in *Efteling* and *Stadium Feyenoord*'s commercial interests to elevate the protection of their visitors. Similarly, at *Hoog Catharijne*, even though the choice of public police patrollers instead of private security guards can by itself be considered a move toward proficient policing, economic (and political) logic still seems to underlie the decision-making.

### 11.2.7 Changes in labor law: A new factor

In the cases of *Efteling* and *Stadium Feyenoord*, the introduction of a labor law strengthening the employment rights of flexible seasonal and on-call workers was an unexpected explanation for numerical changes in private security personnel. Once the Flexi-Law came into force in 1999, temporary staff, especially the lower skilled, became commercially less attractive and were soon replaced by new personnel.

### 11.3 Summary

Based on the case study results, Table 11.1 summarizes the explanatory power of each factor assumed to drive private security growth. The research findings can be summarized as follows. First, *rising crime and related problems* do not account for flourishing private security. In reality, the industry enjoyed rapid growth during years in which recorded crime rates, although still high, stabilized. Moreover, in terms of total manpower, terrorism apparently had no direct impact on the industry's growth. At the local level, except for Efteling, whose management was most keen to suppress disorder for reasons of public relations, the case studies showed the same pattern. There were significant time lags between the occurrence of crime problems and the set up of private security agencies.

Second, *the growth of mass private property* and growing private security are weakly related in the Netherlands, as evidenced by the fact that the spreading of mass private property (e.g., amusement parks, football stadiums) often pre-dates the general demands for private security. Additionally, as the local case studies showed, there was no direct relationship between the enlargement of premises and increasing visitor numbers and private security growth.

Third, *economic rationalities* are important to understanding private security. Specifically, shifts in manned guarding services did relate strongly to economic upturns and downturns. Indeed, the local studies revealed that private security agencies were often established in crisis situations in which company images, and even the survival of organizations, were threatened. Paid guards (as well as privately funded police patrollers) thus became part of risk and safety management strategies for enhancing the attractiveness and commercial viability of venues.

Fourth, *government policy* stimulating bottom-up crime prevention arrangements within civil society closely matches upturns in private security over previous decades. Dutch public authorities have increasingly responsibilized citizens and organizations for their own safety and security, permitting, if not welcoming, the performance of policing activities by private (or privately funded) agents and agencies. This trend was detectable in all three case studies.

**Table 11.1: The influence of explanatory factors**

|  | Netherlands | Efteling | Stadium Feyenoord | Hoog Catharijne |
|---|---|---|---|---|
| **Rising crime and related problems** | - | + | - | - |
| **Growth of mass private property** | +/- | - | - | - |
| **Economic rationalities** | + | + | + | + |
| **Government policy toward private sector participation** | + | + | + | + |
| **An overburdened police force** | +/- | +/- | - | - |
| **Professionalization of private security** | - | - | - | - |
| **New factor: Labor law** | n/a | + | + | n/a |

Fifth, the idea of an *overburdened police force* can sometimes provide explanation for moves away from peripheral functions like patrolling mass private property, which has made private security solutions more attractive. However, there is no evidence for the police being low on resources as a contributory factor. Rather, public satisfaction with police performance has been decreasing in the Netherlands because of lasting incongruities between what police forces can deal with and what society expects them to handle.

Sixth, the belief that the *professionalization of private security* has created positive spirals of popular confidence and support is not sustainable in the Netherlands. Rather, professionalization trajectories proved to be merely an outcome of regulations and individual customer intents, not of self-generating business success.

Seventh, *changes in labor law* – specifically, the 1999 Flexi-Law – did induce a replacement effect of temporary to permanent staff in the cases of Efteling and Stadium Feyenoord. Therefore, this variable can be viewed as a new explanatory factor for shifts in private security employment.

# 12     Conclusions and Discussion: Explaining Private Security

As elsewhere, the Dutch private security market has progressively grown over recent years, and those who were pioneers in manned guarding services have witnessed lucrative returns on their investments. In terms of staff numbers and annual turnovers, private security companies have gradually come to occupy an important position in the policing landscape. However, amazingly, despite this resounding growth, the body of knowledge surrounding paid guards has remained limited because scholars continue to focus primarily on traditional state-led police forces. Yet not taking private security seriously is a grave mistake; this trend could have drastic implications for the future of policing. Therefore, to keep abreast of developments, much greater academic and practitioner attention should be paid to the social and political implications of contract guarding.

    This chapter begins by mapping and explaining the ascendancy of Dutch private security over time by outlining the rise of manned guarding services, assessing the theoretical model and identifying the most important explanatory factors. The subsequent sections critically discuss the nature of manned guarding and the theoretical implications of the research findings, after which the concluding sections address various lines of criticisms put forward in wider academic debates on burgeoning private security. This discussion emphasizes that the democratic state, far from remaining aloof from privatization trends, has a key responsibility as the primary guarantor of collective security interests. This mandate should be borne in mind now that the growth in trends toward the private provision of security is expected to continue strongly through the twenty-first century.

## 12.1 The intellectual puzzle

The main research question of this study was as follows. *How can the growth of private manned guarding services in the Netherlands over the past three decades be explained?* This question breaks down into the following two subquestions:

1.  To what extent have Dutch private manned guarding services expanded over the past three decades?
2.  What explains the growth of private manned guarding services in the Netherlands over the past three decades?

The research aims were twofold: (1) to create detailed knowledge about the size and organization of private security in the Netherlands and identify how the industry has evolved, what private guards do in practice and how they relate to police officers and (2) to elucidate which factors are most important in explaining why private security has grown so large.

The study used qualitative research methods that combined national and local analyses of policing permutations. National data provided a broad matrix of policing and private security developments in which to situate the three focused case studies of amusement park *Efteling*, football stadium *Feyenoord* and shopping mall *Hoog Catharijne*. Together, these icons of leisure facilities in the Netherlands paint a telling portrait of changes in the extent and organization of (private) security forces patrolling mass private property. The three-phase project began with the construction, from an extensive literature review, of a theoretical explanatory framework. The second phase involved data collection (through a mail survey, interviews, documentary sources and preliminary direct observations) to confirm shifts in private security numbers. The final phase analyzed the data to determine which factor is key to understanding current shifts in policing.

### 12.1.1 Shifts in private security

The research findings clearly indicate a substantial increase in Dutch private security. First, combining the data from the multiple sources produced an accurate picture of an industry that has tripled in size over the last 30 years. Specifically, in early 1980, there were approximately 10,000 guards employed in the Netherlands, in contrast to the 30,000 employed today. In addition, contract guards have virtually replaced their in-house colleagues.

Nonetheless, the local case studies tell more complicated stories. At *Efteling*, the in-house security team, after its establishment in 1985, decreased from 12 employees to 9 in 1989 but later expanded to approximately 15 in 2004, the optimal number of security workers needed to safeguard the amusement park's premises. During high seasons, the in-house team was assisted by supplementary contract guards.

In contrast, *Stadium Feyenoord* needed around 600 staff members to keep the sports ground safe and pleasant; however, whereas its in-house team grew from 100 to over 500 between 1993 and 1997, it decreased again to 200 in 2003. Today, Feyenoord employs 300 (more highly qualified) stewards, excluding frequently hired security guards who have come and gone in waves of varying density.

At *Hoog Catharijne*, it was not the hiring of private security staff but the appointment of approximately 5 privately funded police patrollers (1990) that represented the most remarkable shift in policing. This decision was based on a combination of practical reasons related to authority and democratic accountability, but in general, the municipal council considered public foot-patrols better equipped for dealing with security problems than private guards.

### 12.1.2 The explanatory model revisited

This section, which considers the validity of factors that may account for the privatization of policing in the Netherlands (see Figure 12.1), asks how useful the theoretical perspectives are that have shaped current views of manned guarding services. As indicated in chapter 11, government policy toward private sector participation and economic rationalities are most prominent in explaining the mushrooming growth in contract guards. Since the 1980s, Dutch public authorities have actively pushed society to take preventative and protective measures against crime and disorder, a policy that has created room for security solutions in which paid guards could actively participate. The pressing issue has been where public responsibility for policing ends and private responsibility begins. Because security companies have benefited from such tensions ensuing from continual crises in sovereign crime control, they now occupy an increasingly pervasive position in society. Nonetheless, because, in the context of mass private properties, profit-seeking organizations employ contract guards, these latter have inescapably become subject to meticulous financial considerations. Only when government policy, in conjunction with corporate interests, has obliged organizations to invest in security, have they agreed.

### Figure 12.1: The explanatory model

### 12.2 Reflections on flourishing private security

The global flourishing of private security has led to wild speculations about the future of crime control. Some observers have even suggested that state-centered policing models are merely a historical 'blip' (Zedner, 2006b: 81) or 'hiccup' (Shearing, 2005: 62) rather than a long-term reality. There is, however, no need for such theatrical assertions about the impact of paid guarding services on the position of Dutch public police agencies. First, compared with police forces, the *numerical dimensions* of Dutch private security must not be overstated. Thus, even though the provision of exact numbers runs counter to the industry's opaque nature, official statistics suggest that around 30,000 guards are operational in the Netherlands, which equals a 23,630 FTE manpower compared to 53,000 FTE (of which 36,000 FTE is executive staff) for regional and national police forces. Thus, based on total employment figures, private security companies do not outnumber public police forces.

Second, to compare private security guards with police officers is, to a certain extent, to compare apples with oranges. Although both sectors are vested with formal social control activities, their tasks, principles, powers, roles and educational level are *different*: whereas the police's mandate is to bring lawbreakers to justice, profit-seeking security companies are tailored to their customers' interests in crime prevention. Hence, public and private policing sectors represent interpenetrating worlds of organized social control, each with its own appetite for order maintenance and crime-stopping strategies.

Finally, and closely related to the foregoing, security guards *do not replace* the police. Indeed, one noticeable finding is that many internal security guards working as part of a large factory or bank have been outsourced to commercial companies. As a result, the in-house sector has almost been incorporated into the market economy. Moreover, private guards have taken over duties previously undertaken by park keepers or football attendants (not public police officers), a development that Jones and Newburn (2002) referred to as the 'formalization of social control'. This evidence tempers bold claims about the novelty of splintering policing and the role therein of private security. Rather than heralding a new policing era, contract guards have grown out of a longer, sometimes hidden, history of security provision.

One new tendency, however, is that the Dutch government has been increasingly granting contracts guards access to police-like duties as 'street coaches' who discipline youngsters, 'neighborhood managers' who make condominiums safe and clean, sworn-in special constables (*Buitengewoon Opsporingsambtenaren*) who fine parking offenders and custodial officers who guard detainees. Nonetheless, it is as yet impossible to gauge the exact consequences for the division of labor between guards and police officers, the democratic accountability of networks and the steering role of state authorities. Thus, additional research is needed in these areas.

## 12.3 Reflections on explanatory factors

In recent years, scholars have identified various explanations for rising private security around the world but failed to build a conceptual framework. Moreover, present-day police studies suffer from heavily Anglo-Saxon 'ethnocentrism' (Manning, 2005: 32) and so tend to ignore the influences of local histories, policies, economics and cultures on emerging private security industries. In contrast, empirical insights from non-English language countries are barely present in the literature. Recognizing such blind spots, this book challenges dominant assumptions about private security growth.

The first major commonsense assumption refuted by this study's findings is that rising crime has greatly contributed to the increasing demands on private security. Rather, recorded crime rates stabilized and even slightly declined during periods of industry growth. As a result, instead of focusing on numerical waves of felony offences, *ways of thinking* about crime and, in broader terms, insecurity have shifted drastically (Van der Vijver, 2001: 31–32). Specifically, energized by heavy (financial) losses, but also by diffuse (moral) anxieties, the police, entrepreneurs and citizens have joined hands in mutual recognition of 'defined up' deviance, lower tolerance limits and firmer maintenance.

Second, even though long depicted as *the* correct formula, there is no convincing evidence that growing mass private property – for example, shopping malls, football stadiums and amusement parks – triggered private security. This finding confirms Jones and Newburn's (1999: 241) initial doubts that changes in spatial ordering 'should be regarded as the key explanation'. Rather, mass private property often predates the observed boost in private security, and many guards patrol spaces outside the corporate domain.

Third, no support exists for the assumption that a fiscal crisis in public policing explains private guards filling some 'security gap'. On the contrary, the Dutch police have received substantial reinforcement over the years. An alternative explanation may therefore be that rather than a fiscal crisis, there is a *legitimacy crisis* (Garland, 1996). That is, police forces feel overburdened because society's demands for (preferably full) reassurance outstrips police capabilities, which in turn engenders government urgency to stimulate private solutions for crime control.

Finally, the idea that professionalization will create self-enforcing business success does not hold. Yet, it is difficult to dismiss the goal of improving industry quality, even though achieving this aim is not likely to be easy. Indeed, according to critics, buyers generally tend to prefer cheap rather than first-class services, which preference creates vicious circles of low profit margins and limited room for innovative progress (Jones, 2005). In addition, it hampers upgrading of private security guards' skills and qualifications.

## 12.4 Theoretical and research implications

As useful as these new insights are for the Dutch case, further explorations are needed to map out the determinants of private security growth outside the Netherlands. Therefore, an obvious next step would be a longitudinal, in-depth, cross-national study of paid policing using explanations that are robust to the multiple historical, political, economic, geographical and legal factors inherent in diverse privatization scenarios. In addition, researchers might review and compare the competing principles embraced by public police and private security; unravel the precise relationships built by both sectors; and inspect the types of powers, mentalities, resources and working-methods each has available.[1]

Admittedly, such a comparative undertaking, which some judge to be exotic, marginal and even virtually infeasible, will not be easy because substantial national diversity in concepts and data give rise to daunting problems. Nonetheless, despite the substantial caveats, cross-national research has great advantages for expanding knowledge of (mixed) policing systems, for understanding (innovative) changes in security governance, for gaining expertise in best practices and, eventually, for learning about ourselves (Mawby, 1990). Indeed, the maxim that 'nothing is so practical as good theory' should be kept in mind as private security continues to occupy an important place in extended police families around the globe.

### 12.5 Consequences of private security[2]

Based on the empirical evidence, the current increase in contract guards is likely to continue, to the benefit of some but the unavoidable loss of others. Therefore, it is very important to evaluate the possible social and political consequences of trends toward private security in the Netherlands, Europe and beyond. To date, scholars have raised at least four lines of criticism: (1) the exclusionary mandate of security staff, (2) the messiness of policing landscapes, (3) the paradoxes stemming from ever-increasing security provision and (4) the security industry's poor professional image.

First, private security agents are, by legal contract, required to act in an exclusionary manner; therefore, they may selfishly protect only those who can afford their services.[3] However, whereas this indeed be true in terms of denying access to, for example, a football stadium on the basis of house rules, property owners' privileges are still subject to legal constraints. As Mopas and Stenning (2001: 71) emphasized, rather than excluding persons from property 'arbitrarily and for no articulated reason at all', guards can only eject individuals on 'specified and "reasonable" grounds' such as previous misbehavior. Nonetheless, the privatization of policing activities and wider neoliberal policies on individual responsibility for risk reduction (Ericson et al., 2000) do pose serious threats to equal treatment and freedom from discrimination. Private

---

[1]    Bayley and Shearing (2001), Sarre (2005) and Jones and Newburn (2006c).
[2]    This section is based on Van Steden and Sarre (2007).
[3]    Gray (1991), Bottoms and Wiles (1997), Young (1999), Von Hirsch and Shearing (2000) and Crawford (2006c).

security guards are, after all, paid by those who endorse policing activities in favor of their own priorities.

Second, citizens are routinely confronted by cluttered organizations, uniforms and powers as, legal scholars have argued, public/private distinctions have become murky. This lack of distinction serves the security guards' best interest of maintaining an air of authority. In fact, as regards clothing and behavior, many security guards do not mind being confused with police officers and may even pretend to have more powers than they actually possess (Kontos, 2004). As a result, the police, once the central apparatus of power, are slowly becoming intermingled with privatized uses of compulsion (including arrest), search, seizure and eventually exclusion (Terpstra, 2006: 70–72). This diminishment of state primacy together with an accelerating proliferation of alternative (private) order maintainers has produced ambiguous policing patchworks or security quilts (Crawford and Lister, 2004a) that might interfere with democratic values of equality, privacy and legal protection (Terpstra, 2007: 147–148).

Third, several paradoxes persist that cast a shadow on the pursuit of (private) security (Zedner, 2003b). For example, ironically, exclusionary strategies designed to address feelings of anxiety seem to have proven only cumbersome, disappointing and counterproductive. That is, when citizens retreat from wider society into closed fortifications, there is no assurance that their fears will be lessened (Merry, 1981). Such thinking about the communal meaning of safety and security shapes Loader's (1997b) position that policing cannot be left to unfettered market capitalism. Private security, he argued, is 'an oxymoron' (Loader, 1997c: 155) because policing and security are, in themselves, embedded in the rich social texture of close-knit collectivities and the people attached to them.

Intimately allied to the above problem of 'defensive reassurance', private security companies paradoxically engage in fear reduction activities while at the same time taking advantage of people's panic and paranoia. Thus, the persistency of insecurity may stir guards to prompt action, but it also legitimizes them. Moreover, despite the mounting number of security options, societies are not necessarily any safer. Rather, it is an idle hope that either police officers or private guards will ever be able to eliminate crime, and promises to this effect are dangerous and misleading, because 'too much security' (Zedner, 2003b) potentially curtails civil liberties and diminishes individual freedom (Waldron, 2003).

These latter paradoxes relate directly to the fourth and deepest line of criticism: the integrity of an industry that is 'extracting fees and profit from human misery and commodified needs' (Forst and Manning, 1999: 115). Opponents of the private security industry fear that it will give rise to profound social costs, not only in terms of deflation of the trust relations that bind society but also in terms of incompetence, corrupt practices, illegal actions and thug-like behavior (Prenzler, 2004). Admittedly, there is currently no evidence that such problems exist in the Netherlands and, if they do, to what extent; nonetheless, the *vulnerability* of private security work to malpractice and abuse is suspected. In this respect, customers have much to gain from procurement of professional quality, not lowest cost. Hence, companies should better demonstrate that security works – that manned guarding services *are* worth buying.

By definition, taking on such a challenge presumes entrepreneurship and innovation because quality and professionalism can only be improved if the industry assures job enrichment, career advancement and income improvement. At the same time, however, 'professionalization' must not become a code word for elevating private security staff to public police levels. First, it is questionable whether the private security industry will ever be capable of gracing itself with the aura of 'symbolic power' that the police imbue (Loader, 1997a: 8), and in fact such an outcome may be downright undesirable. Second, it should be remembered that much routine policing and private security work does 'not require high levels of expertise and training or the "professional" status which goes with them' (Stenning, 1994: 152). Consequently, although there is always room for professional development in terms of qualifications, competencies and social skills, excessive preoccupation with professionalization is unnecessary.

**12.6 Final remarks**
Even taking into account the above critiques, prohibiting private security companies is not an option; even apart from the fact that security guards have been offered the social and political opportunity to become partners in risk reduction and property defense, it would be absurd to shut down an entire industry that employs tens of thousands of people. Thus, at this point, the most pragmatic solution is to learn to live with private security services by regulating and improving them.

Astonishingly, however, governments – and the Dutch government is no exception – have responded quite sluggishly to such needed regulation and improvement, implying an attitude of indifference and neglect (Prenzler, 2004). Indeed, policy-makers barely have a vision on how to steer and supervise the security industry. In addition, the policing system in the Netherlands has become increasingly diverse, complex and multifaceted, which explains why analysts and practitioners favor better coordination and regulation of the different 'pillars of policing' (Van Steden and Huberts, 2006: 30). Within the European arena, the Netherlands may pay lip service to strict legislation schemes for private security guards, but enforcement is weak and operatives are criticized for proficiency deficits.

In addition, given the EU's preoccupation with liberalization and deregulation, institutionalized statutory pledges nationwide may be altered or replaced by greater emphasis on industry self-regulation. For example, the Dutch association VPB has recently introduced a quality label to indicate its members' professionalism and trustworthiness across the country. Yet, the scope of this accountability mechanism is limited because only a few companies (albeit the largest ones) are affiliated with VPB. Because of these developments, professionalization, transparency and oversight are becoming ever more pressing issues. Therefore, government authorities and security companies should be turning their gaze to appropriate and effective models of cooperation, funding and regulation that represent every player in the nodal networks. Specifically, public policy-makers and private managers alike must govern security in such a way that citizens not only enjoy a satisfactory level of protection but do so in an open, democratic and equitable manner.

# References

Abelson, A. (2006) 'Private security in Chile: An agenda for the Public Security Ministry', *Security and Citizenship Program Bulletin*, 6: 1–10.

Abrahamsen, R. and Williams, M.C. (2005a) *The globalization of private security; Country report: Nigeria*, Aberystwyth, University of Wales.

Abrahamsen, R. and Williams, M.C. (2005b) *The globalization of private security; Country report: Kenya*, Aberystwyth, University of Wales.

Abrahamsen, R. and Williams, M.C. (2005c) *The globalization of private security; Country report: Sierra Leone*, Aberystwyth, University of Wales.

Adang, O. (2001) 'Friendly but firm: The maintenance of public order' (unpublished working paper).

Albanese, J.S. (1989) *Private security and the public interest*, Buffalo, Great Books.

Batelaan, H. and Bos, J. (2003) *De particuliere beveiliging bewaakt? Evaluatie regelgeving particuliere beveiligingsorganisaties* [The guards guarded? An evaluation of legislation on private security], Amsterdam, Regioplan.

Bauman, Z. (2000) *Liquid modernity*, Cambridge, Polity Press.

Bayley, D.H. (1994) *Police for the future*, Oxford, Oxford University Press.

Bayley, D.H. and Shearing, C.D. (1996) 'The future of policing', *Law and Society Review*, 30 (3): 585–606.

Bayley, D.H. and Shearing, C.D. (2001) *The new structure of policing: Description, conceptualization, and research agenda*, Washington D.C., National Institute of Justice.

Beck, U. (1992) *Risk society: Towards a new modernity*, London, Sage.

Becker, T.M. (1973) 'The place of private police in society: An area of research for the social sciences', *Social Problems*, 21 (1): 438–455.

Benn, S.I. and Gaus, G.F. (1983) 'The liberal conception of the public and the private' in S.I. Benn and G.F. Gaus (eds.) *Public and private in social life*, New York, St. Martin's Press: 31–65.

Bijlsma–Frankema, K.M. and Droogleever Fortuijn, A.B. (1997) 'De kwalitatieve datamatrix als analyseinstrument' [A qualitative data matrix as instrument of analysis], *Tijdschrift voor Sociale Wetenschappen*, 42 (4): 448–459.

Bittner, E. (1990) *Aspects of police work*, Boston, Northeastern University Press.

Bottoms, A.E. and Wiles, P. (1997) 'Environmental criminology' in M. Maguire, R. Morgan and R. Reiner (eds.) *Oxford handbook of criminology* (second edition), Oxford, Clarendon Press: 305–359.

Boutellier, J.C.J. (2001) 'The convergence of social policy and criminal justice', *European Journal on Criminal Policy and Research*, 9 (4): 361–380.

Boutellier, J.C.J. (2004) *The safety utopia: Contemporary discontent and desire as to crime and punishment*, Dordrecht, Kluwer Academic Publishers.

Boutellier, J.C.J. (2005) *Meer dan veilig: Over bestuur, bescherming en burgerschap* [More than safe: On governance, protection and citizenship], Den Haag, Boom Juridische Uitgevers.

Braithwaite, J. (2000) 'The new regulatory state and the transformation of criminology', *British Journal of Criminology*, 40 (2): 222–238.

Braithwaite, J. (2006) 'Peacemaking networks and restorative justice' in J. Fleming and J. Wood (eds.) *Fighting crime together: The challenges of policing and security networks*, Sydney, NSW Press: 195–217.

Bryett, K. (1996) 'Privatization – Variation on a theme', *Policing and Society*, (6): 23–35.

Bryman, A. (2004) *The Disneyization of society*, London, Sage.

Burgers, J. (1999) 'Stedelijke landschappen: Over openbare ruimte in de postindustriële stad' [Urban landscapes: On public Spaces in the post–industrial city] in R. van der Wouden (ed.) *De stad op straat,* Den Haag, SCP: 127–148.

Burns, R., Kinkade, P. and Leone, M.C. (2004) 'Bounty hunters: A look behind the type', *Policing: An International Journal of Police Strategies and Management*, 28 (1): 118–138.

Button, M. (2002) *Private policing*, Cullompton, Willan.

Button, M. (2003) 'Private security and the policing of quasi–public space', *International Journal of the Sociology of Law*, 31 (3): 227–237.

Button, M. (2007a) *Security officers and policing: Powers, culture and control in the governance of private space*, Aldershot, Ashgate.

Button, M. (2007b) 'Assessing the regulation of private security across Europe', *European Journal of Criminology*, 4 (1): 109–128.

Button, M., Park, H. and Lee, J. (2006) 'The private security industry in South Korea: A familiar tale of growth, gaps and the need for better regulation', *Security Journal*, 19 (3): 167–179.

Cain, M. (1979) 'Trends in the sociology of police work', *International Journal of the Sociology of Law*, 7 (2): 143–167.

Cachet, A. (1990) *Politie en sociale controle* [Police and social control], Arnhem, Gouda Quint.

Cohen, S. (1985) *Visions of social control: Crime, punishment and classification*, Oxford, Polity Press.

Cools, M. and Verbeiren, K. (2004) *Politie en privébewaking: Samen sterk/Fair face ensemble: La collaboration entre police et gardiennage privé* [Staying strong together: The police and private security], Brussels, Politeia.

COT (1999) *Voetbal en geweld: Onderzoek naar aanleiding van rellen en plunderingen bij een huldiging in Rotterdam (25 april 1999)* [Football and violence: Research on the outburst of riots and looting during an inauguration in Rotterdam (April 25, 1999)], Alpen aan den Rijn, Samsom.

Crawford, A. (1999) *The local governance of crime: Appeals to community and partnerships*, Oxford, Oxford University Press.

Crawford, A. (2003a) 'The patterns of policing in the UK: Policing beyond the police' in T. Newburn (ed.) *Handbook of policing*, Cullompton, Willan: 136–168.

Crawford, A. (2003b) '"Contractual governance" of deviant behavior', *Journal of Law and Society*, 30 (4): 479–505.

Crawford, A. (2006a) '"Fixing broken promises?": Neighborhood wardens and social capital', *Urban Studies*, 43 (5/6): 957–976.

Crawford, A. (2006b) 'Networked governance and the post–regulatory state? Steering, rowing and anchoring the provision of policing and security', *Theoretical Criminology*, 10 (4): 449–497.

Crawford, A. (2006c) 'Policing and security as "club goods": The new enclosures?' in J. Wood and B. Dupont (eds.) *Democracy, society and the governance of security*, Cambridge, Cambridge University Press: 111–138.

Crawford, A. and Lister, S. (2004a) 'The patchwork shape of reassurance policing in England and Wales: Integrated local security quilts or frayed, fragmented and fragile tangled webs?', *Policing: An International Journal of Police Strategies and Management*, 27 (3): 413–430.

Crawford, A. and Lister, S. (2004b) *The extended policing family: Visible patrols in residential areas*, York, Joseph Rowntree Foundation.

Crawford, A. and Lister, S. (2006) 'Additional security patrols in residential areas: Notes from the marketplace', *Policing and Society*, 16 (2): 164–188.

Crawford, A., Lister, S., Blackburn, S. and Burnett, J. (2005) *Plural policing: The mixed economy of visible patrols in England and Wales*, Bristol, Policy Press.

Cunningham, W.C., Strauchs, J.J. and Van Meter, C. (1990) *Hallcrest report II: Private security trends: 1970–2000*, Stoneham, Butterworth–Heinemann.

Cunningham, W.C. and Taylor, T. (1985) *Hallcrest report I: Private security and police in America*, Portland, Chancellor Press.

Decisio (2004) *Freeriderproblematiek en –oplossingen: Naar structurele collectieve beveiligingsmaatregelen voor bedrijven en winkels* [The problem of and solutions for free–riding: Towards structural collective security for companies and shops], Amsterdam, Decisio.

De Jong, M. (2002) 'Peace of mind? Perceptions of contractual security guarding at commercial banks in Saudi Arabia', *Security Journal*, 15 (1): 33–47.

De Lint, W. (1999) 'A post–modern turn in policing: Policing as pastiche?', *International Journal of the Sociology of Law*, 27 (2): 127–152.

De Ruijter, E. (2006) *Evaluatie opleiding beveiliger* [An evaluation of the private security guard training program], Tilburg, Arbeid Opleidingen Consult.

De Wolff, M. (ed.) (1997) *Stadion Feyenoord: Het origineel* [Stadium Feyenoord: The original], Rotterdam, Koppel.

Dekkers, F. (1982) *Eindhoven 1993–1945: Kroniek van Nederlands lichtstad in de schaduw van het Derde Rijk* [Eindhoven 1993–1945: Chronicles of the Dutch 'city of light' in the shadow of the Third Reich], Haarlem, In de Knipscheer.

Dessing, G. (2005) 'Klanten matig tevreden over particuliere beveiliging' [Mediocre customer satisfaction levels with private security], *Security Magazine*, 3: 8–21.

Dessing, G. (2006a) 'Top 12 particuliere beveiliging (manbewaking)' [Top 12 private security companies (manned guarding)], *Security Management*, 9: 4.

Dessing, G. (2006b) 'Klanten meer tevreden over particuliere beveiliging' [Rising customer satisfaction levels with private security], *Security Magazine*, 3: 8–17.

De Waard (1999) 'The private security industry in international perspective', *European Journal on Criminal Policy and Research*, 7 (2): 143–174.

Den Boer, M. (2004) *Out of the blue: Police perspectives on Europe, governance and accountability*, Amsterdam & Apeldoorn, Vrije Universiteit/ Politieacademie.

Dijkstra, G.S.A. and Van der Meer, F. (2003) 'Disentangling blurring boundaries: the public/private dichotomy from an organizational perspective' in M.R. Rutgers (ed.) *Retracing public administration* (volume 7), Oxford, Elsevier Science: 89–106.

Donkers, H. (2003a) *VPB Quickscan: Resultaten voor het kalenderjaar 2002* [VPB Quickscan: Results for the calendar year 2002], Zoetermeer, EIM.

Donkers, H. (2003b) *VPB Branchescan: Resultaten voor het kalenderjaar 2003* [VPB Industry Monitor: Results for the calendar year 2003], Zoetermeer: EIM.

Donkers, H. (2005) *VPB Branchescan: Resultaten voor het kalenderjaar 2004* [VPB Industry Monitor: Results for the calendar year 2004], Zoetermeer: EIM.

Donkers, H. (2006) *VPB Branchescan: Resultaten voor het kalenderjaar 2005* [VPB Industry Monitor: Results for the calendar year 2005], Zoetermeer: EIM.

Downes, D. (1988) *Contrast in tolerance: Post–war penal policy in the Netherlands and England and Wales*, Oxford, Clarendon Press.

Draper, H. (1978) *Private police*, Harmondsworth, Penguin Books.

Eisenhardt, K.M. (1989) 'Building theories from case study research', *Academy of Management Review*, 14 (4): 532–550.

Eggen, A.T.J. (2005) 'Slachtoffers van criminaliteit' [Victims of crime] in A.T.J. Eggen and W. van der Heide (eds.) *Criminaliteit en rechtshandhaving 2004*, Den Haag, WODC: 53–88.

Eggen, A.T.J., Van der Laan, A.M., Engelhard, B.J.M., Blom, B., Broeders, A.P.A. and Bogaerts, S. (2005) 'Criminaliteit en opsporing' [Crime and investigation] in A.T.J. Eggen and W. van der Heide (ed.) *Criminaliteit en rechtshandhaving 2004*, Den Haag, WODC: 89–128.

Elzinga, D.J., Van Rest, P.H.S. and De Valk, J. (1995) 'Een korte geschiedenis van de Nederlandse politie' [A brief history of the Dutch police] in D.J. Elzinga, P.H.S. van Rest and J. de Valk (eds.) *Het Nederlandse politierecht*, Zwolle, W.E.J. Tjeenk Willink: 9–33.

Eppler, E. (2002) *Vom Gewaltmonopol zum Gewaltmarkt?* [From a monopoly of violence to a market of violence?], Frankfurt am Main, Suhrkamp.

Ericson, R., Barry, D. and Doyle, A. (2000) 'The moral hazards of neo–liberalism: Lessons from the private insurance industry', *Economy and Society*, 29 (4): 532–558.

Ericson, R. and Haggerty, K. (1997) *Policing the risk society*, Toronto, University of Toronto Press.

Favarel–Garrigues, G. and Le Huérou (2004) 'State and the multilateralization of policing in post–Soviet Russia', *Policing and Society*, 14 (1): 13–30.

Feeley, M.M. and Simon, J. (1992) 'The new penology: Notes on the emerging strategy of corrections and its implications', *Criminology*, 30 (4): 449–474.

Fleming, J. and Wood, J. (2007) *Fighting crime together: The challenges of policing and security networks*, Sydney, UNSW Press.

Forst, B. and Manning, P.K. (1999) *The privatization of policing: Two views*, Washington D.C., Georgetown University Press.

Foucault, M. (1977) *Discipline and punish: The birth of the prison*. Harmondsworth, Penguin Books.

Frosdick, S. and Marsh, P. (2005) *Football hooliganism*, Cullompton, Willan.

Furedi, F. (2002) *Culture of fear: Risk–taking and the morality of low expectation* (revised edition), London, Continuum.


Gallie, W.B. (1962) 'Essentially contested concepts' in M. Black (ed.) *The importance of language*, Englewood Cliffs, Prentice–Hall: 121–146.

Garland, D. (1996) 'The limits of the sovereign state: Strategies of crime control in contemporary society', *British Journal of Criminology*, 36 (4): 445–471.

Garland, D. (2000) 'The culture of high crime societies: Some preconditions of recent "law and order" policies', *British Journal of Criminology*, 40 (3): 347–375.

Garland, D. (2001) *The culture of control: Crime and social order in contemporary society*, Chicago, The University of Chicago Press.

Garreau, J. (1992) *Edge city: Life on the new frontier*, New York, Doubleday.

Geertz, C. (1973) *The interpretation of cultures: Selected essays*, New York, Basic Books.

George, B. and Button, M. (2000) *Private security*, Leicester, Perpetuity Press.

Geuss, R. (2001) *Public goods, private goods*, Princeton, Princeton University Press.

Giddens, A. (1990) *The consequences of modernity*, Stanford, Stanford University Press.

Gijsbrechts, M. (2004) *Ethic minorities and integration: Outlook for the future*, Den Haag, SCP.

Gill, M. and Hart, J. (1997a) 'Exploring investigative policing', *British Journal of Criminology*, 37 (4): 549–567.

Gill, M. and Hart, J. (1997b) 'Policing as a business: Organization structure of private investigation', *Policing and Society*, 7 (2): 117–141.

Gimenez–Salinas, A. (1999) 'La situation de la sécurité privé en Espagne' [The private security situation in Spain] in J. Shapland and L. van Outrive (eds.) *Police et sécurité: controle social et interaction public/privé/Policing and security: Social control and the public–private divide*, Montreal, L'Harmattan: 115–126.

Gimenez–Salinas, A. (2004) 'New approaches regarding private/public security', *Policing and Society*, 14 (2): 158–174.

Glaser, B.N. and Strauss, A.L. (1967) *The discovery of grounded theory: Strategies for qualitative research*, Chicago, Aldine.

Gounev, P. (2006) 'Bulgaria's private security industry' in A. Bryden and M. Caparini (eds.) *Private actors and security governance*, Zürich, Lit: 109–128.

Grabosky, P.N. (1996) 'The future of crime control', *Trends and issues in crime and criminal justice*, 63: 1–6.

Grabosky, P.N. (2007) 'Private sponsorship of public policing', *Police Practice and Research*, 8 (1): 5–16.

Gray, K. (1991) 'Property in thin air', *Cambridge Law Journal*, 50 (2): 252–307.

Group 4 Securicor (2005), *Particuliere beveiliging: Groeien en grenzen verleggen* [Private security: Growing and expanding], Sensor Special (internal publication).

Guo, T. (1999) 'Private security in China: A note on recent developments', *Security Journal*, 12 (4): 43–46.

Hammersley, M. and Atkinson, P. (2000) *Ethnography: Principles in practice* (second edition), London, Routledge.

Harms, L. (2006) *Op weg in de vrije tijd: Context, kenmerken en dynamiek van vrijetijdsmobiliteit* [On the road to leisure: Context, characteristics and dynamics of leisure mobility], Den Haag, SCP.

Hayes, R. (2000) 'US retail store detectives: An analysis of their focus, selection and training', *Security Journal*, 13 (1): 7–20.

Hayward, K.J. (2004) *City limits: Crime, consumer culture and urban experience*, London, Glasshouse Press.

Heijboer H.J., Vader, J. and Wessels, E.C. (eds.) (1983) *Beveiligingsjaarboek 1983* [Security year book 1983], Arnhem, Noorduijn.

Hiscock, D. (2006) 'The commercialization of post–Soviet private security' in A. Bryden and M. Caparini (eds.) *Private actors and security governance*, Zürich, Lit: 129–148.

Hobbs, D., Hadfield, P., Lister, S. and Winlow, S. (2005) *Bouncers: Violence and governance in the night–time economy*, Oxford, Oxford University Press.

Hobbes, T. (1968 [1651]) *Leviathan*, ed. C.B. Macpherson, Harmondsworth, Penguin Classics.

Hoogenboom, A.B. (1986) *Privatisering van de politiefunctie: Een literatuurstudie over de particuliere veiligheidsindustrie* [Privatizing policing: A literature review on the private security industry], Den Haag, Ministerie van Binnenlandse Zaken.

Hoogenboom, A.B. (1991a) 'Grey policing: A theoretical framework', *Policing and Society*, 2 (1): 17–30.

Hoogenboom, A.B. (1991b) 'The mining police: Dutch private security in historical perspective' in P. Robert and C. Emsley (eds.) *Geschichte und Soziologie des Verbrechens*, Hamburg, Pfaffenweiler: 85–100.

Hoogenboom, A.B. (1994) *Het politiecomplex* [The police complex], Arnhem, Gouda Quint.

Hoogenboom, A.B. (1999) 'Privatisering van de politiefunctie' [The privatization of the police function] in C.J.C.F. Fijnaut, E.R. Muller and U. Rosenthal (eds.) *Politie: Studies over haar werking en organisatie*, Alphen aan den Rijn, Samsom: 549–575.

Hoogenboom, A.B. and Muller, E.R. (2002) *Voorbij de dogmatiek: Publiek–Private samenwerking in de veiligheidszorg* [Beyond dogmatism: Public–private partnerships in security and law enforcement], Zeist: Kerckebosch.

Hope, T. (2000) 'Inequality and the clubbing of private security' in T. Hope and R. Sparks (eds.) *Crime, risk and insecurity*, London, Routledge: 83–106.

Huberts, L.W.J.C. (1998) *Blinde vlekken in de politiepraktijk en de politiewetenschap* [Blind spots in the practice and study of policing], Arnhem, Gouda Quint.

Huberts, L.W.J.C. and Van Steden, R. (2001) 'Naar meer kennis over, voor en van de politie' [Towards more knowledge on, for and about the police], *Tijdschrift voor de Politie*, 63 (1/2): 4–8.

Huberts, L.W.J.C. and Van Steden, R. (2005) 'The Netherlands' in L.E. Sullivan and M.R. Haberfeld (eds.) *Encyclopedia of law enforcement* (volume 3), London, Sage (3 volumes): 1204–1208.

Huberts, L.W.J.C., Verbeek, S., Lasthuizen, K. and Van den Heuvel, J.H.J. (2004) *Paradoxaal politiebestel: Burgemeesters, openbaar ministerie en politiechefs over de sturing van de politie* [Paradoxical police system: Visions of mayors, public prosecutors and police chiefs on police governance], Zeist, Kerckebosch.

Hutchinson, S. and O'Conner, D. (2005) 'Policing "the new commons": Corporate security governance on a mass private property in Canada', *Policing and Society*, 15 (2): 125–144.

Intomart (2005) *Politiemonitor Bevolking 2005: Landelijke rapportage* [Police Population Monitor 2005: National report], Hilversum.

Intomart (2006) *Politiemonitor Bevolking 2006: Beleidsrapport* [Police Population Monitor 2006: Policy report], Hilversum.

Jacobs, J. (1962) *The death and life of great American cities: The failure of town planning*, Harmondsworth, Penguin Books.

Jason–Lloyd, L. (2003) *Quasi–policing*, London, Cavendish.

Joh, E. (2004) 'The paradox of private policing', *Journal of Criminal Law and Criminology*, 95 (1): 49–131.

Johnston, L. (1991) 'Privatization and the police function: From "new police" to "new policing"' in R. Reiner and M. Cross (eds.) *Beyond law and order: Criminal justice policy and politics into the 1990s*, London, MacMillan: 18–40.

Johnston, L. (1992a) *The rebirth of private policing*, London, Routledge.

Johnston, L. (1992b) 'The politics of private policing', *Police Quarterly*, 63 (3): 341–349.

Johnston, L. (1996a) 'Policing diversity: The impact of the public–private complex in policing' in F. Leishman, B. Loveday, and S. Savage (eds.) *Core issues in policing,* London, Longman: 54–70.

Johnston, L. (1996b) 'What is vigilantism?', *British Journal of Criminology*, 36 (2): 220–236.

Johnston, L. (1997) 'Policing communities of risk' in P. Francis, P. Davies and V. Jupp (eds.) *Policing futures: The police, law enforcement and the twenty–first century*, London, McMillan Press: 186–207.

Johnston, L. (1998) 'Late modernity, governance, and policing' in J.P. Brodeur (ed.) *How to recognize good policing: Problems and issues*, London, Sage: 193–214.

Johnston, L. (1999a) 'Private policing: Uniformity and diversity' in R.I. Mawby (ed.), *Policing across the world: Issues for the twenty–first century*, London, ULC Press: 226–238.

Johnston, L. (1999b) 'Private policing in context', *European Journal on Criminal Policy and Research*, 7 (2): 175–196.

Johnston, L. (2000a) *Policing Britain: Risk, security and governance*, Harlow, Longman.

Johnston, L. (2000b) 'Transnational private security: The impact of global commercial security' in J.W.E. Sheptycki (ed.) *Issues in transnational policing*, London, Routledge: 21–42.

Johnston, L. (2003) 'From "pluralisation" to the "police extended family": Discourses on the governance of community policing in Britain', *International Journal of the Sociology of Law*, 31 (3): 185–204.

Johnston, L. (2006) 'Transnational security governance' in J. Wood and B. Dupont (eds.) *Democracy, society and the governance of security*, Cambridge, Cambridge University Press: 33–51.

Johnston, L. and Shearing, C. (2003) *Governing security: Explorations in policing and justice*, London, Routledge.

Jones, T. (1995) *Policing and democracy in the Netherlands*, London, Policy Studies Institute.

Jones, T. (2005) 'Private policing in the United Kingdom: Contemporary trends and future developments' (unpublished working paper).

Jones, T. (2007) 'The governance of security: Pluralization, privatization, and polarization' in M. Maguire, R. Morgan and R. Reiner (eds.) *The Oxford handbook of criminology* (fourth edition), Oxford, Oxford University Press: 841–865.

Jones, T. and Newburn, T. (1995) 'How big is the private security sector?', *Policing and Society*, 5 (3): 221–232.

Jones, T. and Newburn, T. (1998) *Private security and public policing*, Oxford, Clarendon Press.

Jones, T. and Newburn, T. (1999) 'Urban change and policing: Mass private property re–considered', *European Journal on Criminal Policy and Research*, 7 (2): 225–244.

Jones, T. and Newburn, T. (2002) 'The transformation of policing? Understanding current trends in policing systems', *British Journal of Criminology*, 42 (1): 129–146.

Jones, T. and Newburn, T. (2004) 'Comparative criminal justice policy–making in the United States and the United Kingdom: The case of private prisons', *British Journal of Criminology*, 45 (1): 58–80.

Jones, T. and Newburn, T. (2006a) 'The United Kingdom' in T. Jones and T. Newburn (eds.) *Plural policing: A comparative perspective*, London, Routledge: 34–54.

Jones, T. and Newburn, T. (eds.) (2006b) *Plural policing: A comparative perspective*, London, Routledge.

Jones, T. and Newburn, T. (eds.) (2006c), 'Understanding plural policing' in T. Jones and T. Newburn (eds.) *Plural policing: A comparative perspective*, London, Routledge: 1–11.

Kakalik, J. and Wildhorn, S. (1971) *Private police in the United States: Findings and recommendations* (5 volume Rand report for the US Department of Justice), Santa Monica, Rand Corporation.

Kakalik, J. and Wildhorn, S. (1977) *The private police: Security and danger*, New York, Crane Russak.

Kempa, M., Carrier, R., Wood, J. and Shearing, C. (1999) 'Reflections on the evolving concept of "private policing"', *European Journal on Criminal Policy and Research*, 7 (2), 197–223.

Kempa, M., Stenning, P. and Wood, J. (2004) 'Policing communal spaces: A reconfiguration of the "mass private property" hypothesis', *British Journal of Criminology*, 44 (4): 562–581.

Kerr, J.H. and De Kock, H. (2002) 'Aggression, violence and the death of a Dutch soccer hooligan: A reversal theory explanation', *Aggressive Behavior*, 28: 1–10.

Kieckbusch, R.G. (2001) 'Jail privatization: The next frontier' in D. Shichor and M.J. Gilbert (eds.) *Privatization in criminal justice: Past, present and future*, Cincinnati, Anderson: 133–168.

King, M. and Prenzler, T. (2003) 'Private inquiry agents: Ethical challenges and accountability', *Security Journal*, 6 (3): 7–17.

Klein Theeselink, J.J.H. (2003) *Borging van veiligheid in winkelcentrum Hoog Catharijne* [Anchoring safety in shopping mall Hoog Catharijne], unpublished master's thesis, Universiteit Utrecht.

Klerks, P., Van Meurs, C. and Scholtes, M. (2001) *Particuliere recherche: werkwijzen en informatiestromen* [Private detectives: Operations and information flows], Den Haag, ES&E.

Klerks, P., Neijmeijer, P., Bervoets, E. and Van der Wal, R. (2005) *Particuliere recherche: uitbreiding van de reikwijdte van de wet?* [Private investigation: extension of the significance of the law?], Den Haag, WODC.

Kontos, A.P. (2004) '"Private" security guards: privatized force and state responsibility under international human rights law', *Non–State Actors and International Law*, 4 (3): 199–238.

Kooiman, J. (2003) *Governing as governance*, London, Sage.

Law Commission of Canada (2002) *In search of security: The roles of public police and private agencies/En quête de sécurité: Le rôle des forces policières et des agences privées*, Ottawa, LCC.

Lee, C.M. (2004) 'Accounting for [the] rapid growth of private policing in South Korea', *Journal of Criminal Justice*, 32 (2): 113–122.

Leishman, F., Cope, S. and Starie, P. (1996) 'Reinventing and restructuring: Towards a "new policing order"' in F. Leishman, B. Loveday and S.P. Savage (eds.) *Core issues in policing*, Harlow, Longman: 9–25.

Levi, M. (2002) 'Private policing and corruption' in C. Fijnaut and L. Huberts (eds.) *Corruption, integrity and law enforcement*, Den Haag, Kluwer: 441–450.

Livingstone, K. and Hart, J. (2003) 'The wrong arm of the law? Public images of private security', *Policing and Society*, 13 (2): 159–170.

Loader, I. (1997a) 'Policing and the social: Questions of symbolic power', *British Journal of Sociology*, 48 (1): 1–18.

Loader, I. (1997b) 'Thinking normatively about private security', *Journal of Law and Society*, 24 (3): 377–394.

Loader, I. (1997c) 'Private security and the demand for protection in contemporary Britain', *Policing and Society*, 7 (3): 143–162.

Loader, I. (1999) 'Consumer culture and the commodification of policing and security', *Sociology*, 33 (2): 373–392.

Loader, I. (2000) 'Plural policing and democratic governance', *Social and Legal Studies*, 9 (3): 323–345.

Loader, I. (2006) 'Policing, recognition and belonging', *Annals of the American Academy of Political and Social Science*, 605 (1): 201–221.

Loader, I. and Mulcahy, A. (2003) *Policing and the condition of England: Memory, politics and culture*, Oxford, Oxford University Press.

Loader, I. and Walker, N. (2001) 'Policing as a public good: Reconstituting the connections between policing and the state', *Theoretical Criminology*, 5 (1): 9–35.

Loader, I. and Walker, N. (2006) 'Necessary virtues: The legitimate place of the state in the production of security' in J. Wood and B. Dupont (eds.) *Democracy, society and the governance of security*, Cambridge, Cambridge University Press: 165–195.

Lofland, L.H. (1973) *A world of strangers: Order and action in public space*, New York, Basic Books.

Macaulay, S. (1986) 'Private government' in L. Lipson and S. Wheeler (eds.) *Law and the social sciences*, New York, Russell Sage Foundation: 445–518.

Manning, P.K. (1977) *Police work: The social organization of policing*, Cambridge, MIT Press.

Manning, P.K. (2005) 'The study of policing' *Police Quarterly*, 8 (1): 23–43.

Manning, P.K. (2006) 'The United States of America' in T. Jones and T. Newburn (eds.) *Plural policing: A comparative perspective*, London, Routledge: 98–125.

Mans, J.H.H. (1999) *Geld speelt (g)een rol: Eindrapport van de Werkgroep Doorberekening Politiekosten* [Money plays a/no role: Final report of the Study Group on Charging for Police Services] (government report), Den Haag.

Manunta, G. (1999) 'What is security?', *Security Journal*, 12 (3): 57–66.

Manzo, J. (2006) '"You can't rent a cop": Mall security officers' management of a "stigmatized" occupation', *Security Journal*, 19 (3): 196–210.

Marenin, O. (2005) 'Building a global police studies community', *Police Quarterly*, 8 (1): 99–136.

Marx, G. (2005) 'The new surveillance' in T. Newburn (ed.) *Policing: Key readings*, Cullompton, Willan: 761–785.

Mawby, R.I. (1990) *Policing across the world: Issues for the twenty–first century*, London, Routledge.

McLaughlin, E. (2007) *The new policing*, London, Sage.

McLaughlin, E. and Murji, K. (1995) 'The end of public policing? Police reform and "the new managerialism"' in L. Noaks, M. Levi and M. Maguire (eds.) *Contemporary issues in criminology*, Cardiff, University of Wales Press: 110–127.

McLaughlin, E. and Murji, K. (1999) 'The postmodern condition of the police', *Liverpool Law Review*, 21 (2/3): 217–240.

McManus, M. (1995) *From fate to choice: Private bobbies, public beats*, Aldershot, Avebury.

McMullan, J.L. (1995) 'The political economy of thief–taking', *Crime, Law and Social Change*, 23 (2): 121–146.

Meershoek, G. (1999) *Dienaren van het gezag: De Amsterdamse politie tijdens de bezetting* [Servants of the law: The Amsterdam police force under German occupation], Amsterdam, Van Gennep.

Mensen, A.H.H.M. and Rijt–Veltman, W.V.M. (2005) *MKB–locaties: Onderzoek naar de aard en kwaliteit van de bedrijfslocaties van MKB–ondernemingen* [MKB–locations: Research on the nature and quality of small and medium–sized enterprises], Zoetermeer, EIM.

Merry, S.E. (1981) *Urban danger: Life in a neighborhood of strangers*, Philadelphia, Temple University Press.

Michael, D. (1999) 'The levels of orientation security officers have towards a public policing function', *Security Journal*, 12 (4): 33–42.

Micucci, A. (1998) 'A typology of private policing operational styles', *Journal of Criminal Justice*, 26 (1): 41–51.

Minnaar, A. (2005) 'Private–public partnerships: Private security, crime prevention and policing in South Africa', *Acta Criminologica*, 18 (1): 85–114.

Ministerie van Binnenlandse Zaken en Koninkrijksrelaties (1993) *Integrale Veiligheidsrapportage* [Integral safety report] (government report), Den Haag.

Ministerie van Justitie (1977) *Eindrapport Werkgroep Bewaking en Beveiliging* [Final report of the Working Group Guarding and Protection] (government report), Den Haag.

Ministerie van Justitie (1985) *Samenleving en criminaliteit: Een beleidsplan voor de komende jaren* [Society and crime: A policy plan for future years] (government report), Den Haag.

Ministerie van Justitie and Ministerie van Binnenlandse Zaken en Koninkrijksrelaties (2001) *Criminaliteitsbeheersing: Investeren in een zichtbare overheid* [Controlling crime: Investing in a visible government] (government report), Den Haag.

Ministerie van Justitie and Ministerie van Binnenlandse Zaken en Koninkrijksrelaties (2002) *Naar een veiliger samenleving* [Toward a safer society] (government report), Den Haag.

Mommaas, H., Van den Heuvel, M. and Knulst, W. (2000) *De vrijetijdsindustrie in stad en land: Een studie naar de markt van belevenissen* [The leisure industry in the city and at the countryside: A study of the experience market], Den Haag, WRR.

Mopas, M. and Stenning. P.C. (2001) 'Tools of the trade: The symbolic power of private security – An exploratory study', *Policing and Society*, 11 (1): 67–97.

Morré, L. (2004) *Panoramic overview of [the] private security industry in the 25 member states of the European Union*, Brussels, CoESS/Uni–Europa.

Muller, E.R. (2002) 'Policing and accountability in the Netherlands: A happy marriage or a stressful relationship?', *Policing and Society*, 12 (4): 249–258.

Nalla, M.K. and Hereaux, C.G. (2003) 'Assessing goals and functions of private police, *Journal of Criminal Justice*, 31 (3): 237–247.

Nalla, M.K. and Hwang, E.G. (2006) 'Relations between police officers and private security officers in South Korea', *Policing: An International Journal of Police Strategies and Management*, 29 (3): 482–497.

Nalla, M.K. and Newman, G.R. (1991) 'Public versus private control: A reassessment', *Journal of Criminal Justice*, 19 (6): 537–547.

Newburn, T. (2001) 'The commodification of policing: Security networks in the late modern city', *Urban Studies*, 38 (5/6): 829–848.

Newman, O. (1972) *Defensible space: Crime prevention through urban design*, New York, MacMillan.

Noaks, L. (2000) 'Private cops on the block: A review of the role of private security in residential areas', *Policing and Society*, 10 (2): 143–161.

Nogala, D. and Sack, F. (1999) 'Private reconfigurations of police and policing – the case of Germany' in J. Shapland and L. van Outrive (eds.) *Police et sécurité: Controle social et interaction public/privé/Policing and security: Social control and the public–private divide*, Montreal, L'Harmattan: 53–70.

Norris, C. and Armstrong, G. (1999) *The maximum surveillance society*, Oxford, Berg.

O'Conner, D., Lippert, R., Greenfield, K. and Boyle, P. (2004) 'After the "quit revolution": The self–regulation of Ontario contract security agencies', *Policing and Society*, 14 (2): 138–157.

O'Conner, J. (1973) *The fiscal crisis of the state*, New York, St. Martin's Press.

Ocqueteau, F. (2006) 'France' in T. Jones and T. Newburn (eds.) *Plural policing: A comparative perspective*, London, Routledge: 55–76.

Oomen, P., Frederikse, R., Schildmeijer, R. and Zengerink, E. (2004) *Monitor Criminaliteit Bedrijfsleven 2004: Feiten en trends inzake aard en omvang van criminaliteit in het bedrijfsleven* [Trade and Industry Crime Monitor: Facts and trends], Amsterdam, Nipo.

Osborne, D. and Gaebler, T. (1992) *Reinventing government: How the entrepreneurial spirit is transforming the public sector*, Reading, Addison–Wesley.

Ottens, R.W., Olschok, H, and Landrock, S. (eds.) (1999) *Recht und Organisation Privater Sicherheitsdienste in Europa* [Law and private security companies in Europe], Stuttgart, Boorberg.

O'Malley, P. (1997) 'Policing, politics and postmodernity', *Social and Legal Studies*, 6 (3): 363–381.

O'Malley, P. and Palmer, D. (1996) 'Post–Keynesian policing', *Economy and Society*, 25 (2): 137–155.

O'Toole, G. (1978) *The private sector: Rent–a–cops, private spies and the police–industrial complex*, New York, Norton & Company.

Pakes, F. (2006) 'The ebb and flow of criminal justice in the Netherlands', *International Journal of the Sociology of Law*, 34 (3): 141–156.

Papanicolaou, G. (2006) 'Greece' in T. Jones and T. Newburn (eds.) *Plural policing: A comparative perspective*, London, Routledge: 77–97.

Pastor, J.F. (2003) *The privatization of police in America*, Jefferson, McFarland.

Pine, J. and Gilmore, J.H. (1999) *The experience economy: Work is theatre and every business a stage*, Boston, Harvard Business School.

Poulin, K.C. and Nemeth, C.P. (2005) *Private security and public safety: A community-based approach*, Upper Saddle River: Pearson Prentice Hall.

Prenzler, T. (1998) 'La sécurité privée et le problème de la confiance: L'Expérience Australienne' [Contract security and the problem of trust: the Australian experience], *Criminologie* 31 (2), 87–109.

Prenzler, T. (2004) 'The privatization of policing' in R. Sarre and J. Tomaino (eds.) *Key issues in criminal justice*, Unley, Australian Humanities Press: 267–296.

Prenzler, T. (2005) 'Mapping the Australian security industry', *Security Journal*, 18 (4): 51–64.

Prenzler, T. and Sarre, R. (2004) 'Policing' in R. Sarre and J. Tomaino (eds.) *Key issues in criminal justice*, Unley, Australian Humanities Press: 49–79.

Projectgroep visie op de politiefunctie (2005) *Politie in ontwikkeling: Visie op de politiefunctie* [Police in evolution: Vision on policing] (government report), Den Haag.

Putnam, R.D. (2000) *Bowling alone: The collapse and revival of the American community*, New York, Simon & Schuster.

Rawlings, P. (1995) 'The idea of policing: A history', *Policing and Society*, 5 (2): 129–149.

Rawlings, P. (2003) 'Policing before the police' in T. Newburn (ed.) *Handbook of policing*, Cullompton, Willan: 41–65.

Reames, B. (2005) 'Mexico' in L.E. Sullivan and M.R. Haberfeld (eds.) *Encyclopedia of law enforcement* (volume 3), London, Sage (3 volumes): 1186–1193.

Reiner, R. (1992) 'Policing a postmodern society', *Modern Law Review*, 55 (6): 761–781.

Reiner, R. (1997) 'Policing and the police' in M. Maguire, R. Morgan and R. Reiner (eds.) *The oxford handbook of criminology* (second edition). Oxford, Clarendon Press.

Rhodes, R. (1994) 'The hollowing out of the state: The changing nature of the public service in Britain', *Political Quarterly*, 65 (2): 138–151.

Rigakos, G.S. (2002) *The new parapolice: Risk markets and commodified social control*, Toronto, University of Toronto Press.

Rigakos, G.S. and Leung, C. (2006) 'Canada' in T. Jones and T. Newburn (eds.) *Plural policing: A comparative perspective*, London, Routledge: 126–138.

Rigakos, G.S. and Papanicolaou, G. (2003) 'The political economy of Greek policing: Between neo–liberalism and the sovereign state', *Policing and Society*, 13 (3): 271–304.

Rose, N. (1996) 'The death of the social? Re–figuring the territory of government', *Economy and Society*, 25 (3): 327–356.

Rose, N. and Miller, P. (1992) 'Political power beyond the state: Problematics of government, *British Journal of Sociology*, 43 (2): 173–205.

Rothbard, M. (1978) *For a new liberty: The libertarian manifesto*, New York, Macmillan.

Russell, S. (2001) 'Rent–a–judge and hide–a–crime: The dark potential of private
    adjudication' in D. Shichor and M.J. Gilbert (eds.) *Privatization in criminal
    justice: Past, present and future*, Cincinnati, Anderson: 113–122.

Sarre, R. (2005) 'Researching private policing: Challenges and agendas for
    researchers', *Security Journal*, 18 (3): 57–70.
Sarre, R. and Prenzler, T. (1999) 'The regulation of private policing: Reviewing
    mechanisms of accountability', *Crime Prevention and Community Safety:
    An International Journal*, 1: 17–28.
Sarre, R. and Prenzler, T. (2005) *The law of private security in Australia*, Pyrmont,
    Thomson Lawbook.
Schneider, S. (2006) 'Privatizing economic crime enforcement: Exploring the role of
    private sector investigative agencies in combating money laundering',
    *Policing and Society*, 16 (3): 285–312.
SEESAC (2005) *SALW and private security companies in South Eastern Europe: A
    cause or effect of insecurity?*, Belgrade, SEESAC.
Seidensat, P. (2004) 'Terrorism, airport security, and the private sector', *Review of
    Policy Research*, 21 (3): 275–291.
Shapland, J. (1999) 'Private worlds: Social control and security in Britain' in
    J. Shapland and L. van Outrive (eds.) *Police et sécurité: Controle social et
    interaction public/privé/Policing and security: Social control and the
    public–private divide*, Montreal, L'Harmattan: 155–167.
Shapland, J. and Vagg, J. (1988) *Policing by the public*, London: Routledge.
Sharp, D. and Wilson, D. (2000) '"Household security": Private policing and
    vigilantism in Doncaster', *Howard Journal*, 39 (2): 113–131.
Shearing, C.D. (1992) 'The relation between public and private policing' in
    M. Tonry and N. Morris (eds.) *Modern policing*, Chicago, University of
    Chicago Press: 399–434.
Shearing, C.D. (1996) 'Public and private policing' in W. Saulsbury, J. Mott and
    T. Newburn (eds.) *Themes in contemporary policing*, Plymouth, Latimer
    Trend and Co.: 83–95.
Shearing, C.D. (2001) 'A nodal conception of governance: Thoughts on a policing
    commission', *Policing and Society*, 11 (3/4): 259–272.
Shearing, C.D. (2005) 'Nodal security', *Police Quarterly*, 8 (1): 57–63.
Shearing, C.D. (2006) 'Reflections on the refusal to acknowledge private
    governments' in J. Wood and B. Dupont (eds.) *Democracy, society and the
    governance of security*, Cambridge, Cambridge University Press: 11–32.
Shearing, C.D. and Berg, J. (2006) 'South Africa' in T. Jones and T. Newburn (eds.)
    *Plural policing: A comparative perspective*, London, Routledge: 190–221.
Shearing, C.D., Farnell, M.B. and Stenning, P.C. (1980) *Contract security in
    Ontario*, Toronto, University of Toronto.
Shearing, C.D. and Stenning, P.C. (1981) 'Modern private security' in M. Tonry and
    N. Morris (eds.) *Crime and justice* (volume 3), Chicago, University of
    Chicago Press: 193–245.
Shearing, C.D. and Stenning, P.C. (1983a) 'Private security: Implications for social
    control', *Social Problems*, 30 (5): 493–506.
Shearing, C.D. and Stenning, P.C. (1983b) *Private justice and private security: The
    challenge of the 80s*, Montreal, the Institute for Research and Public Policy.

Shearing, C.D. and Stenning, P.C. (1985) 'From the panopticon to Disney World: The development of discipline' in A.N. Doob and E.L. Greenspan (eds.) *Perspectives in criminal law*, Ontario, Canada Law Book: 335–349.

Shearing, C.D. and Stenning, P.C. (eds.) (1987a) *Private policing*, Newbury Park, Sage.

Shearing, C.D. and Stenning, P.C. (1987b) 'Say "cheese!"': The Disney order that is not so Mickey Mouse' in C.D. Shearing and P.C. Stenning (eds.) *Private policing*, Newbury Park, Sage: 317–323.

Shearing, C.D. and Wood, J. (2003) 'Nodal governance, democracy and the new "denizen"', *Journal of Law and Society*, 30 (3): 400–419.

Sheptycki, J.W.E. (2002) *In search of transnational policing: Towards a sociology of global policing*, Aldershot, Ashgate.

Singer, P.W. (2003) *Corporate warriors: The rise of the privatized military industry*, Ithaca, Cornell University Press.

Skolnick, J.H. and Bayley, D.H. (1986) *The new blue line: Police innovation in six American cities*, New York, Free Press.

Stuurgroep Evaluatie Politieorganisatie (2005) *Lokaal verankerd, nationaal versterkt* [Anchored locally, strengthened nationally] (government report), Utrecht.

South, N. (1988) *Policing for profit: The private security sector*, London, Sage.

South, N. (1994) 'Privatizing policing in the European market: Some issues for theory, policy and research', *European Sociological Review*, 10 (3): 219–233.

Spitzer, S. and Scull, A.T. (1977) 'Privatization and capitalist development: The case of the private police', *Social Problems*, 25 (1): 18–29.

Stenning, P.C. (1994) 'Private Policing–Some recent myths, developments and trends' in: D. Biles and J. Vernon (eds.) *Private sector and community involvement in the criminal justice system*, Canberra, Australian Institute of Criminology: 145–155.

Stenning, P.C. (2000) 'Powers and accountability of private police', *European Journal on Criminal Policy and Research*, 8 (3): 325–352.

Stigter, H.W. (2000) *Bedrijfsleven in beeld: Het particulier beveiligingsbedrijf* [Outlook on industry: The private security industry], Zoetermeer, EIM.

Tenge, R., Hesselman, T. and Koenders, A. (2003) *Jaarboek Beveiliging 2003* [Security year book 2003], Alphen aan den Rijn, Kluwer.

Terpstra, J. (2005) 'Models of local security networks: On the diversity of local security networks in the Netherlands', *Crime Prevention and Community Safety: An International Journal*, 7 (4): 37–46.

Terpstra, J. (2006) 'Veiligheidszorg als publiek goed bij een gedeelde verantwoordelijkheid' [Shared responsibility for the public good of security] in L. Gunther Moor and R. Johannink (eds.) *Gedeelde verantwoordelijkheid voor veiligheid*, Dordrecht, SMVP: 63–80.

Terpstra, J. (2007) 'Nieuwe toezichthouders in de publieke ruimte: Geruststelling, fragmentering en vermarkting' [New supervisors in the public domain: Reassurance, fragmentation and marketization] in P. Ponsaers and L. Gunther Moor (eds.) *Reassurance policing: Concepten en receptie*, Brussels, Politeia: 129–152.

Terpstra, J. and Kouwenhoven, R. (2004) *Samenwerken en netwerken in de lokale veiligheidszorg* [Cooperation and networks in local security], Zeist, Kerckebosch.

Tweede Kamer (1990/1991) *Recht in beweging: Een beleidsplan voor Justitie in de komende jaren* [Law in motion: A future policy program for criminal justice] (government report), Den Haag.

Tweede Kamer (2002/2003) *Zicht op taakuitvoering politie* [Gaining insight in police performance] (government report), Den Haag.

Van den Berg, K. and Soffer, I. (2005) *Belevingen en verwachtingen omtrent de politie in Nederland: Kwalitatief perceptieonderzoek onder Nederlandse burgers* [Experiences and expectations of the police in the Netherlands: Qualitative perception research among Dutch citizens], Brandsettters (unpublished report).

Van den Diepstraten, H. (2002) *De Efteling: Kroniek van een sprookje* [Efteling: Chronicles of a fairy tale], Baarn, Tirion.

Van den Brink, G. (2001) *Geweld als Uitdaging: De betekenis van agressief gedrag bij jongeren* [Violence as a challenge: The meaning of aggressive youth behavior], Utrecht, NIWZ.

Van der Graaff, C. and Melchior, C. (2005) *Inzicht in de beveiligingssector* [Insights into the private security sector (position paper), Zoetermeer, EIM.

Van der Graaff, C. and Pleijster, F. (2004) *Zicht op beveiliging: Structuuronderzoek onder de leden van de Vakgroep Beveiliging* [Gaining insight into private security: Research on the members of the Security Department], Zoetermeer, EIM.

Van der Vijver, C.D. (2001) 'Het private toezicht in de publieke ruimte: Ontwikkelingen en discussiepunten in vogelvlucht' [Private security in the public domain: Trends and debates], *het Tijdschrift voor de Politie*, 63 (4): 29–33.

Van der Vijver, C.D., Meershoek, A.J. and Slobbe, D.F. (2001) *Kerntaken van de politie: Een inventarisatie van heersende opvattingen* [The police's core tasks: An inventory of prevailing views], Zeist, Kerckebosch.

Van Dijk, F. and De Waard, J. (2001) *Public and private crime control: Dutch and international trends* (government report), Ministry of Justice, Den Haag.

Van Outrive, L. (1999) 'Morphology des agents and agences privés dans six pays' [The morphology of agents and agencies in six countries] in J. Shapland and L. van Outrive (eds.) *Police et sécurité: Controle social et interaction public/privé/Policing and security: social control and the public–private divide*, Montreal, L'Harmattan: 179–198.

Van Steden, R. (2002) 'Politietaken geen exclusief bezit van het openbaar bestuur' [Policing is no exclusive government property], *Openbaar Bestuur*, 9: 12–15.

Van Steden, R. (2004) 'Particuliere beveiliging in Nederland: een Branche in beweging' [Private security in the Netherlands: A market in motion] in VPB: *Een branche in beweging*, Gorinchem: 13–26.

Van Steden, R. and Huberts, L.W.J.C. (2005) 'Private security industry growth in western countries' in L.E. Sullivan and M.R. Haberfeld (eds.) *Encyclopedia of law enforcement* (volume 3), London, Sage (3 volumes): 1261–1268.

Van Steden, R. and Huberts, L.W.J.C. (2006) 'The Netherlands' in T. Jones and T. Newburn (eds.) *Plural policing: A comparative perspective*, London, Routledge: 12–33.

Van Steden, R. and Sarre, R. (2007) 'The growth of private security: Trends in the European Union', *Security Journal*, 20 (4), 211-221.

Van Swaaningen, R. (2005) 'Public safety and the management of fear', *Theoretical Criminology*, 9 (3): 289–305.

Van Zuijlen, R.W. (2004) 'Veiligheid als begrip: Fundering van de rechtsorde' [Security as a concept: Founding the legal order] in E.R. Muller (ed.) *Veiligheid: Studies over inhoud, organisatie en maatregelen*, Alphen aan den Rijn, Kluwer: 7–24.

Verhoog, J. (2002) *Honderd jaar VNV: De geschiedenis van de beveiliging* [One hundred years of VNV: The history of private security], Noordwijk, Uitgeverij aan Zee.

Vindevogel, F. (2005) 'Private security and urban mitigation: A bid for BIDs', *Criminal Justice*, 5 (3): 233–255.

Visser, J., Frederikse, R. and Hermans, E. (2002) *Slachtofferschap criminaliteit bij bedrijven en instellingen* [Crime victimization amongst business and institutions], Amsterdam, Nipo.

Volkov, V. (2002) *Violent entrepreneurs: The use of force in the making of Russian capitalism*, Ithaca, Cornell University Press.

Von Hirsch, A. and Shearing, C.D. (2000) 'Exclusion from public space' in A. von Hirsch, D. Garland and A. Wakefield (eds.) *Ethical and social perspectives on situational crime prevention*, Oxford, Hart: 77–96.

VPB (2007) *Zelf regelen, beter presteren* [Self regulation, better performance] (policy document), Baarn.

Waddington, P.A.J. (1999) *Policing citizens*, London, Routledge.

Wakefield, A. (2003) *Selling security: The private policing of public space*, Cullompton, Willan.

Wakefield, A. (2005) 'The public surveillance functions of private security', *Surveillance and Society*, 2 (4): 529–545.

Waldron, J. (2003) 'Security and liberty: The image of balance', *Journal of Political Philosophy*, 11 (2): 191–210.

Walker, N. (2003) 'The pattern of transnational policing' in T. Newburn (ed.) *Handbook of policing*, Cullompton, Willan: 111–135.

Weber, M. (1968 [1919]) *Politik als Beruf* [Politics as a vocation], Berlin, Duncker & Humblot.

Weintraub, J. (1997) 'The theory and politics of the public/private distinction' in J. Weintraub and K. Kumar (eds.) *Public and private in thought and practice: Perspectives on a grand theory*, Chicago, University of Chicago Press: 1–42.

Weiss, R.S. (1994) *Learning from strangers: The art and method of qualitative interview studies*, New York, Free Press.

Williams, J.W. (2005) 'Reflections on the private versus public policing of economic crime', *British Journal of Criminology*, 45 (3): 316–339.

Wilson, J.Q. and Kelling, G. (1982) 'Broken Windows', *Atlantic Monthly*, 249 (3), 29–38.

Winkel, L.C., Jansen, J.J.M., Kerkmeester, H.O., Kottenhagen, R.J.P. and Mul, V. (eds.) (2005) *Privatisering van veiligheid/Privatization of security*, Den Haag, Boom Juridische Uitgevers.

Wintle, M. (1996) 'Policing the liberal state in the Netherlands: The historical context of the current reorganization of the Dutch police', *Policing and Society*, 6: 181–197.

Wittebrood, K. and Nieuwbeerta, P. (2006) 'Een kwart eeuw stijging in geregistreerde criminaliteit: Vooral meer registratie, nauwelijks meer criminaliteit' [Increase in registered crime over 25 years: Mostly more recording, hardly more crime], *Tijdschrift voor Criminologie*, 48 (3), 277–242.

Wood, J. and Cardia. N. (2006) 'Brazil' in T. Jones and T. Newburn (eds.) *Plural policing: A comparative perspective*, London, Routledge: 139–168.

Wood. J. and Dupont, B. (2006) 'Introduction: Understanding the governance of security' in J. Wood and B. Dupont (eds.) *Democracy, society and the governance of security*, Cambridge, Cambridge University Press: 1–10.

Wood, J. and Kempa, M. (2005) 'Understanding global trends in policing: Explanatory and normative dimensions' in J. Sheptycki and A. Wardak (eds.) *Transnational and comparative criminology*, London, Glasshouse Press: 287–316.

Wood, J. and Shearing, C.D. (2007) *Imagining security*, Cullompton, Willan.

Wright, A. (2002) *Policing: An introduction to concepts and practice*, Cullompton: Willan.


Yin, R.K. (2003) *Case study research: Design and methods* (third edition), London, Sage.

Yoshida, N. (1999) 'The taming of the Japanese private security industry', *Policing and Society*, 9 (3): 241 261.

Yoshida, N. and Leishman, F. (2006) 'Japan' in T. Jones and T. Newburn (eds.) *Plural policing: A comparative perspective*, London, Routledge: 222–238.

Young, J. (1999) *The exclusive society: Social exclusion, crime and difference in late modernity*, London, Sage.


Zedner, L. (2003a) 'The concept of security: An agenda for comparative analysis', *Legal Studies*, 23 (1): 153–176.

Zedner, L. (2003b) 'Too much security?', *International Journal of the Sociology of Law*, 31 (3): 155–184.

Zedner, L. (2006a) 'Policing before and after the police: The historical antecedents of contemporary crime control', *British Journal of Criminology*, 46 (1): 78–96.

Zedner, L. (2006b) 'Liquid security: Managing the market for crime control', *Criminology and Criminal Justice*, 6 (3): 267–288.

# Appendix 1: Questionnaire survey and interview protocol

**Survey requesting information on the size and extent of private security in the Netherlands (calendar year 2003; translated from the Dutch)**

1.  How large was your private security company's annual turnover (excluding VAT)?

    ........................... in euros, excluding VAT

2.  Who were the customers of your private security company?

    In percentage (%) of annual turnover

    | | |
    |---|---|
    | **Government** | ...................................... |
    | **Business community** | ...................................... |
    | **Nonprofit sector** | ...................................... |
    | **Other** | ...................................... |

3.  How many employees (in full-time equivalency) were employed by your private security company?

    ........................... FTE

4.  Which functions are carried out by the contract guards employed by your private security company?

    In total FTE

    | | |
    |---|---|
    | **Receptionists** | ............................ |
    | **Property protection guards** | ............................ |
    | **Surveillance officers** | ............................ |
    | **Shop supervisors** | ............................ |
    | **Custodial officers** | ............................ |
    | **Immigration and detention officers** | ............................ |
    | **Other** | ............................ |

**Interview protocol for the case studies on private security in quasi-public spaces in the Netherlands (translated from the Dutch)**

**Introduction of the respondent**

1. What is your name?
2. What is your function?
3. How long have you worked for this organization? In what function?

**History of private security**

1. When did your organization establish a private security team?
2. Was this an in-house team or did your organization hire contract guards?
3. What type of functions (e.g. caretakers, janitors, park keepers) were private security guards hired for? What did these employees do?

**Changes in private security**

1. Could you describe shifts in the number of guards employed?
2. Could you describe what guards do and how, if applicable, their job responsibilities have shifted?
3. Could you describe how your private security team is organized and how, if applicable, its organization has changed over time?

**Explanations for changes in private security**

1. Could you recall the major turnings points in (1) the number of security guards, (2) the tasks they perform and (3) the organization of the security team?
2. Could you give me detailed explanations for why changes in (1) the number of security guards, (2) the tasks they perform and (3) the organization of the security team occurred? Possible explanations are (1) rising crime and related problems, (2) the growth of mass private property, (3) economic rationalities, (4) government policy, (5) an overburdened police force and (6) professionalization of private security?
3. Do you have any other relevant remarks about changes in private security and explanations for these changes?

# Appendix 2: Qualitative data matrices

| NATIONAL CASE STUDY | 1980–1990 | 1990–2000 | 2000–2005 | Comments |
|---|---|---|---|---|
| **Shifts in private security** | From about 5,000 to 10,000 guards | From 10,000 to about 22,000 guards | From 22,000 to 30,000 guards | |
| **Rising crime and related problems** | Stabilization of crime rates at around 1,2 mln. cases | Stabilization of crime rates at around 1.2 mln. cases | Increase to 1.4 mln cases followed by downturns to 1.3 mln; terrorists attacks from 9/11 | Stabilization in crime rates, but growth in private security (-) |
| **Growth of mass private property** | E.g., shopping center growth from 350–550 properties | E.g., shopping center growth from 550–750 properties | E.g., shopping center growth from 750–900 properties | Many mass private properties *predate* private security growth (+/-) |
| **Economic rationalities** | Steep economic growth curve from 1985 | Continued steep economic growth curve until 2000 | Flattening out of economic growth; free rider problem (reported in 2004) | Economic waves coincide with the growth path of private security (+) |
| **Government policy toward private sector participation** | 1985 – *Society and Crime* [report] | 1993 – Introduction of an integral safety policy | 2002 – *Toward a safer society* [report] | Public policy aimed at responsibilization of society (+) |
| **An overburdened police force** | n/a | Rising expenditure and manpower, but declining societal satisfaction with police | Rising expenditure and manpower, but declining societal satisfaction with police | No fiscal crisis, but a legitimacy crisis; background condition for public policy (+/-) |
| **Professionalization of private security** | Old legislation dating back to the 1936 Paramilitary Organizations Act; development of new legislation | 1999: The Private Security Providers and Detective Agencies Act | VPB quality label and code of conduct (self-regulation) | Professionalization is an *effect* not a *cause* of growing private security (-) |

| EFTELING | 1952-1980 | 1980-1985 | 1985-1990 | 1990-2005 | Comments |
|---|---|---|---|---|---|
| **Shifts in private security** | No private security staff but park keepers | Army recidivists (1980) replaced by 12 in-house private security guards (1985) | Decline in guards from 12 (1985) to 9 (1989), excluding hired contract guards | Rise in guards from 9 (1989) to 17 (1998); a decline to 13 (2005), excluding hired contract guards | |
| **Rising crime and related problems** | n/a | Disobedient youth and petty crimes | No detailed information available | Slight increases in theft and vandalism (1996) | Efteling very keen on a pleasant atmosphere (+) |
| **Growth of mass private property (size park and visitor numbers)** | n/a | New attractions and rising visitor numbers | New attractions and rising visitor numbers | New attractions, a hotel and golf course and rising visitor numbers | No clear connection with shifts in private security (-) |
| **Economic rationalities of Efteling management** | n/a | Efteling became a private limited company (1990); insurance constraints | Keeping up good customer relations; longer opening hours | Keeping up good customer relations; longer opening hours | Guards seen as crucial in creating a pleasant atmosphere (+) |
| **Government policy toward private sector participation** | n/a | No detailed information available | Establishing closer police contacts with guards until late 1980s, early 1990s | Police retreat (1993), policy toward more responsibility for Efteling | Responsibilization policy felt as important for shifts in private security (+) |
| **An overburdened police force** | n/a | Close contacts with Efteling guards | Withdrawal police from Efteling | Toward an improved public-private partnership | Not an overburdened police per se, but a more critical police (+/-) |
| **Professionalization of private security** | n/a | No interesting developments | No interesting developments | Tightened integral safety structures at the park | An *effect*, not a *cause*, of shifts in private security (-) |
| **Labor law** | n/a | n/a | n/a | Introduction of the Flexi-Law (1999) | Smaller number of guards working longer hours (+) |

| FEYENOORD | 1945-1974 | 1974-1990 | 1990-1997 | 1997-2005 | Comments |
|---|---|---|---|---|---|
| **Shifts in private security** | No private security staff but football attendants | No private security staff but football attendants | Founding of KSS (1991) with 100 in-house stewards; 550 stewards (1997) | Founding of SE&S (2004); number of stewards fell to 300 (2005), excluding hired contract guards | |
| **Rising crime and related problems** | Introduction of hooliganism (1974) | Many stories about incidents | Many stories about incidents | Death of Carlo Picorni (1997) | No immediate link with private security (-) |
| **Growth of mass private property (size stadium and visitor numbers)** | n/a | No interesting developments | Refurbishment of the stadium (1994) | No interesting developments | No direct relations with shifts in private security (-) |
| **Economic rationalities of Stadium Feyenoord** | n/a | Deteriorating stadium, little efforts to counter this trend | New chairman (1991), emphasis on friendly looking stadium | Commercialization of in-house team (2004) to recap costs | Higher quality security staff important for good stadium atmosphere (+) |
| **Government policy toward private sector participation** | n/a | Many government reports | Safety and security guidelines (1990) | Integral safety covenants (1997, 2003) | Responsibilization policy felt as important for shifts in private security (+) |
| **An overburdened police force** | n/a | No detailed information available | Increasing number of officers deployed to Feyenoord | Increasing number of officers deployed, decease after 2005 | Overburdened police no direct cause of improved private security (-) |
| **Professionalization of private security** | n/a | n/a | Gradual discharge of unskilled staff | Hiring of specialized contract staff (2000); introduction of ESOs (2004) | An *effect*, not a *cause*, of shifts in private security (-) |
| **Labor law** | n/a | n/a | n/a | Introduction of the Flexi-Law (1999) | Impetus to discharge unskilled staff (+) |

| HOOG CATHARIJNE | 1973-1982 | 1982-1987 | 1987-2001 | 2001-2005 | Comments |
|---|---|---|---|---|---|
| **Shifts in public and private policing** | Establishment of 40-strong security team and 12-strong police team | No interesting shifts; lots of tensions between the two teams | 1990 police contract: private funding of some 5 public police patrollers | No interesting shifts; calls for better cooperation between the two teams | |
| **Rising crime and related problems** | Unintended attraction of (addicted) homeless and other displaced persons | Rising crime and disorder; *fear* of crime and disorder in particular | Decay of certain parts (or quarters) of Hoog Catharijne; rising crime and disorder problems | Decreasing crime and disorder problems; increasing feelings of safety and security | No immediate link with police contract (-) |
| **Growth of mass private property (size mall and visitor numbers)** | No interesting developments | No interesting developments | No interesting developments | Clean up of Hoog Catharijne; refurbishment of certain quarters | No direct relations with shifts in policing (-) |
| **Economic rationalities of property owner** | Negative public image of the shopping mall | Negative public image of the shopping mall | Security situation goes out of control; local government decides to take the lead (1987) | Improvement of the security situation; keeping up this better atmosphere | Breakthrough when security situation goes out of control (+) |
| **Government policy toward private sector participation** | Local government and private owner quarreling about 'who to blame' | Local government and private owner quarreling about 'who to blame' | Policy experiments (1987) aimed at revitalizing the mall | Toward public-private partnerships: Area Safety and Livability Plan (2003) | Decisive in opting for the police contract (+) |
| **An overburdened police force** | No overburdening, but discussions about sharing responsibilities with security team | No overburdening, but discussions about sharing responsibilities with security team | No overburdening, but discussions about sharing responsibilities with security team | No overburdening, but discussions about sharing responsibilities with security team | Debates more about reasonable public/private working relations than overburdening (-) |
| **Professionalization of private security** | n/a | n/a | n/a | n/a | Professionalization of private security no issue (-) |

# Appendix 3: Summary in Dutch (samenvatting)

# Privatisering van de politiefunctie: de groei van particuliere beveiliging beschreven en verklaard

## Branche in vogelvlucht

Particuliere beveiliging is een groeimarkt die bestaat uit tal van sectoren variërend van manbewaking en recherchebureaus tot leveranciers en installateurs van geavanceerde apparatuur. Het is dus lastig om precies te duiden wat particuliere beveiliging is. Dit proefschrift beperkt zich daarom tot de grootste sector van de markt: manbewaking. Het gaat hier om professionals die de volgende kenmerken gemeen hebben: zij (1) dragen meestal een uniform (2) zijn ongewapend, hoewel het gebruik van honden is toegestaan, (3) hebben zowel private als publieke opdrachtgevers, (4) bieden hun diensten tegen betaling aan en (5) ontlenen hun autoriteit aan huisregels of toegangsvoorwaarden. Beveiligers kunnen bijvoorbeeld optreden tegen illegaal vuurwerk tijdens voetbalwedstrijden en passagiers van een vliegtuig geven impliciet toestemming aan beveiligers voor fouillering en het doorzoeken van persoonlijke bezittingen.

Tussen 1980 en 2007 hebben beveiligingsbedrijven hun personeelsbestand zien groeien van 10.000 naar ruim 30.000. Een drietal (multinationale) ondernemingen domineert de markt. De meeste medewerkers bewaken gebouwen en instellingen, werken als mobiele surveillanten of beveiligen winkels (circa 75%). Een kleiner aantal is actief binnen het gevangeniswezen, werkt als receptionist of verricht andere taken. Het bedrijfsleven is veruit de grootste klant van beveiligingsbedrijven. Daarnaast maken ook de overheid en non-profitinstellingen gebruik van beveiligers. Het aantal beveiligers streeft de politie nog niet voorbij. Geteld in 40-urige werkwerken beschikt de politie over 53.000 fte (36.000 fte executief personeel), terwijl de beveiligingsbranche tot (minimaal) 23.600 fte komt. Toch zijn beveiligers steeds nadrukkelijker aanwezig in de samenleving. Hun zichtbaarheid lijkt die van de politie te (gaan) overtreffen.

## Verwondering

Opvallend genoeg wordt er nauwelijks aandacht besteed aan de opkomst van particuliere beveiligers. Zowel wetenschappers, beleidsmedewerkers en burgers hebben een blinde vlek voor de branche. Clifford Shearing, een gerenommeerde criminoloog, spreekt over een 'stille revolutie' binnen de veiligheidszorg. Beveiligers zijn min of meer sluipenderwijs onze levens binnengedrongen. Hierbij komt dat het bestaande onderzoek een veelal theoretisch, ideologisch en normatief karakter heeft. Empirische studies zijn relatief schaars en worden bovendien door Angelsaksische inzichten gedomineerd. Dit alles roept verwondering op. Verwondering over wie beveiligers zijn, wat ze doen, waar ze vandaan komen en wat hun groeiende aantal kan verklaren. De centrale vraag van het proefschrift luidt derhalve: *hoe kan de groei van particuliere beveiliging in Nederland over de laatste drie decennia worden verklaard?*

De doelstelling van het proefschrift is tweeledig. Ten eerste wordt een beschrijving gegeven van de Nederlandse beveiligingsbranche. Er wordt specifiek ingegaan op de kleurrijke aard, omvang en praktijk van manbewaking. Hoe ziet de sector eruit, hoe groot is zij, wat doen particuliere beveiligers en op wat voor manier werken zij samen met de politie? Ten tweede wil het proefschrift bijdragen aan een beter begrip van drijvende factoren achter het succes van particuliere beveiliging. Tot op heden is er weinig tot geen gedegen onderzoek naar deze factoren verricht. Wetenschappelijke literatuur bevat tal van mogelijke, elkaar overlappende en in elkaar overvloeiende, verklaringen, zonder dat zij zijn gesystematiseerd en bevraagd. Een empirische fundering van geopperde theorieën is daarom belangrijk.

## Onderzoeksmethode
Het onderzoek is opgedeeld in twee fasen. De eerste fase omvat een grootschalig literatuuronderzoek dat uitmondt in een theoretisch verklaringskader. De tweede fase bestaat uit casusonderzoek bestaande uit een enquête, interviews, documentatieverzameling en bezoeken aan praktijkvoorbeelden van beveiliging. Hieronder worden de twee fasen kort toegelicht.

### *Verklaringsmodel*
Vroege wetenschappelijk gefundeerde studies naar particuliere beveiliging stammen uit de jaren zeventig. Amerikaanse onderzoekers schrijven in opdracht van de overheid een vijftal lijvige rapporten ('Rand Reports') om inzicht te geven in de sterk groeiende beveiligingsmarkt. Hun werk wordt begin jaren tachtig opgevolgd door andere Amerikaanse rapporten ('Hallcrest Reports') en Canadees veldwerk ('Contract Security in Otario'). Vooral dit laatste onderzoek heeft veel invloed gehad op het denken over particuliere beveiliging. Naast een overzicht van wat er zoal aan beveiliging bestaat en wat hun rollen alsmede doelstellingen zijn, stellen de auteurs (onder meer de eerder genoemde Clifford Shearing) dat de opkomst van beveiligers sterk samenhangt met grootstedelijke veranderingen. Zij wijzen op onder meer winkelcentra, luchthaventerminals en bedrijvencomplexen ('mass private properties') die in toenemende mate door beveiligers worden bewaakt. Daar het semi-publieke gebieden betreffen, moeten eigenaren voor hun eigen veiligheid zorgen en huren daarom commercieel personeel in.

Deze these is in de jaren negentig door de Britse onderzoekers Trevor Jones en Tim Newburn bekritiseerd. Zij beargumenteren dat 'mass private properties' zoals 'shopping malls' weinig in Europa voorkomen. Daarenboven zijn beveiligers ook buiten deze gebieden actief en kunnen bevindingen niet zonder meer als universeel worden verondersteld. Elk continent en elk land heeft een eigen historische, geografische, politieke, economische, juridische en sociale context. Vanuit dit perspectief clustert het proefschrift een diversiteit aan wetenschappelijke verklaringen. Het gaat om een zestal categorieën, te weten: (1) toename van criminaliteit en gerelateerde problemen, (2) toename van semi-publieke gebieden, (3) economische rationaliteit, (4) overheidsbeleid gericht op verantwoordelijkheidsoverdracht naar private partijen, (5) een overvraagde politie en (6) de professionalisering van particuliere beveiliging. Middels casusonderzoek op zowel nationaal als lokaal niveau wordt de houdbaarheid van voorgaande verklaringen onderzocht.

*Casusonderzoek*
Het empirische onderzoek bestaat uit twee stappen. Op basis van interviews, rapportages, marktonderzoek, statistische gegevens en een enquête onder leden van de Verenging van Particuliere Beveiligingsorganisaties (VPB) is eerst een beeld van de Nederlandse beveiligingssector geschetst. Ten tweede is onderzoek verricht naar concrete cases van particuliere beveiliging. Deze cases omvatten pretpark De Efteling, voetbalstadion Feyenoord en winkelcentrum Hoog Catharijne. Het zijn voorbeelden van semi-publieke gebieden waar beveiligers actief zijn. Ook hier zijn interviews met respondenten – voornamelijk beveiligingsmanagers, beveiligers, politiemensen, politici en beleidsmakers – afgenomen en documenten verzameld.

Het casusonderzoek heeft geleid tot een gedetailleerde beschrijving van veranderingen in de particuliere beveiligingsbranche teneinde deze te kunnen verklaren. Bevindingen zijn nauwkeurig middels kwalitatieve datamatrices geanalyseerd, wat heeft bijdragen aan een systematische totstandkoming van conclusies. Een lastig punt is de generalisatie van resultaten. Door de lokaliteit van cases kunnen bevindingen niet zonder meer naar bredere populaties worden geëxtrapoleerd (statistische generalisatie). Daarom kiest het proefschrift voor analytische generalisatie: worden theoretische noties door empirische observaties ondersteund of niet? Is het antwoord negatief dan worden verklaringen gefalsificeerd, zodat uiteindelijk relevante theorie overblijft.

**Resultaten**
Uit onderzoek naar particuliere beveiliging in het algemeen en naar lokale cases (De Efteling, Stadion Feyenoord en Hoog Catharijne) in het bijzonder blijkt het volgende: overheidsbeleid gericht op verantwoordelijkheidsoverdracht naar

private partijen – het 'responsibiliseren' van de samenleving – alsmede financieel-economische overwegingen zijn de meest prominente verklaringen voor de groei van particuliere beveiliging over de afgelopen 30 jaar.[1] Sinds de jaren '80 heeft de overheid actief de eigen verantwoordelijkheid van de samenleving voor veiligheid gestimuleerd. Binnen deze discussie over verantwoordelijkheidsdeling tussen publieke en private sectoren kon de beveiligingsbranche floreren: burgers en ondernemingen zagen zich genoodzaakt beveiligers in te huren. Tegelijkertijd betekende het krijgen van verantwoordelijkheid niet automatisch dat partijen deze zonder meer namen. Binnen de context van de drie cases bleek dat de inzet van beveiligers onderdeel was van financiële overwegingen. Overheidsbeleid in combinatie met bedrijfseconomische belangen waren doorslaggevend.

De vinding dat toename van criminaliteit en gerelateerde problemen geen direct verband heeft met groeiende particuliere beveiliging is enigszins contra-intuïtief. Criminaliteitscijfers stabiliseerden zich over de afgelopen drie decennia, terwijl de beveiligingsbranche groeide. Ook heeft zich na '9/11' geen opvallende stijging in het totale aantal beveiligers voorgedaan. Wel is het meer algemene thema veiligheid hoog op de politieke agenda gekomen, waardoor het denken over toezicht en handhaving is verscherpt met aannemelijk positieve gevolgen voor beveiligingsbedrijven. Tevens draagt de toename van semi-publieke gebieden niet ondubbelzinnig bij aan de toename van beveiligers. Dergelijke gebieden dateren van (ver) voor de recente vraag naar beveiliging. Voorts wordt de politie niet overvraagd door een tekort aan middelen (financiële crises); budgetten en personeelsbestanden zijn juist vergroot. Er lijkt eerder sprake van legitimiteitscrises, vanwege de enorme vraag naar veiligheid vanuit de samenleving. Tot slot is de professionalisering van medewerkers geen aanleiding maar een gevolg van groeicijfers. Vooruitgang in bijvoorbeeld training volgt ontwikkelingen in de branche.

**Tot besluit**
Overheidsbeleid dat particuliere beveiliging (indirect) stimuleert en faciliteert – dat ruimte laat aan beveiligers – vormt een cruciale factor voor het begrijpen van de vraag waarom de branche snel groeit. Het is des te opvallender dat dezelfde overheid particuliere beveiliging nagenoeg loslaat. Behalve wettelijke vereisten aangaande opleiding en screening ontbreken zicht en controle op particuliere beveiliging nagenoeg. Er zijn wel enige stappen gezet op weg naar publiek-private samenwerking, maar echte interesse in (laat staan visie op) de branche

---

[1]　In de casus van Hoog Catharijne gaat het niet om veranderingen in particuliere beveiliging, maar om een private financiële bijdrage voor extra politiesurveillanten. Deze onverwachte oplossing heeft echter geen gevolgen voor de te verklaren logica achter privatiseringstendensen.

ontbreekt. Een opmerkelijke constatering, omdat veiligheidsbeleid tot de kerntaken van de overheid behoort.

Hoewel de media over een aantal incidenten hebben bericht, lijken zich vooralsnog weinig problemen voor te doen. Nochtans moeten particuliere beveiligers nauwlettend worden gevolgd. Critici wijzen op hun exclusieve mandaat, een dreigende tweedeling tussen 'hyperbeveiligden' en zwakkere groepen, de onoverzichtelijke complexiteit van politie(achtige) beroepen, alsmede de vermenging tussen publieke en private vormen van dwang en drang. Daarenboven is beveiligingswerk niet altijd gemakkelijk. Er wordt veel van medewerkers verlangd, maar ze hebben geen bijzondere bevoegdheden. Particuliere beveiliging is, kortom, een kwetsbare branche.

De laatste observatie is extra prangend vanwege de grote druk op beveiligingsbedrijven. Concurrentie tussen ondernemingen is hevig, de markt zoekt alsmaar nieuwe mensen en gegeven het belang van financieel-economische overwegingen bij opdrachtgevers zijn prijzen vaak laag. Tezamen kan dit de kwaliteit van serviceverlening ondergraven. Alhoewel beveiligingswerk geen topopleiding behoeft, verdient het aanbeveling de nadruk op professionaliteit en betrouwbaarheid te leggen. Zowel de samenleving als de branche zijn gebaat bij integere medewerkers die zijn toegerust op hun taak. Overheid en bedrijfsleven moeten zich derhalve richten op hechtere samenwerking en regulering. Alleen dan blijft het algemene belang van veiligheidszorg voor de toekomst voldoende gewaarborgd.